When Flaming Arrows Fly

Standing Strong in a
Spiritually Exhausting World

Jay Knolls

When Flaming Arrows Fly: Standing Strong in a Spiritually Exhausting World

© Copyright 2023 Jay Knolls

A publication of Wondrous Word Ministries, LLC

Wilmington, NC

All rights reserved. No part of this publication may be reproduced, distributed, or transmitted in any form or by any means, including photocopying, recording, or other electronic or mechanical methods, without the prior written permission of the publisher, except in the case of brief quotations embodied in critical reviews and certain other noncommercial uses permitted by copyright law.

Although the author and publisher have made every effort to ensure that the information in this book was correct at press time, the author and publisher do not assume and hereby disclaim any liability to any party for any loss, damage, or disruption caused by errors or omissions, whether such errors or omissions result from negligence, accident, or any other cause.

Adherence to all applicable laws and regulations, including international, federal, state and local governing professional licensing, business practices, advertising, and all other aspects of doing business in the US, Canada, or any other jurisdiction is the sole responsibility of the reader and consumer.

Neither the author nor the publisher assumes any responsibility or liability whatsoever on behalf of the consumer or reader of this material. Any perceived slight of any individual or organization is purely unintentional.

Unless otherwise indicated, Scripture quotations are from The ESV® Bible (The Holy Bible, English Standard Version®), copyright © 2001 by Crossway, a publishing ministry of Good News Publishers. Used by permission. All rights reserved.

Scripture quotations marked CSB have been taken from the Christian Standard Bible®, Copyright © 2017 by Holman Bible Publishers. Used by permission. Christian Standard Bible® and CSB® are federally registered trademarks of Holman Bible Publishers.

Scriptures marked KJV are taken from the KING JAMES VERSION (KJV): KING JAMES VERSION, public domain.

Edited by Carly Catt and Joanna Kneller

For more information, visit wondrousword.com or email jayknolls@wondrousword.com

ISBN: 979-8-88759-917-5 - paperback

ISBN: 979-8-88759-918-2 - ebook

ATTENTION!

To say thank you for purchasing *When Flaming Arrows Fly*, I would like to offer you a FREE study guide. To claim your copy, please visit wondrousword.com and join my email list.

Dedication

This book is dedicated to two very special people. The first is my beautiful wife, Michelle. For many years, I have talked about publishing a book. Pages and pages of text have accumulated, but I never would have published this work without Michelle's unwavering support. She kindly tolerates my obsession with writing and has the privilege, I suppose, of reading my writing in its raw stages. Hardly a day passes when I'm not tinkering with stories and book ideas. Michelle graciously reads the good, the bad, and the terrible. Thankfully, she catches my ridiculously funny typos before anyone else sees them. Although she's my wife, her assessments are always fair, to the point, and honest. Thanks to Michelle's candid appraisals and encouragement, I keep my pen moving across the empty pages. Thank you, Michelle, for your faithful support, patience, and devotion.

Second, I want to dedicate my first published book to Mrs. Szajewski, who was one of my high school English teachers. Mrs. Szajewski is the person who taught me to love reading, especially classic literature. As a teenager, I never imagined reading anything for enjoyment, and I certainly never expected to choose writing as a hobby. And yet today, I have a library filled with books I have read through the years and a growing list of topics I hope to write on someday. My gratitude for Mrs. Szajewski is deep and eternal. Thank you, Mrs. Szajewski, for investing your time and talents into my life.

Thanks be to God, who gives us the victory through our Lord Jesus Christ.

1 Corinthians 15:57

Table of Contents

Introduction 1

The Problem of Spiritual Exhaustion 13

Biblical Strategies for the Spiritual Battle 40

Strategy One: Understand the Nature of Humanity and the World . 41

Strategy Two: Rest in God's Strength 65

Strategy Three: Dress for Battle 93

Strategy Four: Become Combat-Ready 117

Strategy Five: Put On the Armor of God 139

    Belt: Believe the Truth 143

    Breastplate: Practice Righteousness 164

    Shoes: Lace Up Readiness 184

    Shield: Live By Faith 211

    Helmet: Apply Your Salvation 233

    Sword: Proclaim the Word of God 251

Strategy Six: Pray Without Ceasing 273

Strategy Seven: Stay in the Body 293

Conclusion 317

Appendix: How Does Someone Become a Christian? 320

Acknowledgments 323

Introduction

For I the LORD *do not change.*
Malachi 3:6

One afternoon, a friend of mine presented me with a challenge. He wanted to see if I could catch a flying arrow like a circus performer. Never one to back down from a challenge, I accepted. My first attempt went spectacularly well; like a seasoned pro, I snatched the arrow as it whizzed by. Deciding that arrow-catching was no big deal, I tried again. This time, the point punctured my palm, leaving me in agony. Blood gushing from my hand, we dashed into my friend's house to find his mother. Thankfully, we were elementary kids and my friend didn't have much muscle behind his shot. Watching what appeared to be gallons of my blood washing down the kitchen drain, my buddy's mother asked what happened. I promptly reported that I had fallen and cut my hand on some glass. Pretty good story, I suppose. You can't really see the scar anymore, but I sure remember how foolish I was that day. Arrows are dangerous. By God's grace, I didn't sustain anything more serious than a lacerated hand.

From the Apostle Paul's imagery of spiritual warfare in Ephesians 6, we learn that Satan is hurling fiery arrows at Christians on a regular basis. Faithful followers of Jesus are the target of the devil's attacks. Because we are engaged in a spiritual battle, we must be prepared to stand against evil. In Ephesians 6:16, Paul warns that we need God's shield of faith to provide spiritual protection from the onslaught of the evil one's flaming darts.

In Paul's writings, we find two basic pictures used to describe the Christian life: a race and warfare. The imagery of running a race is used to picture biblical principles such as perseverance and reward for those who run the race well. It's a wonderful illustration to remind Christians that faithfulness to Christ takes effort, grit, and perseverance. Instead of a forty-yard dash, we're running a marathon. With each determined step, we're pressing on toward the finish line where we will be rewarded for faithful service.

While Paul's imagery of running a race is rich in meaning and application, in this book, we will consider the second primary image Paul used: warfare. While talking about war makes many people uncomfortable, it's an effective illustration of the Christian life. No, this is not a radicalized call to take up arms and engage in a new round of Crusades against those who oppose the gospel. This is not a call for any type of violence. This is, however, a plea directed at Christians to understand the nature of the spiritual battle we all face.

Introduction

Before entering ministry, I served in the healthcare industry as a respiratory therapist. In 1995, not long after my wife and I were married, we moved to Vermont where Michelle attended graduate school. Shortly thereafter, I was hired as the director of clinical education at the medical center in Burlington. During these years, I began taking my faith in Christ more seriously. I longed to be a good husband, an excellent employee, and a faithful volunteer in our church. I quickly learned during this time that when we try to obey God, Satan pushes back. Despite my desire to live obediently, my pride, covetousness, impatience, self-protection, and envy didn't die. My insecurities didn't dissolve and become newfound confidence. Past failures were not erased from my memory or the history book of my life. Based on Scripture, I knew that I was a new creature in Christ. Nonetheless, my old nature still tried to dominate my decisions and desires. The devil knew where I was weak and tested my faithfulness to Christ on a regular basis.

The more familiar I became with the Bible, the more I desired vocational ministry. My desire was to assist those struggling in their walk with Christ. Within a few months, God opened doors for Michelle and me to pursue ministry. Three years later, I earned a Master of Divinity degree and was hired as a youth pastor in Orlando, Florida. It was during these years that I received an in-depth education on spiritual warfare. My office was hardly set up when I learned the hard lessons about the sinfulness of people and the wiles of the devil. No seminary professor could have perfectly prepared me for ministry in the trenches of spiritual warfare.

For the first time, I was working closely with people who were addicted to all sorts of sinful habits, such as substance abuse, sexual sins, anger issues, and eating disorders. From close proximity, I watched marriages crumble because of infidelity, alcohol, or abuse. Hearing the stories of emotionally wounded and scarred women, along with a few men, who had suffered through the horrors of abuse at the hands of sinful people was heart-wrenching. Even before entering vocational ministry, I knew sin was always ugly and destructive.

Based on personal experience, I never doubted the existence of evil or that people can be selfish and cruel. In seminary, I had taken several counseling classes to help prepare me for the problems I expected to face in ministry. While these courses were profoundly helpful, learning firsthand how egotistic and sinful people can actually be was difficult to process. Before long, my wife and I were discipling several women who were recovering from years of verbal, physical, and sexual abuse. It was during these sessions that I came to truly comprehend how destructive sin can be. The idea that our sin does not negatively affect others is a misnomer; there is no such thing as a victimless sin. Our wicked hearts are capable of dreadful actions, and I was hearing story after story of people who had been on the receiving end of such atrocities.

In a matter of months, I came to realize that I needed more biblical training to address the increasingly difficult

Introduction

situations coming my way. I started a doctoral program and learned all I could about Scripture and how to communicate it to people in spiritual need. Despite my years of formal theological training, I still don't have all of the answers to life's problems. I'm still learning how to effectively fight this spiritual battle. This book is an attempt to share with you what I'm learning.

Since my time in Florida, I have served as the lead pastor at two churches. The first was in Williston, Vermont. The second is Grace Baptist Church located in Wilmington, North Carolina. As of this writing, I'm still the pastor of Grace. It's a wonderful ministry filled with faithful Christians. But there isn't a perfectly sinless person among our local body of believers—not even me. I'm always careful to not make promises to the people of Grace, especially when I'm uncertain about my ability to keep the commitment. But there is one promise I make regularly and without hesitation: eventually, I will fail, make mistakes, and sadly, even sin against the people God has called me to lead. Sin resides in all of us. Pastors included.

From my perspective, the spiritual battle has grown fiercer during the last few years. That's why I'm writing this book for you. In fact, through the course of this project, I have interacted with six married couples whose marriages are in danger of crumbling due to sinful choices. The battle is intensifying, and I want you to be prepared to stand strong when the fiery arrows of the devil are coming at your heart.

I'm confident that you're struggling with your own spiritual battles. Maybe you're losing ground on some fronts;

most of us are. Perhaps you're battling addiction. Whether it is drugs, alcohol, food, sex, or pornography, the fight quickly becomes discouraging. Maybe your marriage is in a heap of ashes and you're heading for divorce. It could be that you're battling loneliness, depression, anxiety, grief, anger, or doubt. No matter your particular struggle, this spiritual fight can quickly leave us feeling discouraged, passive, disengaged, and even shameful.

During a series of messages I preached on spiritual warfare, I noticed that the topic hit a nerve like none other I had preached. Well, I've hit a lot of nerves before but not always in a positive way. People soaked up the sermons like water to parched soil. Because the series created so many gospel conversations, I decided to rewrite the sermon series into book form. Don't worry; this isn't a collection of boring sermon notes. It's my humble and imperfect attempt to put the lessons I learned through the spiritual warfare series on paper to assist people like you in your fight against temptation and evil.

During my preparation for the sermon series, I came across a term that I would like to share. Yes, I'm a nerd in some ways, and I greatly enjoy reading the definition of a new word each day. The word I want to teach you is *meliorism*. The word is derived from the Latin word *melior*, meaning "better." According to dictionary.com, *meliorism* is defined as "the doctrine that the world tends to become better or may be made better by human effort."[1] In other

---

1 Dictionary.com, accessed February 18, 2023, https://www.dictionary.com/browse/meliorism.

Introduction

words, meliorism erroneously asserts that human beings can, through their hard work and actions, produce an outcome in which there will be steady improvement over the natural course of worldly events.

While meliorism may sound appealing, the Bible teaches that the world's system, by its very nature, is fallen, broken, and heading down a path that will inevitably lead to destruction. The world isn't evolving into a better version of itself. Instead, it's deteriorating into a place where evil is flourishing and righteousness is being pushed to the fringes of society. Don't misunderstand: Christians *can* make a difference in the world through the faithful proclamation of the gospel. We can lead people to the eternal hope found in Jesus. We can disciple believers and help them become more like their Savior. Making and maturing disciples is the calling of every Christian. But no matter our level of effort, humanity will never entirely eradicate evil from the world.

From ancient times until today, every culture has accepted the reality of some type of spiritual world beyond the physical one we can examine with our senses. God created humanity as both physical beings who need to eat, sleep, and work, and spiritual beings who have an innate desire to worship. As spiritual beings, we have no choice but to worship something or someone. You may not be convinced that's true, but as we will discuss later, we all give something or someone preeminence in our lives.

Our desire to worship explains why some type of religion has been found in every culture around the world since the beginning of time. As worshippers, we will allow something or someone to rule our hearts and dictate the direction of our lives. Whether it's an idol crafted from a piece of carved wood, stone, gold, or iron, or an ideology or a pop icon, something will become the object of our worship. In all of creation, people alone are created in God's image and hardwired to worship. Puritan writer Stephen Charnock astutely notes, "The natural inclination to worship is as universal as the notion of a God; idolatry else had never gained footing in the world."[2] For Christians, it is folly to say that we believe in God and yet not humble ourselves in active obedience to his word and worship of him.

Adherence to religious customs and rituals abound all over the globe. During a recent conversation with a friend who is a missionary in Africa, she mentioned that some of the children they have fostered exhibited physical evidence of witchcraft on their bodies, including rows of scars across their chests or ropes tied around their waists, ankles, and wrists by a witch doctor. Two of the babies they cared for were addicted to alcohol and drugs in addition to presenting with visible signs of witchcraft. She told me, "It felt like we went to the edge of hell to fight for their souls."

I have traveled to Haiti where I met people who practice Voodoo. I have visited the Pyramid of the Sun in Mexico where children were once sacrificed and a large Buddhist temple in Shanghai where many ritualistic and superstitious

---

[2] Stephen Charnock, *The Existence and Attributes of God* (Reformed Retrieval), 56.

Introduction

customs take place. I have spent time in France, South Africa, Puerto Rico, and Canada. I have even journeyed through Israel and visited the places where Jesus walked. From what I have seen, religion abounds in every culture because people are spiritual by nature. No government, no matter how totalitarian, has ever or will ever eradicate the innate desire to worship from their citizens. It's impossible.

As Christians, we understand that the biblical record establishes Jesus as the way, the truth, and the life, and that no one is capable of redemption apart from his finished work on the cross of Calvary (see John 14:6; Acts 4:12). Those who reject Jesus as the only way to heaven still practice some form of religion simply because human hearts will always worship something or someone. Everyone worships. Even the staunchest of atheists are worshippers.

The Bible teaches that there is a spiritual battle underway for the hearts of humankind. You may feel comfortable in your nice house and car, but there is a spiritual war taking place all around us. Rather than sitting on the sidelines or hiding from culture, we are called to lovingly engage the world with the gospel.

By God's grace, we are not deployed into this spiritual combat zone alone or ill-equipped. Our Heavenly Father has designed strategies for us to employ during the battle. Satan and his forces are real, and they are powerful, but God's strength far surpasses the capabilities of his enemies.

Before we go any further, I want to reiterate that I fully believe that Satan and his forces are real. Jesus and the writers of Scripture agree with this assessment and make it clear that he is no one to be trifled with. Satan is not a myth or a fairytale created to scare children into obeying their parents. The devil does not wear a red suit with horns, and he is not on par with the Easter Bunny or Santa Claus. He is the enemy of God who is doing all he can to undermine God's redemptive plan for the world. Perhaps Satan's greatest plot is to convince the world that he doesn't exist. If he can trick people into denying his existence, he is well on his way to possessing a devastating amount of influence over the human race.

These are trying times, and the church of Jesus Christ is increasingly in the crosshairs of those who would prefer to eliminate Christianity from the public square and cultural landscape. As faithful followers of Christ, we must be purposeful and intentional in our preparation to engage in the spiritual battle raging all around us. Antagonism toward Christianity is nothing new. No Christian, no matter what time period in which they lived, has ever experienced a culture free of opposition; therefore, as New Testament believers, we shouldn't be surprised when we experience some level of hostility from the world.

When flaming arrows fly, will you be prepared to stand faithfully for Christ?

In the pages to follow, we will study a comprehensive battle plan to assist you in the battle against evil. We will begin our journey studying the dangers of spiritual exhaustion. Then we will consider seven biblical strategies that will provide the proper mindset and weapons necessary to resist the devil and his minions.

Introduction

Before we get started, allow me to share two words of caution. First, if you're looking for seven easy answers to your complicated spiritual struggles, you're going to be sorely disappointed because that book does not exist. This is not an easy-fix self-help book. If you're hoping to find seven proven steps to eliminating the pesky demons in your life, I'm really going to let you down. The Christian life is a battle for righteousness. To fight this battle, we need Scripture, not incantations. It would be disingenuous of me to promise easy answers. So I'm not. What I can promise is that God is faithful, he is all-powerful, his word is sufficient, and he will never leave or forsake you.

Second, while I use the imagery of warfare as implemented in the Bible, I am not, in any way, shape, or form, promoting or condoning acts of physical violence against those with whom we have disagreement or against those who adamantly reject Jesus or the sufficiency of Scripture. As Christians, we do not use violence to preach the gospel; we use love, compassion, and truth. The church's battle cry isn't hate or violence; it's acts of sacrificial love and service. The sword that the church is called to wield isn't one that cuts and kills; it's one that brings healing to the wounded soul and provides eternal life to those who accept the gospel.

In my years of ministry, while I have witnessed a lot of sin, I have also seen people rescued from addiction, bitterness, anger, depression, you name it. I have witnessed broken marriages mended through the power of the gospel, and I have seen lives radically changed. God is still restoring broken relationships, encouraging the brokenhearted, giving joy to the downcast, hope to the hopeless, comfort to the sorrowful, strength to the weak, healing to the sick, restoration to the fallen, illumination to the spiritually blind, and forgiveness to the sinner. The world is a dark place. But in the midst of it all, Jesus shines brighter than the darkness surrounding us.

If you're interested in maturing in your walk with Jesus Christ, don't delay any longer. Life is too short to squander it standing on the sidelines with a clipboard filled with a list of excuses and criticisms. If you long to be a faithful follower of Christ, it's time to get on the field and engage in the spiritual battle. You're going to get cut, bloodied, and bruised. But God's grace and power is sufficient for you.

Christians are called to love God and our neighbors, defend the gospel, live obediently, and stand for righteousness. We stand for Christ on a spiritual battlefield filled with land mines, tanks, missiles, snipers, spies, hackers, and flaming arrows. In this dirty war where deception, temptation, and transgression saturates every crevice of society, we must protect ourselves against Satan's tactics. To do so, we must be immersed in God's word. Flaming arrows will fly. We need to be spiritually ready.

The Problem of Spiritual Exhaustion

The LORD is the everlasting God, the Creator of the ends of the earth. He does not faint or grow weary; his understanding is unsearchable. He gives power to the faint, and to him who has no might he increases strength. Even youths shall faint and be weary, and young men shall fall exhausted; but they who wait for the LORD shall renew their strength; they shall mount up with wings like eagles; they shall run and not be weary; they shall walk and not faint.

Isaiah 40:28–31

As the lead pastor of a local church responsible for a precious flock of God's sheep, I work hard at keeping current with what is taking place in American culture. I read articles and books, listen to podcasts, and stay up on current events. I believe it's my job to stay culturally aware so I can watch for potential issues that could creep into our church. While I don't preach sermons on cultural issues every Sunday,

I do address societal concerns when necessary. I would rather be known as a pastor who consistently preaches Scripture than a political activist or someone who uses sermons to create fear. Because I preach through books of the Bible, I find that I regularly cover appropriate texts that speak to the cultural issues at hand. The Bible contains timeless truth; therefore, it is always timely.

In the spring of 2022, I detected a level of concern, and what I pray was righteous anger, brewing in my soul over the rapidly deteriorating spiritual condition in the United States and in many other parts of the world. With each passing day, we seem to be taking long strides toward a level of cultural apostasy that can't be ignored by the church any longer. Political leaders and cultural influencers in our nation are chipping away historic Christianity's influence in the world, resulting in a rapidly growing moral crisis. I'm no alarmist. But apart from a miraculous awakening, there will be horrific consequences for decades to come if we do not make a course correction.

The unprecedented issues of our day are not merely matters of personal preference—such as Coke versus Pepsi—but of right and wrong. It's a spiritual battle between God's truth and Satan's lies. Our cultural clash is not simply a political dispute between Republicans and Democrats. At the heart of these difficult issues rests a spiritual conflict between the forces of good and evil.

Since the fall of humanity, people have always tried to do that which is right in their own eyes. The period of the Judges, recorded in the Old Testament, serves as a perfect example of what happens when we refuse to follow God's commandments and choose personal autonomy over obedience. As sinners, we prefer setting our own boundaries, creating our own definitions of right and wrong, and blazing our own trails. In Ecclesiastes, Solomon promises that there is nothing new under the sun and that the autonomous mindset is not a recent development. Since the fall, people have always been self-centered, egotistical, self-adulating, and drawn toward autonomy. We must understand, however, that the idea of self-sovereignty is misguided and spiritually dangerous.

As our Creator, God has every right to define what is acceptable behavior and what is not. Over the last few years, the insatiable desire for absolute autonomy has created an environment in which even professing Christians are trying to live independently from God. Increasingly, people don't like being told how to live. This explains why the idea of absolute truth is increasingly rejected. Unfortunately, those who promote the idea of unchanging truth are increasingly viewed with disdain in much of the world. This shift shouldn't create fear in our hearts; it should arrest the attention of every child of God and lead us to the place where we are consistently submitting our lives to Scripture while drawing closer to our Heavenly Father.

Part of my morning routine is catching up on world events. Typically, I briefly check the news and listen to a couple of podcasts. Throughout 2022, there was a long list of pressing issues to monitor. The news was dominated by emotional debates over abortion, gun control, mass shootings, the war in Ukraine, COVID-19, the rising national debt, plenty of political posturing, and a host of LGBTQ+ issues. And with staunch opposition to biblical teaching mounting, there is little doubt that we will soon face a robust collision between secularism and religious liberty. Just writing that list left me feeling spiritually taxed.

Somewhere along the line, the life of an unborn child was deemed irrelevant. Mass shootings became so commonplace, we barely notice them anymore. Aggressors like Putin decided war could be waged without any justifiable reason. Diseases like COVID-19 rattled the world, sparking international lockdowns and economic turmoil. Governmental irresponsibility drove the national debt so high people can't even fathom exactly how much thirty-one trillion dollars actually is, leaving American citizens unable to process the seriousness of our country's indebtedness. God's definition of marriage has fallen under heavy attack. Public schools are discussing sexuality and gender transitions in elementary classrooms. Anyone who challenges the presentation of this material is shamed and labeled all sorts of hateful words.

Not only is all of this spiritually and mentally exhausting, it's preposterous. God's word and commandments have been thrown to the wind because, after all, people are convinced they know better than God and demand to live on their own terms.

On the surface, some of the arguments put forth by today's scholars and activists sound reasonable. As always, there is a nugget of truth in many of the ideas culture promotes. For instance, God's love and loving our neighbors as ourselves is often invoked as a means of defending the moral revolution taking place. From a biblical point of view, we must acknowledge that of course God is loving, and obviously we're commanded to love our neighbors as ourselves. After all, Jesus himself said in Mark 12:30–31, "You shall love the Lord your God with all your heart and with all your soul and with all your mind and with all your strength. The second is this: You shall love your neighbor as yourself. There is no other commandment greater than these." These two commandments are the foundational truths of Christianity, and they teach a valuable principle: we cannot love our neighbors sacrificially until we love God supremely. In addition to understanding these two indispensable commandments, we must also consider the theological doctrine of God's unity.

God's Unity

There is no debating that Christians are commanded to love God and others. Nevertheless, we must keep in mind a theological principle known as the unity or simplicity of God. The unity of God rightly explains that God cannot be divided into parts. While we see God's various attributes highlighted throughout Scripture, this does not suggest that one of God's attributes supersedes another. Theologian Wayne Grudem explains the unity of God this way: "When Scripture speaks about God's attributes it never singles out one attribute of God as more important than all the rest.

There is an assumption that every attribute is completely true of God and is true of all of God's character."[3] The point is simple: God is incapable of setting aside one of his attributes to fit the distorted agendas of mankind. We may try to redraw God's boundaries by overlooking or minimizing certain attributes, but this is an intellectually futile exercise. It's impossible to divide God into parts and rearrange his attributes in the order we like best.

Few Christians think of themselves as theologians, but every believer is a theologian to some degree. The majority of believers will never darken the door of a seminary, but all people, even the nonreligious, have a theological grid through which they view the world. Practically speaking, all of us are theologians because we all have a view of God. As we think about Scripture's description of God, it's essential that we keep his unity at the forefront of our minds.

Here's why the unity or simplicity of God is so important: when people highlight God's love so they can promote ideologies that contradict the rest of his character, they are stepping out on extremely thin ice. God is perfectly loving. That's true. He never stops being love, and he never stops loving. God is also perfectly holy. He never stops being holy. God is also perfectly just and is incapable of being unjust.

God loves the world; that's why he sent his Son to die on the cross for our sins. Because of the Father's love for us, Jesus was ruthlessly crucified so that we can enjoy eternal life

---

[3] Wayne Grudem, *Systematic Theology* (Grand Rapids, MI: Zondervan Publishing, 1994), 178.

in God's presence. The Lamb of God took upon himself the brutality and harsh punishment that we deserve. We were not the ones nailed to a cross. Out of love, the Father sent his Son to satisfy his holy wrath against sin. Jesus was crucified because of our rebellion against God. As John wrote in his gospel, "For God so loved the world, that he gave his only Son, that whoever believes in him should not perish but have eternal life" (John 3:16). That, my friend, is love.

Here is where our understanding of God often goes off the rails. God's love for humanity does not afford us the right to live however we choose, especially when it means blatantly disregarding Scripture's clear commandments. Because God is equally holy and just, he will hold people accountable for their sins and judge them accordingly. God is indivisible; therefore, we cannot concentrate on God's love and mercy to the neglect of his perfect holiness and justice. Using God's love as an excuse to violate Scripture is as foolish as a person who sets himself on fire believing his skin will never be burned. All Christians should rest in God's love, but we cannot ignore his holiness and justness in the process.

Sin is so opposite of God's nature that even the tiniest drop of iniquity would taint his holiness, making him no longer God. All forms of wickedness are incompatible with his character. In his word, God has revealed to us how we are to live. Because of his perfect holiness and justice, he will hold us accountable for every decision we make. Where God's word is clear, it's imperative that we live accordingly.

The Danger of Unrestrained Feelings and the Misuse of Scripture

Rather than being angry over the moral condition of culture, Christians should be consumed with concern and compassion for the world. All people, even those with whom we disagree, are created in the image of almighty God and deserve to be treated with kindness, dignity, and respect. Seeing so many precious souls blinded by the morally insane cultural narrative should drive a stake of Christlike love and empathy through our hearts. Rather than standing in condemnation of the world, we are to take the truth of the gospel to our culture in love.

While we need not feel despondent, a realistic assessment of the world is in order. The mounting threat to Christians and churches posed by cultural degradation is the reason to be prepared to stand for biblical truth. Already Christians are falling prey to the rapidly secularizing culture. As Albert Mohler, the president of The Southern Baptist Theological Seminary notes, "The secular temptation confuses beliefs with emotions, suggesting that all that matters is feelings and fulfillment. As the society has become more secular, even faithful church members unwittingly adopt strange and unbiblical ways of thinking and believing."[4] Whenever we allow our feelings about a particular subject to take over our decision-making process, we are prone to theological error and choosing disobedience to God over obedience. Feelings

---

4 Albert Mohler, *The Gathering Storm* (Nashville, TN: Thomas Nelson Publishing, 2020), 21.

are real and powerful, but they do not always direct us to what is true. Whenever we are controlled by unrestrained feelings, we are tempted to twist Scripture to fit the cultural narrative or to justify our own sinful actions.

For example, when it comes to the issue of sexual purity, too many Christians disregard God's commandments concerning sex and marriage because their feelings and emotions have slipped into the driver's seat. Infatuation, and the powerful feelings that come along with it, is behind the vast majority of adulterous relationships. I would suggest that the statistics on sexual sins among Christians closely mirror that of the world because we are more focused on how people make us feel than on God's commandments to be sexually pure before and after marriage.

Through the years, I have had many Christians try to explain to me why their adultery, or *fling* as they typically prefer, was acceptable to God because the new person produced much stronger feelings, emotions, and desires than their spouse. On several occasions, I have been shown emotionally charged texts and emails that were exchanged in the early stages of an inappropriate relationship that fed the flames of lust and eventually led to full-fledged adultery. Sometimes these marriages ended in divorce. Emotions and feelings are God-given, but when they become the basis for moral decisions, we are proving that we are more interested in serving ourselves than sacrificially loving others. We can claim to be Christians all we want, but when we foster unrestrained emotions and twist Scripture, or outright ignore it, to justify our sinful choices, we are in big trouble.

Living in an increasingly immoral culture can be spiritually exhausting, and I'm afraid too many Christians have become spiritually anemic or indifferent to what is taking place. Worn down by the onslaught of morally corrupt propaganda, many Christians are in danger of caving to the firestorm of cultural pressure. Feeling ostracized by those who vehemently oppose the gospel, many Christians are turning a blind eye to the moral decline of our day. Even more troubling, some believers are twisting or ignoring Scripture to justify their acceptance of what is taking place. Unrestrained feelings are never an excuse for misusing Scripture to alleviate intimidation or derision. In the Sermon on the Mount, Jesus teaches, "Blessed are you when others revile you and persecute you and utter all kinds of evil against you falsely on my account" (Matthew 5:11). Being ridiculed and threatened is never enjoyable; it can leave us feeling afraid or rejected. Knowing that Jesus promises his blessing upon those who face such persecution should drive us to be faithful to him, even when our feelings and emotions beg us to make an easier and less costly decision.

Buying into the secular worldview dominating the public debate will undoubtedly bring immediate relief from the degrading attacks of the moral activists attempting to erase God's commandments from society. But Christians must beware. The peace enjoyed by embracing the anti-God agenda will be shallow and short-lived. Most importantly, accepting the culture's moral agenda places us at odds with our Creator.

Flaming arrows are flying. Are you up for the fight?

The Will to Fight

We all know the squeaky wheel gets the grease. The principle is simple: those who complain or cause the most problems are more likely to receive attention than the ones who quietly do what is expected without creating drama. Like loudmouthed students who force their opinions on a classroom, the culture is stiff-arming Christians and trying to bend the church to its will.

Over time, raucous people wear down their opponents and win an argument because they break down the will of their adversary one forceful and intimidating word at a time. Weary of the conversation, many throw up their hands in frustration and cave to the demands of the domineering individual. It's hard to stay faithful when we're constantly accused of being the problem and browbeaten to accept the culture's ungodly ideology. I stand for the biblical definition of marriage, yet I do not harbor hatred for anyone who denies that marriage is only between one man and one woman. But according to the vocal influencers of our time, defending God's definition of marriage automatically makes me hateful and close-minded. Being called a hater is wearisome, but regrettably it has become the norm for those living according to scriptural principles. We may grow tired of being wrongfully labeled, but we must never compromise God's truth on the altar of personal comfort.

Oftentimes military conflicts, like the one in Ukraine, become wars of attrition. One by one, soldiers are picked off. Cities are laid to waste. Food and water supplies are disrupted. A blitzkrieg is slowed to a methodical campaign in which one army is forced to surrender. Dwindling resources, a lack of able-bodied soldiers, and a loss of the will to fight leave an army hopeless. War is wearisome. Knowing soldiers can only fight for so long, armies try to force their adversary into submission one relentless day at a time.

War of attrition is equally true in spiritual warfare. Inside our hearts, we may feel like we are breaking into tiny pieces. Sometimes, the daily grind of spiritual warfare crushes our will to fight. When we are too spiritually exhausted to stand against evil, we feel guilty. Scores of vocal politicians and influencers want Christians to believe that Christianity is the problem. According to some, if Christians would surrender the fight and allow people to live without the confines of God's moral law, all the wrongs in our world would be corrected. Meliorism could become reality. It's the fictitious utopian world John Lennon sang about in the song "Imagine." Without religion, the world would be allowed to come together and be one. According to the cultural elites, it's committed followers of God's word who are standing in the way of moral progress and keeping the world from experiencing lasting peace and happiness.

All of the cultural reveries about global tranquility are nice sentiments, but as we'll see in Strategy One, the utopian world John Lennon envisioned will never happen apart from the Lord Jesus Christ's return. Fantasies about harmony between good and evil are dangerous and futile. As the great preacher Charles Spurgeon warned, "Peace between good and evil is an impossibility; the very presence of it would, in fact, be the triumph of the powers of darkness."[5] Because evil and holiness are categorically incompatible, there will never be a truce between Satan and Jesus Christ. In the midst of this ferociously fought spiritual battle, Christians are called to faithfully obey God—no matter what the culture demands or how loudly they scream their venomous intimidation. The world is a very different place than those spearheading the cultural revolution understand it to be. As Christians, we must keep God's word as the lamp unto our feet and continue following the path of obedience. No matter the cost.

Encouragement from Isaiah 40:28-31

Perhaps you're feeling spiritually frazzled, as if you're hanging by a thread. Times of spiritual exhaustion can leave you discouraged and hopeless. When the world is pressing against us, it's easy to feel abandoned by God. One of the biblical passages I find particularly encouraging is Isaiah 40:28-31. I've included the verses at the beginning of the chapter. I pray the following observations are an encouragement to you.

First, there is great reassurance in knowing that the Lord is the everlasting God who never grows faint or weary. We will discuss resting in God's strength in Strategy Two, but for now I encourage you to dwell on the comforting truth that the eternal one who created you possesses inexhaustible strength. God's power is endless, and it's readily available

---
5 Charles Spurgeon, *Morning and Evening* (Peabody, MA: 1991), 671.

to those who trust in him. As Puritan theologian Stephen Charnock writes, "The power of God is that ability and strength, whereby he can bring to pass whatsoever he please; whatsoever his infinite wisdom can direct, and whatsoever the infinite purity of his will can resolve."[6] While we all have lingering questions concerning evil's continued existence in the world, the Bible clearly teaches that the power, aptitude, and strength of almighty God far surpass Satan and his forces as they oppose God's redemptive plan. There is great hope and confidence found in knowing that God is never too weak to act on our behalf.

Second, because God's understanding is unsearchable, he is never unaware of what is taking place in this world or in our lives. In Isaiah 40:27, Isaiah asks, "Why do you say, O Jacob, and speak, O Israel, 'My way is hidden from the Lord, and my right is disregarded by my God'?" In light of God's unwavering power and infinite knowledge, we should never believe he has forgotten us or that he is unaware of our difficulties. Throughout Scripture, God demonstrated his ability to deliver his people in their time of need. God is eternally incomparable and indescribable (see Isaiah 40:25–26); therefore, there are no grounds on which his power and authority should be questioned or doubted.

Our Heavenly Father knows the name of every star in the sky, and he knows every one of your fears and doubts. His knowledge and wisdom far surpass even the most intellectually gifted genius this world has to offer. Humans have

---

6 Charnock, 417.

nothing to teach God; we have no wisdom to offer and no information he does not already possess. God is never confused or forgetful. He alone knows all of the answers. Likewise, our God knows our circumstances, and he will never forsake those he has graciously adopted.

Third, because God is omnipotent, he is powerful enough to provide strength to the faint and weak. Because we are all frail flesh and blood, we do not possess infinite strength. Isaiah reminds us that even the young, known for their vibrancy, eventually grow weary and exhaust all their energy. While people in their youth are typically the strongest and most energetic citizens in society, even they need rest at some point. Living in a culture that celebrates youthfulness, self-sufficiency, and self-reliance makes it difficult for most people to admit weakness, especially when it comes to sin and temptation.

I struggle with being an overachiever and find taking time off to rest very challenging. There are also times when I become mildly self-righteous when it comes to how few hours I sleep. Admitting that I'm tired or that I need a nap, even when I'm sick or emotionally drained, is unacceptable in my sinfully self-sufficient mind. Even when I can hardly think straight or write a coherent sentence, I try to power through and get more done. Typically, my prideful refusal to admit that my brainpower and physical strength have been depleted only makes matters worse. Sin regularly blinds us to many of our destructive choices, and for me that sometimes comes in the form of refusing to admit my need for rest.

We typically avoid acknowledging any sign of vulnerability, even simply admitting an honest mistake, so we don't appear fragile. This is particularly true when it comes to confessing sin. Admitting physical weakness is hard enough, but divulging sin is next-level difficult. But remember, because we are finite and imperfect, there's no shame in admitting weakness, exhaustion, or even sinful choices. It takes courage to admit when you're physically or spiritually exhausted. Admirable people take responsibility when they're wrong. Only the brave admit their sin and ask for forgiveness. The honorable are honest about the temptations that persistently test their hearts. Seeking help from a trusted Christian friend or pastor when you're feeling under conviction, broken, downcast, shunned, angry, hurt, guilty, tempted, or alone is a sign of spiritual maturity, not weakness. In fact, acknowledging your spiritual and/or physical depletion allows God to strengthen you and provides the body of Christ with the opportunity to offer support and encouragement. As David wrote in Psalm 62:8, "Trust in him at all times, O people; pour out your heart before him; God is a refuge for us."

When faced with enemies on every side, David cried out to the Lord, "For you equipped me with strength for the battle" (Psalm 18:39). With God's help, David prevailed over his enemies and became the greatest king in Israel's history. I love Psalm 116:7, which says, "Return, O my soul, to your rest; for the Lord has dealt bountifully with you." Spiritual exhaustion only clouds our minds and leaves us feeling anxious, confused, and discouraged. Acknowledging your vulnerability and weakness is the first step in experiencing the rejuvenating power of God's glorious strength.

God will strengthen us for the spiritual battles we all face, but the church plays an important role as well. As New Testament believers, we are commanded to "Bear one another's burdens, and so fulfill the law of Christ" (Galatians 6:2). The body of Christ is expected to support and encourage one another when a member is weighed down by the overwhelming, soul-crushing burdens of life. It's important to note, however, the church cannot biblically assist a member when no one is aware of the problem. Until you swallow your pride and seek help from someone who loves you and cares about you, you will live in fear, isolation, shame, and despair. Your struggle is not unique to you. I promise. Humbly admit your weakness and seek out the help you desperately need to find the necessary strength to fight your personal spiritual battle.

During my years in ministry, I have been made privy to some of the darkest secrets and struggles of countless people. At the end of many of these difficult conversations, individuals have begged me not to think differently of them because of the information they shared. Truth is, I *did* see all of these individuals differently afterward: my level of respect for each and every one of these dear Christians only grew stronger. It takes a lot of strength, courage, and honor to admit weaknesses, temptations, struggles, and sins. You don't have to stand alone in this battle. To be clear, I don't have all of the answers to people's problems. No person possesses that kind of wisdom, insight, or ability. But Jesus does.

In God's wisdom, he has called his church to be his hands, feet, eyes, ears, and mouth to assist one another as we bear the heavy burdens that weigh us down. It's never easy addressing spiritually devastating and demoralizing issues. The process is always messy. But by God's grace, the strength you require to face your spiritual battle is available through the power of God's word and the Holy Spirit.

Finally, this passage reminds us that those who long to have their strength renewed must patiently wait for the Lord. Because the Old Testament was originally written in Hebrew, it's important to note that *wait* is translated from the Hebrew word *qavah*. This Hebrew word means "to look for eagerly, to hope, or to expect." While waiting on God requires patience and faith, we can look eagerly to the Lord and trust that he will provide the necessary strength required during times of spiritual depletion and exhaustion. Waiting on the Lord is not a passive action. It's unacceptable for a believer to seek God's intervention then simply sit idly by, expecting God to remedy the problem. Christians are called to actively stand against the evil permeating the world while seeking the Lord's direction and strength in the battle.

Isaiah includes a beautiful picture of the strength God provides to his people. The prophet says that those who the Lord strengthens "shall mount up with wings like eagles." *Mount up* is translated from the Hebrew word *awlaw*, meaning "to go up, to ascend, to climb." The sense of the word is to go up and over—like an eagle flying over a mountain. Don't miss the magnitude of this picture. When we are strengthened by the Lord, we have the ability to run, not crawl, and to never grow weary. Those who wait on the Lord will soar like eagles and find the indispensable strength to face the forces of evil.

While waiting on the Lord, we are to continue obeying our Heavenly Father and looking to him to provide as he deems best. Prolific Christian author Warren Wiersbe observes, "The greatest heroes of faith are not always those who seem to be soaring; often it is they who are patiently plodding. As we wait on the Lord, he enables us not only to fly higher and run faster, but also to walk longer."[7] Faithfully walking with Christ requires us to persevere, one patiently waiting step at a time.

A Potential Source of Spiritual Exhaustion

Every pastor I know has soapbox issues they like to harp on; I definitely have a couple of my own, and I would like to address my biggest one with you. One of the potential sources that may be feeding your spiritual exhaustion is the media you're consuming. Whether it's television, news, podcasts, YouTube, or social media, a constant intake of media can quickly have a negative impact on your spiritual condition. In older adults, it's typically through a constant diet of their favorite news channel. Whether it's CNN, MSNBC, or Fox News, filling your mind with sensationalized news coverage is not spiritually healthy. In younger

---

[7] Warren Wiersbe, *Be Comforted* (Colorado Springs, CO: David C Cook, 1992), 133.

individuals, these influences generally come through social media sources. While older people prefer Facebook, and often spend substantially too much time there, younger individuals generally prefer apps like Instagram, Snapchat, or TikTok. Of course, YouTube holds tremendous sway over the younger generations as well. While I'm not ignoring the positives that come with technology and social media—they certainly exist—I'm gravely concerned over the impact media has over our culture.

One of the significant challenges in our day is the proliferation of information via podcasts, the internet, television, and social media. The bombardment of content can be a demoralizing distraction from those activities that would be spiritually profitable. Some of the information we consume is true, and we need that, but most of it is opinion and baseless speculation. That's why I personally spend very little time listening to talking heads proclaiming hours of opinion and speculation as if they were fact. Subjecting ourselves to hypothetical and dramatized opinions on a regular basis creates an unhealthy anxiousness and negativity that can rot our souls. There's no denying the world is in a tangled web of adversity. We have big problems to address, both here in the United States and around the world. I'm not advocating burying our heads in the sand and ignoring what is taking place, but I am pleading with you to spend less time worrying and obsessing about that which you cannot change. Rather than stewing over the news and social media, invest time serving others and equipping yourself for the spiritual battle we're fighting.

We never want to ignore or deny the facts of current events, but we don't need to invest time fretting over the feelings and conjectures of speculative people. Spending hours consuming news, even from conservative outlets, is not spiritually healthy. Rather than feasting on a constant diet of breaking news, consume God-honoring content that will draw you closer to the Lord. If you're wasting valuable time on media, cut back. Way back, if necessary. You won't be missing anything. When something truly newsworthy happens, I promise you'll find out soon enough.

The voices of this world are demanding the right to tell you how to think about the world and morality. Followers of Christ must understand that the vast majority of the cultural influencers are not speaking from a distinctly biblical worldview. Sprinkling in a Bible verse on occasion doesn't make the commentator doctrinally sound. Be extremely careful with the media you consume.

We are all influenced by those around us, and this undoubtedly includes those with whom we interact online. In our super-connected world, we are often shaped by people we have never even met. Online influencers can greatly affect how we see the world and how we interact with friends and family. That's why we must carefully analyze the voices speaking into our hearts and minds. There are innumerable possibilities as to the opinions influencing your thought patterns. Take time to analyze your friendships. Evaluate the relationships you have online and in person. The people we surround ourselves with will have tremendous influence on how we think about the world and how we interact with it.

We cannot control every individual who enters our lives, but we can regulate who gains intimate access to our hearts and minds. Through the years, I have known scores of toxic people. By God's grace, I have learned to protect myself against the negative influence of noxious individuals. Sometimes this meant distancing myself from those who were filled with negativity and malice. If you're feeling spiritually exhausted, it is possible there are poisonous people speaking into your life through interpersonal friendships or via social media. If that's the case, prayerfully and wisely address these negative relationships before these individuals create more discouragement in your life.

Social media has value, but there are also great dangers. Consuming too much social media can place you at risk for spiritual exhaustion. Author Tony Reinke rightly notes, "Digital technology is most useful to us when we limit its reach into our lives."[8] If social media is draining your soul of hope, love, and joy, make some substantial changes to your media habits. Here are some examples of how you might reduce your media intake: (1) Refrain from looking at your phone first thing in the morning. Read your Bible, pray, and go outside for a few minutes before you even touch your phone. If you use the alarm on your phone, buy an old-fashioned alarm clock for your bedroom so you don't have to touch your phone right away. (2) Set a time limit to keep yourself from scrolling for hours on end. I did this with

---

8 Tony Reinke, *12 Ways Your Phone Is Changing You* (Wheaton, IL: Crossway, 2017), 199.

Amazon a few years ago when I realized how much time I was wasting searching for new books. I would give myself five minutes to browse the new releases, then close the website. (3) Put accountability software on your computer that has the ability to limit your time online and the websites that you visit; we used these with our children. (4) Delete apps if you have to. With our children, we set their phones to where they needed permission to add an app. (5) Give up your smartphone and go back to a flip phone. (6) Eliminate technology you can't control. I know men who no longer own personal computers because of their struggle with pornography.

These suggestions may seem silly, but in Matthew 5:29–30, Jesus implemented hyperbolic language to describe the radical amputation that may be necessary in order to keep ourselves from sin. Your spiritual well-being is far more important than keeping up to date with what's happening on social media or on the news or on your favorite website. It's far more advantageous to be spiritually healthy than culturally informed.

Takeaways

Before we leave this chapter, I want to encourage you to consider the following seven takeaways. I believe these are important issues that we must evaluate in order to defend ourselves against spiritual exhaustion.

1. Assess your emotions and make sure that your decisions are not being made by unrestrained

feelings. When our emotions and feelings become the driving force in our lives, we are in danger of making horrible, ungodly, life-altering decisions that will produce destructive consequences.

2. Assess your view of Scripture, which contain God's eternally true commandments. Do not fall into the trap of allowing your view of Scripture to be determined by your feelings or by the cultural pressures of the day.

3. Assess your level of resolve to fight in the spiritual warfare. Throughout the rest of this book, we will study strategies to stay faithful to the Lord in the midst of this battle. But for now, take time to analyze your willingness to stand for Christ in this increasingly secularized culture.

4. Assess your reliance on the Lord for strength. We all grow weary in this fight, but God has promised to provide strength to those who trust in him. Wait upon the Lord, and he will renew your strength.

5. Assess your willingness to humbly admit your weaknesses, vulnerabilities, struggles, failures, and sins. The first step in receiving God's strength is admitting that you need it. Acknowledging your need for help is also the first step in receiving help and support from the body of Christ.

6. Assess your social media consumption. If you are addicted to social media and other forms of media, resolve right now to take whatever steps necessary to

break the hold media has over your life. Be specific in your goals and find someone to help keep you accountable.
7. Assess your friendships, both online and in person. Determine those who are toxic and drawing you away from the Lord. If there are people robbing you of your spiritual joy and peace, take the appropriate steps to remedy the situation. Before making any rash decisions, seek counsel from a spiritually mature friend, pastor, or Christian counselor.

With a better understanding of what's at stake, we will now turn our attention to seven strategies that will equip you to spiritually flourish even in a culture that rejects the gospel. Whether you're feeling spiritually susceptible at the moment or not, the following chapters will strengthen your relationship with the Lord and prepare you to face the challenges of our day. Identifying the problem lays the groundwork for our battle plan. Now, we need to develop a specific strategy to stand strong in the battle. Knowing there will be flaming arrows coming our way, we must begin our preparation by properly understanding the nature of humanity and the world.

Key Point: Spiritual exhaustion is a dangerous condition that can develop because of the culture war taking place, often leaving Christians feeling defeated, isolated, and numb.

For Further Consideration

1. Which of the cultural issues facing the world are you most anxious over? Why do these particular issues trouble you?
2. How have your feelings, emotions, and the cultural pressures of this age affected your view of Scripture, the world, and people?
3. Have you adopted any strange or unbiblical ways of thinking and believing? If so, what are they? Find Scriptures that speak to these issues and use them to correct your perspective.
4. What encouragement can you glean from Isaiah 40:28–31?
5. Take careful inventory of your media habits and implement necessary changes and limits.

Biblical Strategies for the Spiritual Battle

Strategy One
Understand the Nature of Humanity and the World

That you may be blameless and innocent, children of God without blemish in the midst of a crooked and twisted generation, among whom you shine as lights in the world.

Philippians 2:15

On a typical Friday in the fall of 2022, I was at home writing a sermon. It was a pleasant day in southeastern North Carolina. The cooler temperatures provided the opportunity to open our windows after months of oppressive heat and humidity. In the quietness of the midday, I was consumed with a biblical text when I was startled by what sounded like a booming clap of thunder. There were a few clouds dotting the sky, but nothing that would indicate we were in store for a major thunderstorm.

Minutes after the bang rattled our windows, the sound of blaring sirens pierced the stillness of the neighborhood. Through our glass sliding door, I saw plumes of black smoke billowing into the crystal-blue sky. Hearing the sirens closing in, I did what every good—okay, *nosey*—neighbor does: I hopped in my car and drove down the street behind our house to see what happened.

Sitting in one of the driveways, I saw a work van that looked like it had been struck by a falling bomb. A sea of orange and red flames aggressively melted the metal like a Popsicle on a hot summer day. I never heard exactly why the vehicle exploded, but explode it did.

As I drove away from the scene, I turned my thoughts to those living in Ukraine being regularly bombed by the Russian military. What happened in my neighborhood was an accident, but in many parts of the world, warfare is a common experience that Americans are not accustomed to. Centuries of human history have proved that warfare is a destructive and prevalent part of the human experience. History books are filled with accounts of brutal conflicts ranging from localized disputes to world wars. While some wrongly believe war can be eradicated, the horrific events taking place in Eastern Europe are painful reminders to the contrary.

Even the pages of God's word are stained with the blood of those who were killed during times of military conflict. In Matthew 24:6, Jesus promised there would be wars and rumors of wars throughout this age. We shouldn't be surprised when swirling threats of war or military conflict happen.

The gruesome images of maggot-infested corpses, mass graves, orphaned children, bombed apartment complexes, rocket shells strewn all over fields and city streets, and traumatized citizens make most of us cringe in revulsion. It's difficult to imagine an activity that displays the depravity of humankind more vividly and grotesquely than the gory act of war. Given the depths of our depravity, Jesus warned that wars and rumors of wars are simply to be expected.

Daily Warfare

Like the vast majority of people, I have never been on a physical battlefield. By God's grace, I have never been shot at by an enemy nor have I experienced the ghastly sights, sounds, and smells of warfare. As someone who grew up during the Cold War, the threat of a nuclear attack loomed heavy in my soul. I lived with the haunting images of people's faces melting off and entire cities being laid to waste by a nuclear weapon. So the threat and rumors of wars, I understand. But when it comes to actual battlefield experience, I have none.

And yet, I fight in a spiritual war every day. Although it's not a physical battle fought with guns, tanks, airplanes, ships, and nuclear weapons, it's a difficult, bloody, and exhausting fight against the agents of evil. This war isn't unique to me. It's the same conflict against evil that has been raging since the fall of humanity. Whether you acknowledge it or not, you're in the crossfire. This fight is for our hearts and for the hearts of our children and grandchildren.

There are days when I, probably like you, feel spiritually and emotionally exhausted from the fight. Don't misunderstand; I'm not referring to the malaise most Americans experience because of the frantic chase-our-tails-in-circles-until-we-drop lifestyle. No, the exhaustion I'm referencing is something far deeper and substantially more dangerous. Defending God's truth is hard work. That's why I fear too many Christians are on the verge of giving up the fight.

Minutes before one of my writing sessions, I perused the news. Allow me to share the first four headlines I saw. They startled me. Perhaps they will startle you as well. They read: "Man shoots ex-boss to death over typo on paycheck"; "Ex-principal guilty of sexually abusing 21 students"; "Girl, 16, found shot to death was missing for 2 months"; and "Mom charged in death of 5-year-old found in suitcase." Not the most encouraging way to start a writing session, but these headlines serve as a snapshot of what's taking place in our world.

If you're feeling discouraged, afraid, overwhelmed, or defeated right now, please don't throw your hands up in despair and quit. There are at least two reasons to stay faithful in the fight against evil. One, you are not alone. All over the globe, there are scores of faithful Christians facing the same spiritual attacks. And two, there is hope in the Lord Jesus Christ. You can have joy, courage, peace, and consistent spiritual growth in this fallen world. But you cannot experience the joy of your salvation without coming to a biblical understanding of the world and humanity.

Serving as Salt in a Decaying Culture

Many Christians I know are experiencing spiritual depletion simply because we live in a fallen and broken world where Jesus Christ and the Bible are no longer welcome—particularly not in the public square. Living during a time when the voices of evil are shouting from every rooftop and screaming from every nook and cranny of the internet is enough to drive countless Christians to the sidelines where they can live in the delusional coma of false peace by cowering on the edges of society.

Hiding from culture is not God's will for any person who claims the name of Jesus. Expecting the whole world to love Christians, embrace them, and accept the gospel with open arms is unrealistic. Ever since the fall of mankind, the majority of people have disobeyed God and his commandments. In recent years, however, there has been a substantial spike in resistance to historic Christianity. Little by little, many cultures have steadily grown biblically illiterate, hostile to the concept of absolute truth, and curiously intolerant of those who are not falling in line with the moral revolution. Intriguingly, the most vocal advocates for tolerance are often the most intolerant of biblical Christianity. As the world has become increasingly connected through the internet and social media, the number of people who vehemently oppose Christianity have mushroomed into a wave of fiery opposition against God and his church.

Admittedly, the church has not been blameless in this increased antagonism. In recent years, the atrocious scandals that have plagued the church undoubtedly hurt the church's standing in the world. When these moral controversies are combined with the disdain for absolute truth and the intensifying level of spiritual and moral insanity present in today's society, a heated disagreement is inevitable.

Many years ago, I wrote my doctoral dissertation on the role of cultural changes in the church. Since completing that project, the situation has only deteriorated. We're living in a scary time; it's an age in which evil is running rampant, and there is no indication that it's going to retreat into the shadows anytime soon. To be fair, debauchery has infiltrated this world since Satan deviously swindled Adam and Eve in the garden. This is not the first time in history unrestrained evil has permeated the world. The two world wars alone prove the earth has always been heavily influenced by sin. What is different in recent years is the level to which wickedness is being shamelessly promoted and applauded in practically every culture. We're living in days that increasingly resemble the time before the flood and the period of the Old Testament Judges.

Turn on the television for five minutes or swim in the shark-infested waters of social media for a little while and you'll be slapped in the face with bold messages that stand in blatant opposition to the clear teachings of Scripture. Should you dare to oppose the cultural elites and influencers, you'll be labeled as a hater and categorically dismissed as a mindless religious zealot unfit for an intelligent cultural conversation.

It's time for Christians to face the music; today's rapidly secularizing culture would prefer to keep Christians where we belong: cowering on the periphery of society with our heads between our knees, trying to survive the barrage of Satan's arrows flying in our direction. We're expected to stay in our pews or hide in our homes. For the Christians who courageously share their faith publicly, a heavy dose of ridicule and shame awaits.

Jesus Christ didn't establish his church to cower in a corner and hide from culture. He called his followers to serve as salt and light in this fallen world while holding fast to the word of life (see Matthew 5:13–14; Philippians 2:16). Serving as salt and light in this depraved world cannot be done in hiding or while sitting on the sidelines sipping on Gatorade. According to Jesus, Christians are to be salt in this rotting culture.

Only God's word can curb the moral decay taking place all around us. We must also serve as light in the darkness, shining forth the good news of Jesus Christ. In order to stand strong in this decaying culture, Christians must faithfully obey God even when the battle escalates. In John 17:15–18, Jesus prayed, "I do not ask that you take them out of the world, but that you keep them from the evil one. They are not of the world, just as I am not of the world. Sanctify them in the truth; your word is truth. As you sent me into the world, so I have sent them into the world." Despite the ferocious opposition he faced, Jesus never cowered from culture. Instead, he lovingly confronted the spiritual blindness of those around him with the truth and compassionately called sinners to repentance. As followers of Christ, our mission is to follow in his footsteps.

Judging by the headlines, it sometimes feels as if the world is spinning off its axis. Many Christians are left wondering if God is still paying attention. While we're seemingly outnumbered and outmatched, hunkering down someplace safe and letting the world rot seems like a reasonable plan. But this is not why God chose to leave his people in this world. As sojourners and exiles, we must understand that the world is not our friend or home (see 1 Peter 2:11). According to God's redemptive plan, he left us in this world to serve as ambassadors for his kingdom (see 2 Corinthians 5:20), entrusted with the task of being salt and light. Our mission and responsibility is to faithfully share God's glorious plan of redemption with the world.

An Explanation of Philippians 2:15

Today's disturbing events should not come as any surprise to those faithfully following Jesus. On the one hand, denying the challenges of this age is foolish and dangerous. But on the other hand, despair is not the right response either. We are not to live as if all hope is lost. Despite the world's glaring imperfections, the Apostle Paul calls God's people to live "without blemish in the midst of a crooked and twisted generation"

(Philippians 2:15). We are commanded to live obediently to God's perfect and absolute standards, no matter how far the world strays from them. God is fully independent of his creation and is the sovereign ruler over it, making him free to do as he pleases and govern the world according to his holy character. God alone has the absolute authority to define what is good, beautiful, and true. Our duty is to obey his decrees and bring glory to his magnificent name.

As we seek to faithfully obey God's commandments, we cannot overlook the two descriptive words Paul uses to describe the state of the world in Philippians 2:15. While Paul urges Christians to be blameless and innocent, it would be unwise and dangerous to ignore the cultural setting in which the pursuit of righteousness occurs. Reading the words *crooked* and *twisted* should set off numerous alarms in our minds. Given the nature of the world, living without any blatant ethical blemishes will never be easy. Both adjectives provide helpful insight as to why living faithfully to Christ is often spiritually and emotionally exhausting. When we grow weary, we must remember David's profound words in Psalm 18:32, where he declared it was "God who equipped me with strength and made my way blameless." We can never be blameless in our own strength. That's why we need God's sustaining grace to keep us standing strong in the battle.

When Christians conduct themselves according to God's commandments, they stand in stark contrast to the crooked and twisted world. Like bright lights on a moonless night, believers should stand as beacons of hope calling sinners to place their faith and trust in Christ. In the immediate textual context of Philippians 2, Paul argues that part of being blameless is living without complaining and murmuring. According to this text, Christians who are known as complainers and murmurers ruin their testimony. Their light is extinguished, and their saltiness is diluted.

Because the New Testament was originally written in Greek, a brief explanation of the words translated as *crooked* and *twisted* is in order. The first word, translated as *crooked* in English, is from the Greek word *skolios*. This term likely sounds familiar; it's the word from which we get the English word *scoliosis*. In Greek, *skolios* means "crooked or curved." The word can also be used to describe something that is "perverse, wicked, or unscrupulous." In the context of Philippians 2:15, Paul uses *skolios* with the sense of perversion and wickedness.

Paul's second descriptor is the word *twisted*, which is translated from the Greek word *diastrepho*. This Greek word means "to distort, pervert, or corrupt." In Acts 20:29–30, Luke uses this same word to record Paul's warning to church elders. The text reads, "I know that after my departure fierce wolves will come in among you, not sparing the flock; and from among your own selves will arise men speaking twisted things, to draw away the disciples after them." Like in the days of Paul, error is creeping into the church today through infiltration of the twisted culture's ideology and through wolves wearing sheep's clothing and teaching false doctrine.

Today's radical sexual revolution is a clear example of how our twisted culture is distorting what God intended in order to satisfy their own aberrant desires. In sinful humanity's demand for autonomy, people will always attempt to distort God's creation to meet their own definition of what is acceptable. There's no better place to start than with an assault on God's original design for sexuality. The normalization of unnatural sexual behaviors is an aggressive attempt to undermine God's authority. By twisting the truth, people attempt to make the Bible fit their own agenda so they can ignore God's commandments with a clear conscience.

When put together, these two adjectives painfully and accurately describe our current cultural context. Once again, there has never been a time in history when moral corruption was absent. But Paul's description should serve as a stern reminder that our world is undeniably distorted and corrupted by sin. Societies are brimming with wickedness because the world is populated by sinners. According to the biblical record, all people are born sinful and fall short of God's perfect holiness (see Romans 3:23). In the New Testament, *sin* is a translation of the Greek word *hamartia*, meaning to "miss the mark." Sin is coming short of God's absolutely righteous standards. Only the crucifixion of the spotless Lamb of God could pay the ransom for our sins (John 1:29; 1 Timothy 2:5–6).

In the biblical sense, *hamartia* indicates the act of missing or wandering from the path of uprightness. Sin, therefore, is to deviate from God's commandments and to violate them in thought, word, *or* action. Notice, sin is not merely something that we do with our hands. Sinful speech, like gossip, murmuring, complaining, and lying, readily flows from our mouths. Wicked and carnal thoughts often consume our minds, keeping us from meditating on God and his word. Author and pastor Paul David Tripp explains sin this way: "Sin is by its very nature anti-authority and antisocial. At its core, sin doesn't care who is in charge and how others are affected."[9]

While some erroneously believe that people are inherently good but are capable of sinful actions, Scripture teaches that all individuals are inherently sinful and sin because they are sinners. In fact, the Bible teaches that even our good works are filthy rags before our holy and righteous Creator (see Isaiah 64:6). Sin mars everything we do, leaving black stains on even our best intentions.

An Introduction to Heart Idols

The prophet Jeremiah calls our hearts (i.e., our innermost being) deceitful and desperately sick or wicked (see Jeremiah 17:9). Our sinful hearts are easily drawn away to worship idols of our making. I can probably guess what you're thinking—there's no piece of rock, wood, or metal in your house that you bow down to and beg to provide rain, food, money, or health. But don't read too hastily past the first of the Ten Commandments. The very first commandment given to Moses strictly forbids having any other gods before God. Despite what you may believe, we've all failed this commandment.

---

9 Paul David Tripp, *Reactivity* (Wheaton, IL: Crossway, 2022), 46.

Understand the Nature of Humanity and the World

All of us can name something or someone that has taken God's place in our hearts and consumes our thoughts, time, and affections. When something found in creation, even a good thing, becomes an ultimate thing and surpasses God in our hearts, it has by definition become an idol. Once we find an idol we like, we cling to it, believing it will provide lasting joy, contentment, and satisfaction. Remember, Satan lacks the power to control a Christian, but he can tempt, trick, and tantalize us into worshipping idols, which can control our lives with categorically destructive results. Some of the most popular idols include comfort, material possessions, acceptance, pleasure, control, appearance, intimacy, respect, safety, glory, and affirmation. When we consider this brief list, it becomes evident that no one can even get by the first commandment without falling flat on their face. We choose idolatry and sin because we believe Satan's lie that there is something in this world that can mend the gash in our souls and provide the happiness, pleasure, and gratification we think we deserve.

Sports always came easily to me while growing up. When I was four years old, my parents bought football equipment for me so I wouldn't get injured playing with my older brothers and their friends. I started playing baseball somewhere around the third grade. I felt at home on the baseball diamond and quickly became one of the most feared hitters in our league. When I came to the plate, kids would chant my name. I was a perennial all-star and dreamed of having my name on the back of an MLB jersey. I longed for the glory of the big leagues. The money. The fame. The entourage. In my idolatrous heart, I wanted to be worshipped for my athleticism. I could see the world at my feet, casting glory before me for my wondrous existence.

More on this later, but at sixteen years of age, my good and gracious Heavenly Father started to prune my idol of fame and admiration from the soil of my self-centered, glory-seeking heart. Because God loves me, he humbled me through an illness that almost took my life in order to save me from my counterfeit god—myself. Being the expert idolater that I am, I foolishly refused to give up on god Jay all that easily. I arrogantly longed to sit on the throne of my own heart, and I wasn't willing to allow God to take his rightful place as ruler of my life. By his merciful hand, he humbled me and taught me that he alone is God.

When my sports dream died, I exchanged athletics for academics. In college, I became obsessed with grades and attending medical school. I went from an average student to one who excelled in the classroom. I would like to say that my plan of being a physician was totally driven by a compassionate desire for taking care of sick people, but that would be dishonest. Caring for the sick was part of the reason, but not the only one. I was also motivated by big houses, fast cars, and of course, the glory.

While my outward actions shifted from bats to books, my false god hadn't changed. I was still worshipping the idols of fame, money, my precious reputation, and glory. I wanted all the credit. I selfishly desired to have all of the glory, praise, and admiration cast at my feet rather than the Lord's. Fear of man and perfectionism began eating away at my soul. Depression soon followed because I never received the amount of glory I believed I deserved.

Sad to say, but in my early days of ministry, I preached about the Messiah coming to die for our sins. Meanwhile, deep in my heart, I believed that I was a messiah who deserved all the glory that rightfully belonged to the true Messiah. By God's perfect grace, I got the wind knocked out of my sails early in the pastorate. I was still seeking glory, but the hard knocks of ministry humbled me pretty quickly. Oh, I still have moments where I crave praise and admiration, but thankfully, they come around far less often than they once did. I'm still learning that a heart filled with my own glory has no room for God's glory. Thanks to our idolatrous hearts, some of us like the spotlight to be on ourselves. But when we worship God alone, we allow all the praise, adoration, and glory to be his.

I'm not alone in my idolatry; false worship certainly didn't originate with me. Ever since the fall of humankind, the world has been under the curse of sin and has groaned under the devastating consequences (see Romans 8:22). In the opening chapters of Genesis, we read about Adam and Eve's original sin in the garden and God's chastisement that followed. Part of Satan's deceptive plot to entice Adam and Eve into sinning against their Creator was to slander God's character when he told Eve, "For God knows that when you eat of it your eyes will be opened, and you will be like God, knowing good and evil" (Genesis 3:5). The serpent craftily implied that God was withholding knowledge from Adam and Eve, limiting their ability to enjoy life and preventing them from becoming as knowledgeable as the Creator. In response to Satan's temptation to eat from the forbidden tree, Eve "saw that the tree was good for food, and that it was a delight to the eyes, and that the tree was to be desired to make one wise, she took of its fruit and ate, and she also gave some to her husband who was with her, and he ate" (Genesis 3:6).

Notice the three characteristics of the fruit that arrested Eve's attention: (1) it was good for food, it would satisfy her desire for physical pleasure by being enjoyable to eat; (2) it was delightful to her eyes, it was visually pleasant and appealing; and (3) it would provide the power to become wise, knowing good from evil. Believing they were deserving of the pleasures the fruit offered and fit to be coequals with God in knowledge, Adam and Eve ate. These three temptations coincide with John's teaching in 1 John 2:16, "For all that is in the world—the desires of the flesh and the desires of the eyes and pride of life—is not from the Father but is from the world." The desires of the flesh and eyes, combined with pride of life, provide insight into three of the most common idols of our day: pleasure, beauty, and knowledge. The cravings of our sinful hearts readily make gods out of those things that we foolishly believe will gratify the lusts of our flesh, satisfy the inordinate desires of our eyes, and quench the insatiable aspiration for all the world offers.

Understand the Nature of Humanity and the World

King David, who Scripture describes as a man after God's own heart, wrote in Psalm 14:1, "There is none who does good." Many times in his life, David proved this verse to be true. While considered to be a righteous king, one to whom the other kings of Israel would be compared, David was a depraved man with sinful cravings and an idolatrous heart. The most infamous illustration of this in his life was when he lusted after Bathsheba, coveted her beauty in his heart, tore her away from her husband, Uriah, had illicit sex with her, and eventually killed Uriah to cover his tracks after Bathsheba announced she was pregnant with his child (see 2 Samuel 11).

David, the man through whom Jesus would eventually be born, chose to follow his lust and idolatry over obedience to God. Peter, one in Jesus's inner circle, chose the god of comfort when he denied the Lord three times (see Luke 22:54–62). Judas, another one of Jesus's disciples, chose the god of silver when he betrayed Christ over remaining faithful to God (see Matthew 26:14–16). Not long after the Exodus, the Israelites asked Aaron to make gods for them. After Aaron fashioned a golden calf, they falsely proclaimed, "These are your gods, O Israel, who brought you up out of the land of Egypt" (Exodus 32:4). David's words in Psalm 14:3 underscore the depths of our depravity: "They have all turned aside; together they have become corrupt; there is none who does good, not even one." King David, along with every human being who has ever been born, was corrupt and incapable of perfectly following God. Throughout human history, there is only one exception to David's words. Only God's Son, the Lord Jesus Christ, has ever lived free from idolatry and sin.

All Have Sinned?

Perhaps you remain suspect of the notion that all people are born sinners. To those who question the sinfulness of humanity, I encourage you to consider children for a moment. Like many of you, I'm a parent. All three of my children have discovered consistent and creative ways to sin against God and others. Without being formally taught on the finer points of sinful behaviors, they quickly became black-belt-ninja-level sinners. Children may be adorable on the outside, but they're as putrid and rotten on the inside as the rest of us.

Admittedly, some sins are easier to detect than others. But remember, those children who silently harbor a defiant attitude and stiff-necked pride in their hearts are as culpable for their sins as kids who steal another person's belongings or blatantly lie to a parent. In the book of James, we find a sobering warning. James writes, "For whoever keeps the whole law but fails in one point has become accountable for all of it" (James 2:10). Even one violation of God's law is sufficient to condemn us. If we were to count how many times we break God's commandments in word, thought, or deed during the course of a day, we would realize how wicked our hearts really are. Our innate rebelliousness is why teaching children to lie, steal, covet, cheat, or dishonor their parents isn't necessary for them to know how to do it; sinning against God and others comes naturally to each and every one of us.

Understand the Nature of Humanity and the World

In 1 John 1:8, we read, "If we say we have no sin, we deceive ourselves, and the truth is not in us." From cover to cover, the Bible confirms the sinfulness of mankind. As the great reformer Martin Luther noted, "Men are altogether without any virtue in which they may glory (*before God*). They have no righteousness at all of which to boast before God."[10] Any wrongdoing, no matter how seemingly insignificant, makes us sinners deserving of God's judgment. Our transgressions separate us from our holy God, placing us in danger of eternal separation from him. Only by the shed blood of Jesus can we be redeemed from our sin. Because the wages of sin is death, we are unworthy of salvation on our own merits (see Romans 6:23). God's gracious gift of eternal life is only found through faith in the spotless Lamb of God.

Overcome by our depravity, and lost in our sin, we needed a Redeemer to pay the penalty for our sins. Pastor and theologian John Piper writes, "This means that what must change fundamentally is God's anger toward us because of our God-dishonoring sin."[11] Since we are incapable of changing God, God mercifully intervened on our behalf and sent his Son to take the wrath we rightfully deserve upon himself. Only by God's grace are we saved, and not of ourselves lest we fall into sinful pride (see Ephesians 2:8–9). Only those who humble themselves before God, repent of their sins, and place their faith in Jesus alone for redemption are truly Christians. Once God's grace saves us from our sin,

---

10 Martin Luther, *Commentary on Romans* (Grand Rapids, MI: Kregel Publications, 1976), 77.

11 John Piper, *God Is the Gospel* (Wheaton, IL: Crossway, 2005), 43.

the gospel transforms us bit by bit so that we increasingly resemble Jesus. If you want more information about how to become a Christian, or if you want to be sure that you are a genuine believer, I invite you to read the appendix at the back of the book.

Given the systemic fallen nature of the world, we must conclude that the idea of meliorism, which I introduced earlier, is an illusion. Mankind is incapable of solving the world's sin problem; only Jesus has the power and authority to accomplish that miracle. Because we are immersed in an evil age where millions of people reject the gospel, it's easy to see why Christians so often feel spiritually depleted and exhausted. It's tiresome living day in and day out with people who consistently and blatantly refuse to believe that Jesus is the Lamb of God who came to take away the sins of the world. The glorious gospel is available to all, but sadly, the majority will reject it.

Takeaways

Perhaps you're tired of the fight and don't feel like standing for righteousness any longer. As ambassadors for Christ, however, we are not excused from the spiritual battle. Ignoring the world and its spiritual blindness is unthinkable. Those who claim the name of Christ are commanded to live blamelessly in this world so that we can effectively proclaim the gospel to those in need of redemption.

Remember, the biblical writers were not super-humans who lived in utopian societies. When the Apostle Paul wrote many of his epistles, he was sitting in prison. Places like Corinth were known for their idolatry and carnality. Jesus's disciples were called to serve in a culture ruled by immoral Roman politicians, not a Christian culture. And yet, the early church flourished even during times of intense persecution. If Christians in the early days of the church could thrive in less-than-ideal circumstances, so can we. To spiritually flourish in this evil age, there are three important choices we must make.

1. Because people are sinners by nature and the world is inherently corrupt, you must intentionally choose vigilance. When we talk about the world in this context, I am referencing the system of ideas, values, morals, and practices that permeates the culture and systematically influences people's thoughts, beliefs, decisions, morality, and priorities. According to Scripture, Satan holds tremendous sway over the world's operating system. Giddy optimism unwisely dismisses the evil tendencies that saturate the culture and the troublesome problems facing society. Meanwhile, cynical pessimism overlooks the many blessings that God graciously bestows upon humanity and the world. Rather than being blind to the world's wickedness or indifferent to the wonders of God's creation, we must see the world through a biblical perspective and understand it for what it is. Although the world is fallen, God's grace affords us the opportunity to flourish and enjoy his creation.

2. Because you live in a world where sinners will sin against you, you must choose to forgive those who do so. Ephesians 4:32 commands Christians to, "Be kind to one another, tenderhearted, forgiving one another, as God in Christ forgave you." Forgiving those who sin against you protects your heart from harboring resentment and bitterness. Pride feeds the belief that people should never sin against you. Remember, God's Son lived a perfect life and was still egregiously sinned against. Jesus is the spotless Lamb of God who came to take away the sins of the world, and people still opposed him, belittled him, and rejected him. The world did not understand or accept Jesus; that's why the world will never understand or accept his followers. Because God has forgiven you for your sin, you must obediently forgive those who sin against you.

3. You must repent of your own sins. For starters, if you haven't done so already, you must repent of your sins and believe in the Lord Jesus Christ for salvation. Assuming that you have already made a profession of faith, you must now focus on seeking your Heavenly Father's forgiveness when you break fellowship with him through your sinful choices. Because you're still imperfect, sin will be part of your life until the moment of your final breath. Because your gracious Heavenly Father is faithful, he will always forgive you (see 1 John 1:8–10). You must also repent and

seek forgiveness from those you sin against. Taking personal responsibility for your sin, without making excuses, is a sign of spiritual maturity and is necessary for fostering a growing relationship with God and others.

Understanding the nature of humanity and the world is rudimentary to living a blameless life while engaged in spiritual warfare where Satan's flaming arrows fly. You're likely wondering how to remain faithful to Christ in the midst of this crooked and twisted generation. In the pages to follow, we will discuss this challenge. In order to live as a light in the dark world, you must first understand the enemies you will inevitably contend with in this fallen world. In Strategy Two, we will begin our journey through Ephesians 6:10–20. In this passage, the Apostle Paul offers lifesaving instruction for those brave enough to engage in spiritual warfare and stand strong when Satan's fiery darts come our way.

Key Point: By nature, the world is perversely wicked and dreadfully corrupt because it is populated by sinners in desperate need of redemption through Jesus Christ.

For Further Consideration

1. Are you truly a Christian? Can you describe the moment in which you placed your faith in Jesus Christ for salvation? If not, please read the appendix at the back of the book where I describe how you can know for sure that you are a Christian.

2. Read through the Ten Commandments (Exodus 20:1–17) and the Sermon on the Mount (Matthew 5–7). Take note of how your thoughts, words, and actions compare to God's perfect standards.
3. Look up Galatians 3:13 and 1 Peter 2:24 and explain these verses in your own words.
4. Christians are to live blamelessly in this fallen world. Because perfection is impossible on this side of heaven, think about the areas in which you are not blameless and make a list of applicable Scriptures to help you mature in these areas.
5. What specific circumstances or individuals are causing you to feel spiritually depleted or exhausted?
6. In what areas of your life have you grown complacent in your Christian walk?
7. Have you retreated from the spiritual battle? What specific steps do you need to take in order to re-engage the world?
8. Are there people you need to forgive? Are there individuals you have sinned against and need to seek their forgiveness?

Strategy Two
Rest in God's Strength

Finally, be strong in the Lord and in the strength of his might.
Ephesians 6:10

Each weekday morning at five, I meet two close friends, Adam and Jeff, at the gym for some old-school weightlifting. Since high school, I've enjoyed weight training and the challenge of lifting as much weight as possible. Since turning fifty, I've noticed a gradual decline in the amount of weight I can lift without destroying what's left of my shoulders and knees, but I keep trying to get better. It pains me to admit it, but I'm not as strong as I was years ago. More problematic is the harsh reality that the downward spiral is going to continue because my body is aging. Even at my strongest, I could never have matched the strength of The Rock. But, as strong as Dwayne Johnson may be, his strength still pales in comparison to God's.

Believing you're strong enough to face the devil and this sinful world on your own places you in grave danger of becoming a spiritual casualty. During my years of pastoral ministry, I've seen my fair share of individuals who have fallen prey to the pressures of the culture and the schemes of the devil. Many of these professing Christians foolishly believed they were strong enough to withstand temptation on their own. Some spent months or even years sinning behind closed doors. But eventually, their sin was discovered. It always is. In one fell swoop, they lost far more than they had gained from their sin.

Because of God's general revelation and common grace, not all of society is offensive to his holiness and forbidden by his word. In fact, many wondrous aspects of culture reflect God's beauty and bring glory to his name; therefore, they can be enjoyed by faithful followers of Christ. Fine art, music, and literature are three examples. Nonetheless, since the gravitational pull of society is toward that which violates God's commandments and feeds our inclination toward self-indulgence, we must persistently assess the cultural influences that we permit into our lives to be sure we are not becoming desensitized to what Scripture forbids and God deems sinful. If you're dabbling in sin, making excuses for compromises, or actively affirming sinful behaviors, I plead with you to wake up from your spiritual malaise and flee from the deceptiveness of the twisted and idolatrous world.

False Religions in the Ancient City of Ephesus

One of the passages of Scripture that I've found particularly helpful in my life is found in Ephesians 6:10–20. Paul's letter to the church at Ephesus was written in approximately AD 62 while he was imprisoned in Rome. During Paul's time, Ephesus was a thriving harbor city near the western shores of modern-day Turkey. Located near the Aegean Sea, the city's harbor brought ships from around the Mediterranean, making Ephesus a place of great importance in biblical times.

In 334 BC, Alexander the Great took control of Ephesus. The Romans took possession of the city in 133 BC when Attalus III, king of Pergamum, bequeathed the city to Rome. Beginning with Caesar Augustus, Ephesus entered a time of great prosperity, reaching a population of over 400,000 people by the New Testament era. It became one of the major cities in the Roman Empire.[12]

In Acts 19, we learn that Paul's preaching of the gospel in Ephesus produced severe opposition from those who practiced false religions, which included occultism. In verse 11, Luke uses the Greek word *tugchano* to describe Paul's miracles, implying these miracles were exceptional in comparison to the others recorded in the book of Acts. Through the power of Christ, Paul was able to perform miracles that far exceeded the cultic magic associated with the worship of the goddess Artemis. God was doing miraculous work through Paul's

---

12 James S. Jeffers, *The Greco-Roman World of the New Testament Era* (Downers Grove, IL: InterVarsity Press, 1999), 267.

ministry, but his ministerial successes were not without spiritual hostility.

These wondrous works were not intended to bring glory to Paul but rather to authenticate him as an apostle and to draw people to the resurrected Messiah. As a result of Paul's preaching and miracles, some of the itinerant Jewish exorcists began invoking the name of Jesus in their confrontation of evil spirits as if it were a magic formula. Contrary to Paul, who was humbly relying on God's miraculous power to work through him, these exorcists believed they could bend the will of the gods for their own financial gain.

Because these magicians had no relationship with Jesus, they were publicly and hilariously humiliated. These spiritual charlatans offered their spells and incantations as a means through which their customers could be cured and blessed. For a fee, of course. New Testament scholar John Polhill writes, "The more exotic the incantation, the more effective it was deemed to be."[13] Passages like Acts 19 remind Christians that the one true God will never be manipulated or controlled by the religious and spiritual rituals of self-serving people. The gospel always stands in opposition to selfish manipulation and distortion of God's absolute truth.

Jesus is not a circus show or a birthday party trick. He is not for sale, and his name is not a magical incantation. Our Creator isn't going to bend his will to anyone. Even the demon possessing the man in Acts 19 attested to the fact that these exorcists were fake; only Jesus and his apostles had

---

13 John B. Polhill, *Acts* (Nashville, TN: Broadman and Holman Publishers, 2001), 403.

authority over evil spirits. The sons of Sceva were proven powerless against the forces of hell (see Acts 19:14–20).

Ephesus was also home to the temple of the Greek goddess Artemis, who was the goddess of the moon, chastity, and hunting. In Roman mythology, Artemis was known by the name Diana. During Paul's time, Artemis was one of the most worshipped deities in the Roman Empire. Located throughout the empire, there were at least thirty-three shrines built to honor the goddess. While Artemis wasn't the only deity worshipped in Ephesus, she was the most prominent.[14]

Because of its architectural beauty and grandeur, Artemis's temple was named one of the seven wonders of the ancient world. Her temple was obviously a place of worship, but it also became the hub of Ephesus's economic life. The temple conveniently served as a bank where people from all over the empire deposited money. As scholars Stambaugh and Balch observe, "It would be safe there since no one would dare to violate the holy place."[15]

Due to the foot traffic the temple produced, Artemis worship became a profitable business. As Polhill writes, "Ephesus was considered to be *the* center of the cult, and pilgrims flocked from all over the empire to worship at its famous temple, especially during the spring Artemision."[16] Much like today, religion became a lucrative enterprise in

---

14 Gerald F. Hawthorne, Ralph P. Martin, and Daniel G. Reid, eds., *Dictionary of Paul and His Letters* (Downers Grove, IL: InterVarsity Press, 1993), 250.

15 John E. Stambaugh and David L. Balch, *The New Testament in Its Social Environment* (Philadelphia, PA: The Westminster Press, 1986), 150.

16 Polhill, 409.

Ephesus. When business was threatened by Paul's bold proclamation of the gospel, people responded in anger.

Throughout Ephesus, many people turned from false worship and placed their faith in Jesus. Because people were forsaking their worship of Artemis when they accepted Jesus as Savior, revenue was declining for the vendors selling replicas of her temple (see Acts 19:23–41). As business dried up in the marketplace, those making high profits off Artemis's worshippers were infuriated. Theologian Craig Keener notes, "As often, religious piety becomes a thin cloak for personal economic interests."[17] The gospel always becomes controversial when it hinders economic profitability.

Unlike the vendors making money off worshippers, a group of repentant magicians willingly sacrificed their expensive books as a testimony of their newfound faith in Jesus (see Acts 19:19). Those making a good living off Artemis, however, had no interest in tolerating a loss of income. As a result, a local craftsman by the name of Demetrius incited a riot when he pointed out the recession created by Paul's proclamation of the gospel.

It was to the citizens living in this idolatrous culture that Paul penned his letter to the church at Ephesus. While preaching in the city, he witnessed spiritual opposition from those profiting from the city's idol market. Based on Paul's firsthand experience in the city, he understood the spiritual challenges facing the Ephesian church. As a result, he offered

---

17 Craig S. Keener, *The IVP Bible Background Commentary: New Testament* (Downers Grove, IL: InterVarsity Press, 1993), 379.

these believers a letter filled with rich doctrine combined with compassionate encouragement to stay faithful to the gospel.

Paul's Letter to the Ephesian Church

In the opening chapters of Paul's epistle, he describes how one becomes a genuine follower of Christ. He also reminds the church that all people are born dead in trespasses and sins and that those who repent of their sins are redeemed through the grace of God by faith in Christ alone rather than by works of righteousness (see Ephesians 2:1–13).

In the second half of Ephesians, Paul presents the characteristics that are indicative of faithful Christians. One verse of Scripture that is worth noting here is Ephesians 4:1, where Paul urges Christians to "walk in a manner worthy of the calling to which you have been called." Genuine followers of Jesus Christ will bear lasting spiritual fruit by faithfully living in accordance with Scripture.

Living as a faithful Christian in this sinful world is undoubtedly a tall task that can leave believers spiritually confused, fearful, and exhausted. It's important to remember that conflict between Christians and culture is nothing new. Concerning the city of Ephesus, scholars Elwell and Yarbrough write, "If religious life was dominated by emperor worship, idolatry, and the black arts of occultism and spiritism, moral life was typical of a Greco-Roman city: A large brothel stood at one of the major intersections."[18] Given

---

18 Walter A. Elwell and Robert W. Yarbrough, *Encountering the New Testament* (Grand Rapids, MI: Baker Books, 1998), 309.

the idolatry, materialism, and moral bankruptcy in Ephesus, being a first-century Christian in the city wasn't radically different from what we experience today.

Everything Paul previously discussed in Ephesians is summarized in the closing section of the book. Ephesians 6:10 notably begins with the telling term *finally*. This word not only indicates a new paragraph, it also functions as an effective transition to the concluding portion of the letter. Every directive Paul has offered must be carried out in a particular context—a battlefield. Paul commands us to walk worthy of our calling in the midst of a ferocious spiritual battle fought against Satan and his forces.

As Paul brings his letter to the church at Ephesus to a pointed conclusion, he presents some necessary requirements for remaining steadfast in this perverse generation. Christians are ill-equipped to navigate the treacherous waters of this turbulent culture relying on their own wisdom and a battle plan roughly sketched on the back of a napkin. Not only is our knowledge and preparation inadequate to thwart Satan's arrows, we're also too spiritually weak to survive the battle in our own strength. This is why Paul's final instructions are so important.

At the beginning of Paul's conclusion, he shares an important ingredient for flourishing in the midst of this wicked age. The commandment found in Ephesians 6:10 is straightforward and simple: "be strong." Although the commandment is easy to understand, it's difficult to apply. When we lack strength, faithfulness and courage quickly evaporate like a puddle on a hot summer day.

Old Testament Examples

What Paul orders in Ephesians 6:10 echoes several key passages found in the Old Testament. Rather than providing an exhaustive list, here are three occasions in which God commanded leaders to be strong and courageous.

1. Moses's instruction to his successor, Joshua

    The context of this instruction is the passing of leadership from Moses to Joshua. Moses, arguably the most influential leader in the Old Testament, is nearing the end of his life and offers his final words to the people of Israel and to the man who will soon take his leadership position.

    In Deuteronomy 31:6, Moses addressed the people of Israel and said, "Be strong and courageous. Do not fear or be in dread of them, for it is the LORD your God who goes with you. He will not leave you or forsake you."

    In Deuteronomy 31:7, Moses addressed Joshua and said, "Be strong and courageous, for you shall go with this people into the land that the LORD has sworn to their fathers to give them, and you shall put them in possession of it."

2. God's instruction to Joshua

    Once Joshua officially became Israel's new leader, God commanded him to demonstrate courage and strength. God's plan for Joshua was not an easy one to follow; he was commanded to lead God's people into the Promised Land where he was to drive out those living there.

In Joshua 1:6–7, we read, "Be strong and courageous, for you shall cause this people to inherit the land that I swore to their fathers to give them. Only be strong and very courageous, being careful to do according to all the law that Moses my servant commanded you."

In Joshua 1:9, we read, "Have I not commanded you? Be strong and courageous. Do not be frightened, and do not be dismayed, for the Lord your God is with you wherever you go."

3. King David's instruction to his successor and son, Solomon

The context of this passage is also the passing of leadership from one leader to the next. In this case, it's King David passing the crown to his son. David had unified the people of God. Under his leadership, the nation of Israel prospered. Now, it was Solomon's turn to reign.

In 1 Kings 2:1–2, we read, "When David's time to die drew near, he commanded Solomon his son, saying, 'I am about to go the way of all the earth. Be strong, and show yourself a man.'"

I cannot imagine how Joshua and Solomon felt as they assumed the positions of leadership once held by two of the greatest leaders in Old Testament Israel. Talk about big shoes to fill. According to God's redemptive plan, Joshua's leadership career was one of war and conquest. Solomon's kingship was defined by building God's temple in Jerusalem and capitalizing on the successes of his father's reign. Given the challenges both men faced, they had legitimate reasons to feel uncertain and afraid.

It's interesting to note the close connection between the need for strength and for courage. One of the mistakes many Christians make is believing the heroes of the faith were perfect people living in a perfect world with perfect intentions, implementing perfect action plans to produce perfect results. After all, when we talk about men like Moses, Joshua, David, and Solomon, we're talking about four of the greatest leaders who have ever lived. If Old Testament Israel had created their own version of Mount Rushmore, these are the four men who would have had their faces chiseled in the rock. Despite their prominent places in Israel's history, however, all four men were sinners in desperate need of God's grace, and they teach us a valuable lesson.

Despite their major accomplishments in God's redemptive plan, influential men like Moses, Joshua, David, and Solomon were prone to fear and timidity. These profoundly gifted leaders faced physical enemies who were intent on destroying them along with the people they were called to lead and protect. When left to their own abilities, they were categorically out of their depth. They desperately needed God and his sustaining power. Consider the challenges each of these men faced.

When God called Moses to lead the people of Israel out of slavery and bondage in Egypt, Moses offered plenty of excuses as to why God was making a terrible mistake asking someone like him to stand up to Pharaoh. Eventually, Moses obeyed. After the miracle at the Red Sea, Moses had the *privilege* of leading thousands of critical, backbiting, stubborn, and insubordinate people through the wilderness for forty long, miserable years. Yup, Moses lived the dream. Far from perfect, and faced with insurmountable problems, Moses was filled with doubt, anger, and a whole heap of fear. But he faithfully rested in God's power and sustaining grace, and he refused to allow his insecurities to keep him from fulfilling God's plan for his life. Whenever God calls us to a task we feel inadequate to accomplish, we must humbly seek God's infinite strength.

Following the Exodus, Joshua was closely associated with Moses and was one of the twelve spies chosen to survey Canaan. Ten of the spies believed it was folly to enter the land. Joshua, however, was eager to obey God, even when it meant facing difficult challenges. While Joshua proved to be a brave warrior, God had to command him to have the necessary courage to obey what the Lord asked. Honestly, Joshua is one of the few people in Scripture who lacked glaring flaws. Despite God's promised victory in Canaan and Joshua's years of experience serving with Moses, he still needed the strength and courage only God could provide to overcome his lingering fears of facing powerful armies that wielded physical swords and arrows. Faithful leaders like

Joshua refuse to allow fear to hold them hostage and choose to trust God to do as he promised in his way and in his time. When we are facing circumstances that make us fearful, we must allow God's boundless strength to provide the courage we need to obey.

David is also one of the most recognizable names in the Bible. He was the young shepherd boy who courageously killed the giant Goliath with nothing more than a sling and a rock. On multiple occasions, David was surrounded by enemies who wanted him dead. Some of his fiercest enemies were his own sons. After taking the throne, David became an adulterer and a murderer. At times, he displayed both arrogance and fear. When afraid, however, David acknowledged his weakness and sins, and fell on his face before God, beseeching God to provide him with strength. Unlike so many of the other kings of Israel, David humbled himself and asked God for forgiveness (see Psalm 51). When fleeing from his son Absalom, David penned Psalm 3, where he writes, "I will not be afraid of many thousands of people who have set themselves against me all around" (v. 6). Like Moses and Joshua, David was imperfect and incapable of following God's commandments in his own strength. Apart from God's omnipotent hand guiding his steps, David would have been unable to withstand the adversity he faced. We can all learn from David's example. In our times of fear and weakness, we must also seek God's inexhaustible power.

David's successor was his son Solomon, who God called to build the temple in Jerusalem. When God appeared to

Solomon in a dream and offered him whatever he wanted God to provide, Solomon, understanding that he was young and lacked the necessary wisdom and experience to be an effective king, answered, "Give your servant therefore an understanding mind to govern your people, that I may discern between good and evil" (1 Kings 3:9). Solomon understood that his inexperience and lack of wisdom would hinder him as a leader; therefore, he didn't selfishly ask God for a long life, the death of his enemies, or wealth. In 1 Kings 3:12, God answered Solomon's request for wisdom, promising, "I give you a wise and discerning mind, so that none like you has been before you and none like you shall arise after you." Solomon was astute in asking God for the necessary wisdom to be a good king. He wanted to know right from wrong because he longed to be a godly leader who would accomplish all God intended.

Under Solomon's wise leadership, Israel's economy flourished, allowing him to become arguably the wealthiest man in history. Despite Solomon's profound wisdom, he eventually wandered away from God's word and became a sinful and idolatrous king. Surrounded by the blessings of success, he enjoyed unprecedented opportunities to use his wealth, wisdom, power, and influence to lavish himself in any pleasure imaginable. Solomon used his affluence and status to get whatever his selfish heart desired. According to Ecclesiastes, Solomon collected mores houses, vineyards, gardens, pools, slaves, possessions, herds, flocks, treasures, wives, and concubines than any one person would need in a hundred lifetimes. From 1 Kings 11:3, we learn that Solomon had seven hundred princesses as wives and three hundred concubines. The last phrase of the verse is a sad commentary on his life. It tells us that "his wives turned away his heart." Rather than fearing God and keeping his commandments, as he later wrote in Ecclesiastes 12:13, Solomon sought pleasure above all else. By the end of his life, Solomon discovered that his illustrious pursuits of pleasure, possessions, and power were nothing but foolishly chasing the wind. How often do we pursue the same list to the neglect of God? Rather than resting in the Lord's power for the strength to withstand temptation, Solomon repeatedly tried living in his own strength and failed miserably. Not only is the Lord's strength necessary on the physical battlefield, as it was for Joshua, it is also needed on the spiritual battleground.

What is it that is drawing you away from the Lord? Is it pleasure? Possessions? Power? When we feel the world's temptations tugging at our hearts, we must seek the Lord's unfathomable strength if we are going to successfully resist the vanity of this world.

No matter the specifics of the conflict, all four of these men had to remain strong and courageous in order to faithfully follow God's path for their lives. Undoubtedly, there were moments when each of them felt like giving up the fight. But through God's strength, they were able to bravely stand against their enemies and accomplish magnificent successes for God's glory. If Moses the liberator, Joshua the conqueror, David the giant slayer, and Solomon the wise needed God's strength, there is no doubt the rest of us do as well.

Fear and Courage

As New Covenant believers, we're not standing at the end of machine guns and rocket launchers when we enter the arena of spiritual warfare. As we'll soon discover, our enemy is fighting against us in a more clandestine and cunning way than a platoon of soldiers storming a city. Rather than standing against a physical army on a bloodstained battlefield, we're pitted against the forces of evil, which are actively and purposefully influencing our society. Although the enemy we face cannot be tracked by radar, sonar, or satellite imagery, the forces of evil are maneuvering against Christians in a calculating manner.

Fear and weakness reside in the sinful heart of all of us. That's why we need to emulate people like Moses, Joshua, David, and Solomon. All people fear something; otherwise we wouldn't see the persistent commandment to be strong and courageous scattered throughout the Bible. Where there is an absence of fear, there is no need for courage. The opposite of courage isn't fear; nor is fear the opposite of courage. These two emotions always coexist, jockeying for control of our heart and minds. Courage is present when we're riddled with fear but choose to do what God requires anyway.

For many years, our daughter, Jaelyn, has been involved in drama, speech, and music. Like me, she can use her speaking gifts in front of a large crowd without batting an eye. We both blossom on the stage. I don't write that out of arrogance or self-promotion, but because God, by his grace, wired us to serve him in that capacity. Most people break out into a cold sweat imagining themselves standing on a stage with hundreds of eyes watching their every move and expecting them to deliver a speech or sing a song. Jaelyn and I thrive on it.

One day, I asked Jaelyn to name the most common fear people share. Although I don't recollect her answer, I do remember her puzzled response when I told her that most people rank public speaking as their greatest fear. With squinted eyes and a wrinkled nose, she confusedly asked, "Why?" The fear of public speaking makes no sense to either of us. Nonetheless, I know several individuals who get so nervous in front of people, they can't form a sentence.

Fears come in many different shapes and sizes, but we all have them. I don't fear speaking in front of hundreds of people every week, but I do fear rejection and heights. If you are deathly afraid of public speaking, you most likely will never be a public speaker by trade like I will never be a roofer, thanks to my unreasonable fear of ladders. Part of God's giftedness to me is public speaking. That does *not* mean, however, that fear has not negatively affected my speaking ministry.

For years, I struggled with the fear of rejection. Early in my ministry, I would feel physically ill after most of my speaking times. While a gifted speaker who never shies away from an opportunity to talk, I feared that people hated my sermons, lessons, and classes. I have never been afraid to speak in front of anybody, but I have definitely feared rejection by those whom I was called to teach.

Should I ever allow my fear of rejection to keep me from doing what God has called me to do, I would be disobedient and outside of God's plan for my life. I don't pretend to know God's will for your life, but I wonder if you're allowing fear to keep you from being all God has called you to be.

No matter your areas of giftedness, there will always be reasons to fear using them. Moses was afraid to speak, but God gifted him to lead a massive group of refugees. Joshua was afraid of the battle he was called to fight, but God gifted him to conquer the Promised Land. David was afraid of his enemies, but God gifted him to unify a nation. Solomon was afraid he lacked the wisdom necessary to be an effective king, but God gifted him with the wisdom and discernment needed to lead Israel and build God's temple. All four of these men were gifted leaders, but each of them fostered lingering fears in their hearts that could have hindered their accomplishments had they not turned to the Lord for strength and guidance.

If I had not died to myself and stopped obsessing about possibly being rejected, there is no way I would have ever dared to write this book. I can't name your greatest fear, but I'm guessing you can. Seek the Lord right now. Allow him to quiet your fears and strengthen you for the mission he has called you to fulfill.

Fear of the Lord

Psalm 112 is a wisdom psalm that explains the blessings that come from fearing God and keeping his commandments. The second part of Psalm 112:1 reads, "Blessed is the man who fears the Lord, who greatly delights in his commandments!" As the writer begins this psalm, he boldly declares that the one who fears God is a blessed man, which we will discuss shortly. Properly fearing God, and submitting ourselves to his authority, does not drive us away from his presence in terror. Instead, it draws us to the Lord, to the one in whom we find grace, mercy, forgiveness, and strength. Motivated by an attitude of reverential awe, we humbly approach him, trusting in his infinite goodness, grace, and wisdom. The one who is blessed sincerely respects God's holiness and authority, understanding that God is God and we are not. Fearing God and delighting in his eternal word changes our character and makes us increasingly virtuous.

According to verses 4 and 5 of Psalm 112, the person who fears God and faithfully obeys his commandments is gracious, merciful, righteous, generous, and conducts his affairs with justice. The fear of God is the only type of fear that makes us more like Christ and keeps us trusting in him.

Generally speaking, we fear people more than God. Rather than fearing God and keeping his commandments, we fear people and give them a degree of influence over us that should belong to God alone. That's why Proverbs 29:25 forewarns, "The fear of man lays a snare, but whoever trusts in the Lord is safe." Being controlled by what people think about us or what they will do if we disappoint them, like reject us, keeps us in spiritual bondage and from becoming all God created us to be. A stark contrast to the dangers of fearing people is offered in Proverbs 14:26–27. It says, "In the fear of the LORD one has strong confidence, and his children will have a refuge. The fear of the LORD is a fountain of life, that one may turn away from the snares of death." Proverbs 19:23 adds, "The fear of the LORD leads to life, and whoever has it rests satisfied." Fearing man brings entanglement, chaos, insecurity, and grief. Fearing God, however, produces safety, confidence, life, rest, and satisfaction.

Fearing God is a holy fear that leaves us trembling before him in reverential awe of his majesty, holiness, and sovereignty. In Psalm 119:120, we read, "My flesh trembles for fear of you, and I am afraid of your judgments." Approaching God with a casualness fit for an old college buddy is never pictured in Scripture. Even Moses, the man who spoke directly with God, was told to remove his shoes because, as the Lord told him, "the place on which you are standing is holy ground" (Exodus 3:5).

Properly fearing the Lord acknowledges him as the omnipotent Creator and sustainer of the glorious and mysterious universe in which we live. We must never contemplate or approach God, the one who controls the seas and knows the future, with disrespect or flippancy. The reverential fear of God is awed by the wondrous truth of the gospel. It marvels at the fact that a holy, just, and loving God would take on flesh and die on the cross for our sins so we can enjoy eternal life in his magnificent presence. The fear of the Lord brings wisdom, joy, satisfaction, and abundant life. Fearing God reminds us that in our almighty Heavenly Father, we have an unshakable fortress and impenetrable shield as our protector. It's the reverential awe of God that drives us to him because in his presence we find peace, comfort, rest, wisdom, and contentment. When we properly fear God, we cry out with the psalmist, "The LORD is my portion!" (Psalm 119:57).

Fearing man is sinful because it places humankind on the throne of our hearts, making pleasing people more important than pleasing God. It guides our relationships and determines our friendships: "Whoever walks with the wise becomes wise, but the companion of fools will suffer harm" (Proverbs 13:20). When we fear mankind, we are controlled by their opinions and allow the misguided wisdom of people to dictate our decisions and priorities. Being the companion of fools leads us away from Christ, and produces a slew of regrettable consequences.

When Moses met with the Lord on Mount Sinai in Exodus 34, he illustrated what the fear of God looks like when he "quickly bowed his head toward the earth and worshipped" (Exodus 34:8). Like Moses, we are to reverently bow our hearts and lives before God's awesome presence. Those who fear God are called blessed and are able to enjoy the peace, joy, safety, confidence, and abundant life that comes with pleasing God above all else.

Experiencing God's blessings is something all believers long for. In Psalm 112:1, the psalmist uses the Hebrew word *ashre*, translated as *blessed* in the ESV, which means "satisfied, content, and whole." *Ashre* is a positive judgment made by God that declares that the one who fears him is the kind of individual who has his approval. Think about that for a moment. Whose approval do you readily seek? Man's? Or God's? The world, along with our counterfeit gods, promise lasting joy and contentment, but neither can deliver on their promises. Only fearing God and delighting in his commandments can produce a genuinely satisfied and content life.

In Psalm 112:7–8, we discover another spiritual benefit of fearing God over humans. The verses read, "He is not afraid of bad news; his heart is firm, trusting in the Lord. His heart is steady; he will not be afraid." I love that! Believers who fear God and trust in him will not experience sinful and debilitating fear even when bad news or threatening reports come their way. Fearing God produces a sturdy confidence that refuses to back down when the spiritual battle grows heated and Satan's flaming arrows target our hearts.

When our hearts are firmly planted on God's commandments, he will establish us and we will never be shaken by fear or threats. Even when trials come, we will not be afraid. Actively trusting the Lord produces the kind of confidence and courage we need in this spiritual warfare. The fear of *man* brings devastating consequences into our lives, but living in reverential awe of *God* keeps us from choosing the path of destruction and walking off the battlefield. When we make God the centerpiece of our lives, temptation to sin does not overcome us and our circumstances do not discourage us.

When we properly fear the Lord, sin loses its appeal.

God-fearing individuals do not seek self-glory. They are not held hostage by the opinions of others, nor do they fear those who stand in opposition to the gospel. God-fearers are immovable during times of adversity because their hearts are anchored and secured by almighty God. From Psalm 112, we learn that the source of true courage comes from fearing God and trusting in his strength.

God's Strength

Because sinful fear is woven into our fallen DNA, we must pay close attention to Paul's simply stated commandment found in Ephesians 6:10: "Be strong." While this directive is brief, there is an important nuance to this statement that we must consider. Learning to read Greek isn't necessary to understand the New Testament; there are occasions, however, when it's helpful to consult the original languages to gain a fuller understanding of the text. The commandment found in Ephesians 6:10 is one such example.

In this verse, Paul uses the Greek verb *endunamoo*, meaning "to be strong" or "endure with strength." The word's basic meaning is simple enough to comprehend, but what is important to highlight is Paul's usage of what is called the passive voice. Without being bogged down with linguistic technicalities, I want you to understand that the passive form means this commandment is best understood as "to be made strong" or "to be strengthened."

I'm a huge proponent of comparing solid English translations of the Bible to gain a more accurate understanding of the original languages. The verses quoted in this book are from the ESV version. But when it comes to Ephesians 6:10, I particularly like the CSB translation. It reads, "Finally, be strengthened by the Lord and by His vast strength." In this instance, the CSB beautifully captured the essence of the passive voice.

Here's the amazing point that I want you to glean from Paul's usage of the passive voice in Ephesians 6:10. This verbal form indicates that because we are flesh and blood, we are incapable of empowering ourselves for the spiritual battle we are facing. In our finiteness, we sleep, cry, break bones, bleed, get sick, and ultimately die. Because we lack the crucial resources needed to defeat the evil principalities wreaking havoc in today's culture, we need God's assistance. Although overpowering the agents of evil in our own strength is impossible, we still foolishly try. When we are tempted to trust in ourselves, we need to remember that relying on our own inadequate abilities will leave us spiritually vulnerable to Satan's attacks.

Our finite abilities are woefully insufficient for the battle, placing us in grave danger of caving to the pressures and temptations of this age when we rely upon our own strength. But the strength of almighty God is inexhaustible and always sufficient in the battle against evil. God is omnipotent; we are not. God can create a universe from nothing by his spoken word; we cannot. Nonetheless, more often than not, we place our confidence in our own strength, guaranteeing eventual defeat.

Takeaways

I tend to be a bit of a control freak. My sinful pride tries to convince me that I can do all things through the power of almighty Jay who is able to strengthen himself. Yeah, that doesn't typically go well. Apart from God strengthening me, I'm prone to making a big mess of my life while heartily sinning along the way. Our treasonous hearts believe we know more than God and that we can sufficiently handle the fiery arrows of the evil one on our own. But when we rest in our own laurels and capabilities, we eventually fail. Here are three ways in which we fail when we rest in our own strength.

1. We will not authentically conduct our lives in a manner worthy of our calling. Like the Pharisees, we can clean up the outside of our lives and portray a façade of piety while still walking in the flesh and in our own power. For those who grew up around church, we know the lingo; we know how to convince people that we're walking with Jesus. We've memorized the cliché Christian words, and we know when to use them. We're smart enough to sprinkle in an *amen* or two, call someone brother or sister, mention prayer, or quote a Bible verse that seems fitting for the occasion. When we consistently implement these churchy actions, we can fool a lot of people. We may even make the Christian-of-the-month list in our discipleship group. But when we're living distantly from the Lord in our hearts, we're not actually walking worthy of our calling. We're nothing

but fakes when we use our limited abilities to clean up the outside of our lives. Others may buy the act, but our omniscient God knows what is truly residing in our hearts.

2. We will quickly find ourselves overcome by fear and timidity. Israel's big four were incapable of following God's plan for their lives in their own strength. When they tried, even these great men failed. Like the rest of us, these four servants of God were only strong and courageous when they allowed the Lord to strengthen them. Only in God's power were they capable of fulfilling the Father's bidding. When they chose to trust the Lord, they were mightily used in God's redemptive plan. Thousands of years later, we're still reading about how God miraculously used them for his glory.

3. We will become spiritually vulnerable and at risk for allowing temptation to gain access to our hearts. In our self-sufficiency, we can reach the place where we believe we're strong enough to withstand the temptations that will inevitably come our way. I have met with people addicted to drugs, alcohol, pornography, sex, etc., who have been caught in their sin. They are often broken, weeping, and promising to never fall into these temptations again. All of them started off well with keeping their promise. Sadly, those who chose to remain disconnected from Jesus and his church eventually chose to return to their previous

lifestyle. A couple of individuals that come to mind left their families and haven't been seen since. Apart from the Lord's strength and support from fellow believers, we are susceptible to following the same path to spiritual destruction.

Resting in God's strength is necessary to fight the forces of evil. But allowing God to strengthen us is only the beginning. We must also get dressed for battle. Because when flaming arrows fly, we had better be well protected. In the next chapter, we will turn our attention to the armor of God.

Key Point: Because we're prone to spiritual exhaustion, which often produces fear and timidity, we must allow the Lord to strengthen us through the power of his Holy Spirit.

For Further Consideration

1. According to Ephesians 4:1, you are commanded to conduct yourself in a way that is worthy of your calling. In what area(s) of your life are you falling short of this goal? How can you procure assistance in your struggle?
2. Read and meditate on these additional verses:
   1 Samuel 30:6
   Psalm 28:7–8
   Zechariah 10:12
   Acts 9:22
   1 Timothy 1:12
   2 Timothy 2:1
   2 Timothy 4:17

3. Which of the following are your worst fears?

   Rejection

   Embarrassment

   Intimacy

   Bodily harm

   Being alone

   Being ridiculed

   Sharing your faith

   Financial hardship

   Suffering loss

   Meeting new people

   Standing for what God defines as morally acceptable

   Public speaking

4. Invest some time studying Moses, Joshua, David, and Solomon. Once you have an overview of their lives, summarize how they managed to overcome fear during times of trial.

5. In what area(s) of life are you relying on your own strength?

6. What is preventing you from trusting in God's strength?

Strategy Three
Dress for Battle

Put on the whole armor of God, that you may be able to stand against the schemes of the devil.

Ephesians 6:11

While my family currently lives in a North Carolina beach town, I love the western part of our state. There's something about being surrounded by mountains covered with leafy trees that calms my spirit. Our daughter is currently attending Montreat College, providing us with a good reason to visit the mountains on a regular basis. During one of our visits, our youngest son, Jordan, was exploring a stream while my wife and I sat on a boulder, watching the water rippling by. After a few minutes, a little boy ran over to announce that he had spotted a venomous snake in the stream.

Curiously, I watched the young informant. He was lingering by the riverbank with a group of kids; they were intently looking at something on the ground. I decided to have a look. When I reached the bank, everyone had left but one girl who was sitting on a large rock. I asked what she was watching, and she pointed to a large rattlesnake curled up on the stream's edge, only a foot or so from the large rock where she sat. A decent-sized fish was clutched in the snake's clenched jaw. Already dead from the injection of lethal venom, the fish was slowly being digested.

The little girl explained that she had been sitting on the rock with her bare feet dangling over the edge, watching the fish swimming near the shoreline. Unbeknownst to her, the rattlesnake was hiding beneath the rock hunting for lunch. When the fish swam inches from the bank, the snake struck and snatched its prey from the water.

Like that unsuspecting fish, we are also being stalked by dangerous enemies of our own. Sure, we could be bitten by a rattlesnake or attacked by a bear, but I'm far more concerned about the daily attacks that come from our spiritual enemies. As illustrated in our discussion on Acts 19, Christians have always lived in a world where enemies of the cross abound.

As we learned from Paul's experience in Ephesus, even the most faithful Christians are not exempt from spiritual opposition. No matter our level of spiritual maturity, spiritual warfare will be waged in our homes, workplaces, communities, and churches. In an attempt to wreak havoc in the lives of God's people, Satan seeks an opportunity to gain a foothold in our hearts so he can draw us away from the Lord. When the old serpent tries to sink his fangs into our souls, we're in for a fight.

Like a snake, the devil lurks in the shadows and hides under rocks. He disguises himself as an agent of light, attempting to take advantage of our anger, bitterness, resentment, jealousy, covetousness, lust, greed, fear, and rebelliousness to draw us into sinful actions. Right now, Satan and his agents of evil are diabolically plotting to destroy as many Christian marriages, homes, businesses, and churches as they can. Because we are up against a formidable foe, we must be dressed in God's armor and ready to fight.

The Nature of the Christian Life

Despite the popular teaching of many pastors today, the Christian life is not a picnic, a walk in the park, a piece of cake, a bed of roses, or the yellow brick road to unlimited health and wealth. Instead of a stroll down easy street, the Christian life is a struggle against temptation and evil. Following Christ will forever be, on this side of heaven, a spiritual battle. I'm growing increasingly concerned that many Christians are either too disinterested, too indifferent, or too spiritually exhausted to fight against evil any longer.

Whenever we decide to faithfully serve Christ, we are going to be confronted by spiritual adversaries. As well-known pastor and prolific author, John MacArthur, wisely observes, "A Christian who no longer has to struggle against the world, the flesh, and the devil is a Christian who has fallen either into sin or into complacency. A Christian who has no conflict is a Christian who has retreated from the front lines of service."[19] To those professing Christians not experiencing the oppressive pressures of living in the crossfire of this spiritual conflict, you may want to reread the previous quote. Make sure you have not given in to complacency or retreated from the front lines to live in comfort while everyone else presses on in obedience to Christ. If you are a genuine follower of Christ, you are called daily to take up your cross and faithfully follow him (see Matthew 16:24–26). If you're complacent or hiding from the fight, you may feel comfortable now, but the battle will eventually draw you in. Because of Satan's ruthless assaults and barrage of fiery darts, Christians must dress themselves in the armor of God so they can withstand his inevitable attacks.

Walking worthy of our calling in the midst of this crooked and twisted generation over the long haul requires putting on and taking up the armor of God. Before considering the specific pieces of God's armor, we need to take a closer look at our enemies and how to resist them. Ephesians 6:11 is an important verse to understand as we prepare to take our stand against evil.

Get Dressed

Proper preparation is essential for living the faithful life Paul describes in the book of Ephesians and illustrates in the book

---

19 John MacArthur, *Ephesians* (Chicago, IL: The Moody Bible Institute, 1986), 332.

of Acts. Unprepared believers are easy prey for the powers of darkness. In Ephesians 6:11, we learn why we must allow the Lord's power to reside in our lives and strengthen us to stand against Satan's strategies. Concerning the craftiness of the devil, author Max Anders writes, "He stands ready to whisper venomous accusations to us in our quiet moments and hurl demonic defamations in our busy ones."[20] There is never a time when we do not need to be on guard against the old serpent's flaming arrows. Putting on the armor of God is the means by which we stand strong in the Lord in the midst of this crooked, twisted, and evil generation.

Paul's straightforward commandment *put on* comes from the Greek verb *enduo*, meaning "to sink into (clothing)" or "to clothe oneself." The imperative mood indicates a sense of permanence, meaning we are to clothe ourselves in the whole armor of God and never take it off. God's armor is not a uniform to be worn during certain hours of the week or on game day; it must be worn at all times.

My wife and I both have doctorates. Michelle received hers long before I completed mine. For years, I have joked that I only bothered getting a doctorate for two silly reasons. One, because I grew weary of getting mail addressed to Mr. and Dr. Knolls. And two, so that I could wear a funny hat during our high school's graduation ceremonies—one like Martin Luther's.

---

20 Max Anders, *Galatians, Ephesians, Philippians, and Colossians* (Nashville, TN: Holman Reference, 1999), 193.

As the president of a Christian school, I have the privilege of participating in commencement each spring. During this formal event, I wear my distinguished-looking doctoral robe and weird hat. For 364 days of the year, my very expensive graduation regalia remains wrapped in a plastic cover, hanging in the back of my closet. For all but one day out of the year, I retrieve my clothes from my closet and completely ignore my regalia. I take the robe, hat, and hood out for one evening, and once the ceremony is finished, I put it right back where I found it. There it stays for another 364 days.

How I utilize my regalia is not how Christians are to approach the armor of God. The Lord didn't provide us with his armor to only pull it out of our spiritual closet when we think we might need it. Paul's instructions are clear: we're commanded to clothe ourselves with the armor and keep it on at all times because we never know when a spiritual attack will take place. Without God's armor, we'll be left unprotected against the spiritual raids that will predictably come, making us easy targets.

Sinking into the full armor of God means that we are to put on the complete set of defensive and offensive weapons. Paul's imagery brings to mind a soldier who is fully equipped for the battlefield. This armor, translated from the Greek word *panoplia*, includes a shield, sword, lance, helmet, greaves, and breastplate. *Panoplia* indicates that complete protection is required when entering the arena of spiritual warfare.

In all likelihood, Paul was chained to a Roman soldier when he penned his letter to the Ephesians. Because of his faithfulness to Christ and unapologetically bold proclamation of the gospel, he found himself in the company of soldiers following each of his arrests. Although the commandment to put on the full armor of God likely caused Paul's readers to picture the armor worn by a Roman foot soldier, this imagery is not limited to a Roman soldier. I would suggest that Paul's imagery primarily calls to mind the Old Testament armor of Yahweh and the promised Messiah.

The comfort and encouragement of this picture is that the armor Paul had in mind belongs to none other than God himself. In the Old Testament, we find examples of God pictured as a fully equipped warrior who forgives sin while simultaneously standing in righteous judgment against it. Two examples would be the following:

"He put on righteousness as a breastplate, and a helmet of salvation on his head; he put on garments of vengeance for clothing, and wrapped himself in zeal as a cloak" (Isaiah 59:17).

"And his delight shall be in the fear of the LORD. He shall not judge by what his eyes see, or decide disputes by what his ears hear, but with righteousness he shall judge the poor, and decide with equity for the meek of the earth; and he shall strike the earth with the rod of his mouth, and with the breath of his lips he shall kill the wicked. Righteousness shall be the belt of his waist, and faithfulness the belt of his loins" (Isaiah 11:3–5).

These two Old Testament illustrations demonstrate that the armor of God as presented in Ephesians coincides with the armor previously worn by God in his judgment against evil. This armor empowers Christians to stand against the forces of evil that are in defiant opposition to God's redemptive plan. The Greek word *histemi* (translated *stand*) was used in military contexts in reference to a soldier holding a critical position while facing an attack.

Like soldiers standing their ground against an enemy's assault on a physical battlefield, God's armor allows Christians to stand against the schemes of our spiritual enemies. It was necessary for Roman soldiers to be the type of men who could be relied upon to stand their ground even when under a ferocious attack. Likewise, Christians are to develop the character and fortitude required to stand their ground even when the forces of evil are moving against us.

Satan and His Diabolical Methods

Satan is a real enemy who Paul describes in Ephesians 2:2 as "the prince of the power of the air, the spirit that is now at work in the sons of disobedience." The word *prince* is a translation of the Greek word *archon*, meaning "ruler, commander, chief, or leader." Paul's description denotes Satan's immaterial nature and the vastness of his influence. He is the evil one who is diligently working in those disobeying God.

Prior to coming to Christ, the Christians in Ephesus were living under the power and influence of three daunting forces: the world (see Ephesians 2:2), the devil (see Ephesians 2:2), and the flesh (see Ephesians 2:3). Concerning their former lifestyle, they were not as free as the world told them.

In fact, they were in bondage to sin. New Testament scholar Peter O'Brien writes, "Those outside of Christ are not only subject to the pervasive bondage of the present evil age; they are also inspired and empowered by personal evil forces."[21] The one ruling these evil forces is none other than the fallen and rebellious angel known in Scripture as Satan. Since his rebellion against God, the old serpent has been God's archenemy, determined to oppose God and the church until the end of the age.

Elsewhere in Scripture, Satan is described as a roaring lion, a serpent, the father of lies, the tempter, and the accuser. First John 3:8 reminds us that "The devil has been sinning from the beginning. The reason the Son of God appeared was to destroy the works of the devil." Individuals who continually live a lifestyle contrary to God's commandments are revealing themselves to be children of the devil (see 1 John 3:9–10).

Although Satan's powers are limited, he is too powerful for Christians to resist and defeat in their own strength. Notice the craftiness of our enemy. Paul commands Christians to stand against the devil's "schemes" or "wiles" (KJV). The Greek word translated as *schemes* is *methodeia*, from which we get the English word *method*. In Greek, *methodeia* means "cunning arts, deceit, craftiness, trickery, or deception." Paul's usage of this word reminds us that Satan rarely, if ever, attacks Christians overtly. The father of lies typically lures

---

21 Peter T. O'Brien, *The Letter to the Ephesians* (Grand Rapids, MI: William B. Eerdmans Publishing Company, 1999), 159.

believers away with deception and duplicity as he craftily uses our fleshly desires to charm us into disobedience.

Interestingly, *methodeia* was used to describe a wild animal stalking its prey before ambushing its target. Much like the rattlesnake hiding under the rock waiting for its opportunity to attack, Satan lurks in the darkness, clandestinely searching for God's sheep who are wounded and vulnerable or have wandered from the fold and are isolated. Rather than attacking openly, the old serpent typically prefers to carry out his strategies incognito as he shrewdly plays on people's doubt, disbelief, loneliness, and insatiable desire for freedom and autonomy. Whenever the devil senses weakness or susceptibility, he unleashes his flaming arrows of temptation and entices us with the promise of freedom and satisfaction in the sinful pleasures of this world. In following his schemes, we fall in sync with his cunning plans and desires.

The concept of immoral desires and actions certainly does not mean that all pleasures are sinful or forbidden. God isn't a killjoy determined to keep all sources of enjoyment from his followers so they lead bleak and miserable lives. This does not mean, however, that all of our desires are equal. Some of our desires are beneficial and life-sustaining, while others are destructive and soul-crushing. God fashioned people with senses that afford us the opportunity to enjoy the innumerable pleasures provided in the theater of God's creation. The colorful spectacle of every beautiful sunset, the melodious sound of birdsong, every whiff of a sweet-smelling flower, the gentle touch of a cool breeze, and each succulent morsel of food point to God's wondrous and creative work.

Judging by the splendors of creation, our gracious Heavenly Father isn't opposed to recreation or pleasure—far from it; that's why he provides us with wondrous sights, tastes, smells, sounds, sensations, and wholesome activities to enjoy (see Ecclesiastes 3:11–13; 1 Timothy 6:17). Nevertheless, God is opposed to sinning to experience pleasure and participating in activities that are strictly forbidden. In his wisdom, he also forbids indulging in pleasure to the point it becomes our all-consuming reason for living. God has created many magnificent provisions for us to enjoy for our physical and spiritual benefit. However, unrestricted use of these provisions causes much harm. When pleasurable things like food, sex, exercise, and leisure are used outside of God's boundaries or to excess, they become sinful. Satan even twists and uses the good provisions found in creation to lead us away from God and bring us under sin's bondage. God does not call us to stand against pleasure but rather against sin.

Many people today view God as a cruel and tyrannical being who is only interested in squelching the pleasurable longings of our hearts and keeping us from enjoying ourselves. Rather than basking in the goodness, holiness, and graciousness of God, they stew in bitterness and resentment, considering God and his divine word to be injurious to their liberty. We must recognize, however, that it is out of God's unfathomable love, immeasurable mercy, and fatherly compassion that he places wise and well-defined boundaries in our lives. God provides these restrictions so we are afforded the opportunity to truly enjoy all that is pure, lovely, and pleasing to him in this world without guilt, shame, or the fear of judgment.

Despite today's popular opinion, God desires for humans to enjoy his creation (see Ecclesiastes 5:18–19). Nevertheless, it is impossible for God to retain his absolute holiness, unstained righteousness, and marvelous love without hating iniquity, rejecting immorality, and judging sin according to his perfect standard as recorded for us in the pages of Scripture. Our culture repeatedly tries to relieve God of his deity and authority so that people are free to live however they choose with no concern for consequences. In God's word, however, we find a clear delineation of what behaviors are acceptable and which ones are not. Our responsibility as Christians is not to force our opinions onto God's perfect word but to humbly obey all he commands.

According to Paul's description, Satan is shrewdly plotting and deceptively scheming against God's people. He tries to convince people that God is not good and that his boundaries are unreasonable and too restrictive. While readily acknowledging the intensity and craftiness of Satan's powerful assaults, we must remember that he is not omniscient or omnipotent. Although his knowledge is limited, he does have millennia of experience surveying mankind. From the devil's careful observation, he knows what makes people tick. More specifically, he knows where your flesh and mine are weak and what temptations we find particularly attractive. As the roaring lion prowls about, he is noting what temptations work on individual Christians. Prowling the perimeter, Satan looks for a weak point to expose and exploit. While not omniscient, the devil has observed our previous patterns of sinfulness and cunningly capitalizes on these sinful desires to draw us away from God and into various forms of wickedness.

The schemes of the devil are insidious; they are perfectly tailored, baited, and camouflaged traps waiting to ensnare and destroy those who are not spiritually prepared. Because of Satan's deceptiveness, evil rarely looks unattractive or repulsive. Sin is always wrapped in an attractive package—one that appeals to our appetites. Whenever temptation gives way to disobedience, Satan gains an upper hand. That is why we must fear God, delight in his commandments, and resist temptation.

The Reality of Temptation

Temptations I find appealing are not necessarily the ones you're susceptible to. For instance, I can drive past a liquor store and not give the place a second look. But for some of my friends, it's a white-knuckle event every time they come within a mile of one. When I smell tobacco, I become nauseated. To some, smelling tobacco is like enjoying the wonderful aroma of steak cooking on the grill. For people living in chronic discomfort, painkillers become attractive. Sometimes this leads down the dark road of drug addiction.

While alcohol, tobacco, and drugs are not attractive to me, I assure you that I have my share of temptations that are daily struggles. One of which is my regular battle with perfectionism. Now that may not sound so terrible to you, but I assure you it's toxic and destructive. Based on the damage perfectionism has caused in my marriage and in other relationships, there's little doubt that this besetting sin is one Satan loves to exploit in my life.

Perfectionism started early in my life, and sports exacerbated the problem. In college, perfectionism drove me to the goal of not only straight A's but to perfect 100s on every test, homework assignment, project, and paper. To score anything less than a perfect score was, in my mind, a failure. Going three-for-four in a baseball game was not perfect enough, nor was a 99 percent on a test; therefore, I failed.

When the flames of perfectionism are burning hot in my soul, I become miserable to be around (you can ask my wife). Walking the perfectionism tightrope over the canyon of failure has kept me from trying a lot of things, like publishing books. I often wonder what I could have achieved for the cause of Christ if I hadn't allowed my flesh to pursue the illusion and ever-moving target of perfection. Satan likes to whisper in my ear the lie that to be loved, accepted, and respected, I have to be perfect. Combine the deceiver's sweet song of temptation with an idolatrous heart that craves acceptance, respect, and glory, and I'm a breath away from coming unglued. The problem with walking on tightropes over a canyon is when you fall, you fall to your own demise.

At times, I can be spiritually weak and susceptible to temptations. Same as you. In an attempt to isolate and discourage us, the deceiver tries to sell us the lie that we are the only ones who experience temptation. He also tries to convince us that our sin will never hurt anyone, that we deserve to indulge in our pet sin, or that the temptation is too strong to resist, so there's no reason to try. But in 1 Corinthians 10:13–14, Paul reminds us that "no temptation has overtaken you that is not common to man. God is faithful, and he will not let you be tempted beyond your ability, but with the temptation he will also provide the way of escape, that you may be able to endure it. Therefore, my beloved, flee from idolatry." Encouraging words, but far too often we don't believe them or apply them to our daily lives.

From 1 Corinthians 10, we learn that temptation is a common part of the human experience. We are also promised that no matter how overpowering the temptation may feel, God is faithful and will provide a way of escape. Part of Satan's cunning scheme is to persuade us that Paul's words in verse 13 are fallacious.

Honestly, there are times when Paul's instruction does feel acutely untrue. Here's why. First, God's promised escape may not include the removal of the temptation. In these instances, he will provide the spiritual strength necessary to endure our particular cravings for evil. The problem is we need to seek his strength in order to stand against the temptation; oftentimes we rely on our own strength, so we fail. Second, sometimes we're caught flat-footed and unsure how to defend ourselves against temptation. Like Joseph in Genesis 39:11–12, there are times when we have to urgently flee from temptation and idolatry. Third, the path of escape is often a road we're unwilling to take. Jesus taught that radical measures sometimes need to be taken to stay pure. According to his teaching, there are times when extreme actions like tearing out your eye and cutting off your hand are necessary to stay clear of temptation (see Matthew 5:29–30). Jesus's hyperbolic language is not commanding us to dismember ourselves. Please don't cut off any body parts.

He is, however, instructing us to take whatever steps necessary to stay away from sin. This may include ending relationships, canceling the internet, taking an alternate route home from work, leaving your place of employment, or some other inconvenient measure in order to flee temptation and idolatry. Because temptation and idolatry are constantly luring us away from obedience to God's commandments, we desperately need the armor of God.

Standing against the Devil

Early in my ministry, I boldly and imprudently declared that I don't have an addictive personality. With time and experience, I have come to realize that everyone has an addictive personality. All Satan needs is the right bait, and he can hook us like a bass. The alluring enticements the deceiver uses against us are an attempt to convince us that we deserve the delicious delights of sin for a season in the comforts of his palace of pleasure. But as Spurgeon warned, "Satan's house has a front chamber full of everything that is enticing to the eye and bewitching to the sensual taste; but there is a back chamber, and no one knoweth, no one hath seen the whole of its horrors."[22] Believing we will be afforded the opportunity to enjoy the savory taste of sin without suffering the gut-wrenching consequences, we follow the desires of our sinful flesh like an ox to the slaughter (see Proverbs 7:22).

Unfortunately, our brains only remember the short-term pleasure sin brings. Oh, how quickly we forget the shame, frustration, pain, and guilt sin produces. We often use our pet sins to medicate the pain in our hearts, to cover our insecurities, or to gain relief from the stress of life. But once we satisfy our desires, we realize that we have once again disappointed God and created a mess.

Satan always works in conjunction with our sinful flesh and idolatrous hearts to skillfully entice us into sin. Despite Satan's involvement, however, we cannot blame him for our choices. Satan and his evil forces cannot force us to do anything; therefore, we are fully culpable for our decisions. Please scratch the phrase "the devil made me do it" from your vocabulary. You are responsible for your sin, not the devil.

In James 1:13–14, we read, "Let no one say when he is tempted, 'I am being tempted by God,' for God cannot be tempted with evil, and he himself tempts no one. But each person is tempted when he is lured and enticed by his own desire." Did you notice the last sentence? We are tempted because we are easily enticed by the sinful desires residing in our imperfect hearts. You cannot blame God for your sin. Nor can you blame others.

---

22 Kerry James Allen. *Spurgeon's Quotes: The Definitive Collection* (Kress Biblical Resources, 2018), 403.

Truthfully, standing against temptation and the schemes of the devil while constantly fleeing from idolatry is spiritually exhausting. There are days when I don't feel like fighting anymore. I erroneously believe that I could find relief from temptation and my idolatry by finding a cabin deep in the woods where I can escape and hide myself away. But there's a major problem with my fantasy; I would be lugging my sin nature and idolatrous heart right along with me. No matter how far I remove myself from society, my sin nature and idolatry would find a way to break through the solitude, and I would still violate God's commandments. I'm that wicked. And so are you.

None of us can leave home without our sin nature. It follows us wherever we go, promising that if we give in to temptation, we will be satisfied, fulfilled, and perfectly content. Because we are prone to believing Satan's lies and caving to the temptations he places before us, we must follow Paul's instruction offered in Ephesians 6:13. Paul writes, "Take up the whole armor of God, that you may be able to withstand in the evil day, and having done all, to stand firm." Without God's armor, we cannot stand firm against the schemes of the devil and we cannot keep ourselves free from idolatry. The day of evil in this text likely describes the age leading up to Christ's return as well as critical times in which Satan's conspiracies will be intensified as Christ's second coming approaches. The evil day does not, however, overlook particular times in which individual Christians fall under a barrage of Satan's attacks.

Biblical scholars William Cook and Chuck Lawless astutely note, "Times may come when a person is physically or emotionally drained and therefore highly susceptible to enemy temptations, or when a believer is overconfident in his spiritual strength and lowers his guard, failing to sense his need to be strengthened by the Lord."[23] There is coming a critical time in which evil will violently assault God's people. That's why we cannot grow weary in doing what's right and open the door for the devil and his evil forces. Overconfidence will also place us in harm's way; therefore, we need God's protection against Satan's schemes.

A Defeated Enemy

While we never want to overlook or dismiss the power of Satan, we must keep him and his influence in perspective. Yes, he is walking about like a roaring lion seeking whom he may devour (see 1 Peter 5:8). Keep in mind, however, Jesus Christ has already defeated Satan on the cross. Because God's adversary is a defeated enemy, he knows his time is short. This explains why Satan is relentlessly trying to cause as much chaos, heartache, and devastation as possible.

According to Ephesians 1:20–23, Christ has already defeated the forces of evil; therefore, we have no need to fear Satan or his operatives. This does not negate Satan's ability to influence people living in this wicked age. As Christians, we are not called to win the ultimate victory over Satan.

---

23 William F. Cook III and Chuck Lawless, *Spiritual Warfare in the Storyline of Scripture* (Nashville, TN: B&H Academic, 2019), 147–148.

Jesus already delivered the knockout blow when he died on the cross for the sins of the world. Rather than defeating Satan, Christians are called to withstand his deceptive and destructive attacks.

As culpable agents, we have the choice of granting authority to whomever we trust. The devil has no influence over us except for the authority we foolishly grant him by believing his lies. Neither the devil nor his demons can possess those who have the Holy Spirit of God residing in their hearts. Although Christians cannot be demon possessed, they can permit evil forces to influence their decisions. Permitting the forces of darkness to hold sway over us entrenches the vices of this world deep in our hearts. It's imperative, therefore, that we stand resolutely in the victory secured by the Lord Jesus Christ on the cross of Calvary and not allow Satan to have any influence over our lives.

Living in the time between what Christ has already accomplished on the cross and what he will accomplish when he returns, we are prone to spiritual exhaustion, frustration, and discouragement. Life is war, but don't lose heart because the ultimate victory has already been won by the Messiah, Jesus Christ. Bible scholar Frank Thielman notes, "Paul urges his readers to defend the position that the Messiah has won for them by putting on the armor of God and standing firm against the devil and other invisible evil powers."[24] The question is not whether or not you will be in the battle; the question is whether or not you will be prepared to hold the

---

[24] G. K. Beale and D. A. Carson eds., *Commentary on the New Testament Use of the Old Testament* (Grand Rapids, MI: Baker Academic, 2007), 830.

ground Jesus has claimed through his death, burial, and resurrection. We are not thrown into this spiritual battle against the forces of evil unprotected from enemy fire. God has provided his armor to protect us from the schemes of the devil and to enable us to hold the ground Jesus won. But it's up to us to put it on.

Takeaways

My family likes visiting zoos. One warm spring afternoon, we were exploring the zoo in Greenville, South Carolina. When we came upon the lion enclosure, I was profoundly disappointed when I saw the lazy-good-for-nothing lions sleeping on a hill some distance from the glass. They were visible, but from our vantage point they were difficult to see. In frustration, I whined to my wife that I wished I had brought a BB gun. Confused, Michelle asked what I planned to do with a BB gun. Thinking the answer was obvious, I was equally befuddled. In exasperation I explained that I wanted a BB gun to sting the lions' backsides so I could see them rearing up and charging the glass.

Not sure what to say to her husband's foolish and—according to her—mean idea, she simply reminded me that lions were dangerous and asked why I would ever want one to charge me. I simply pointed to the thick layer of impenetrable glass between us and the lions. Sure, the lions could roar, charge, growl, claw, and attack, but they couldn't touch me. I was perfectly safe behind the glass.

That's the way I see our spiritual enemy. Satan can roar all he wants. He can tempt and taunt me. He can growl and flash his teeth, and even inflict pain and suffering in my life within God's sovereign will as he did in the life of Job. While the great dragon can create disruption and difficulty, he can never destroy my eternal soul because I am protected by the shed blood of Jesus Christ. If you know Jesus as your Savior, Satan can't spiritually destroy you either. While we await Christ's return and stand against evil, we also have access to God's armor.

Before you leave this chapter, there are three simple steps I would like you to take in your walk with Christ.

1. Clothe yourself in the armor of God and rest in its protection. I know we haven't studied each piece of the armor in detail yet, but even a cursory reading of Ephesians 6:10–20 provides enough information to put on God's armor. As we inspect each article of armor, you'll come to a better understanding of Paul's imagery.

2. Replace your anxiety, sinful fear, and defeated spirit with one of peace, confidence, courage, and assured victory. Satan's schemes are destructive; therefore, we must be properly dressed in God's armor. Satan and his forces are formidable, but they are limited.

3. Become mindful of which of Satan's carefully crafted bait successfully entices you most often. I can name my bait. Can you name yours? Again, Satan has observed your actions long enough to know where you're spiritually weak and vulnerable. He knows how to expose the cracks in your defenses. Even a short assessment of your most recent spiritual failures

should be enough for you to identify your areas of susceptibility. Once your weaknesses are identified, bolster your defenses in those areas.

I have given you a lot to think about in this chapter. Take some time to reflect on the information and answer the questions below. In the following chapter, we will go a little deeper into why preparing for spiritual combat is so important.

Key Point: Because of Satan's deceptive nature, we must clothe ourselves in the whole armor of God so we can firmly stand against his enticing schemes.

For Further Consideration

1. In what area(s) are you particularly vulnerable to temptation?
2. How do Ecclesiastes 3:11–13 and 1 Timothy 6:17 influence your understanding of pleasure? Describe how and when God's good provisions become sinful.
3. Which of the following schemes of the devil do you find most alluring? What is it about these schemes that you find especially attractive?

   The promise of avoiding sin's consequences

   The myth of greener grass

   The seduction of worldliness

   The invigorating invitation of pride

   The illusion of self-reliance

   The therapeutic lie of rationalizations and excuses

   The intoxicating guarantee of endless pleasure

The unwavering assurance that you deserve what you desire

The falsehood of God's indifference and/or absence

The propaganda that you deserve the right to run your own life on your terms

4. Look up the following verses and write an explanation of each.

Matthew 16:17–19

Ephesians 4:25–29

Colossians 2:13–15

Hebrews 2:14

Revelation 20:10

Strategy Four
Become Combat-Ready

For we do not wrestle against flesh and blood, but against the rulers, against the authorities, against the cosmic powers over this present darkness, against the spiritual forces of evil in the heavenly places.

Ephesians 6:12

Early one morning, a few minutes after four, I was making my usual trip to the gym. As I merged onto the main road, I checked my mirrors for cars and only saw one set of headlights well behind me. I entered the right lane and paid little attention to the vehicle trailing me. A few moments later, I was startled when the approaching car slammed into the back of mine, hard enough to snap my head against the headrest. By God's grace, I didn't spin out of control or end up in the ditch.

Given the increasing rate of violent crimes in our country, I was unsure how to respond. Knowing that there have been setups where people hit someone on purpose to get the driver to stop in order to rob them, or worse, I carefully considered my options. My car at the time was old and the least of my worries. A dent on my rear bumper was irrelevant. Thankfully, the contact happened a hundred yards or so from the church where I pastor. Once I reached the driveway, I pulled off the road and watched as the car stopped behind me. I had positioned my car at the end of the driveway where I could escape through the parking lot if needed.

Expecting the car doors to fly open and attackers to rush my vehicle, I cautiously opened my door with my eyes fixed on the other car. With my blood pressure sky-high, jaw and fists clenched, I waited to see what would happen next. Should the situation turn violent, I was combat-ready and equipped with a plan. I was ready to either zip away or stand my ground and fight. Either way, I was prepared to take action.

Understanding Satan and the Forces of Evil

Satan spends much of his time working behind the scenes, testing the waters, and laying traps. But there are also occasions in which he hides in plain view. In 2 Corinthians 11:14, we read, "Satan disguises himself as an angel of light." The devil masterfully makes that which will cause spiritual destruction glitter like gold. God's adversary is capable of making even the most heinous of sins appear attractive to the spiritually vulnerable. If sin appeared gross, there would be no desire to chase after it. That's why the deceiver makes sure to present sin in a way that will draw us in and appeal to our carnal appetites.

When I was a kid, our church showed a movie one evening about hell. Because the content was graphic, the kids were sent to the nursery to play while the adults watched the movie. Of course, back in the 1970s, the older children were often left unattended in the nursery. Curious about the movie, some of the kids peeked through the curtain covering the nursery window and watched. I was one of those little spies. While I didn't see all of the movie, what I did see is still etched in my mind.

Looking back as an adult, the film was pretty ridiculous and not very biblical. From what I remember, the devil had a multicolored face and sharp, pointy horns. It was the quintessential image of Satan seen on the streets of Halloween night. He carried something that looked more like a shovel than the classic pitchfork and meandered through the pit of hell randomly whacking people with it.

Some forty years later, I no longer picture Satan the way the movie director presented him in that 1970s film. Because the biblical writers were never inspired to record exactly what Satan looks like, I can't accurately describe him. As a fallen angelic being, possibly one of the archangels, I now imagine Satan appearing in a more physically favorable manner. I'm confident of this much: the roaring lion isn't roaming about disguised in a red suit with a pointy tail, yellow horns, and a pitchfork. Satan's apparel is far more sinister. In Homer's classic *The Odyssey*, sirens were creatures with angelic singing voices who used their intoxicating melodies to entice sailors. Once the voyagers were hypnotized by their sweet songs, the sirens would lure them into the cove to drown them.

Like sirens singing their enchanting songs to entice and hypnotize their prey, Satan conceals himself as a suitable and beguiling alternative to God. The accuser presents himself as an angel of light, convincing wayward believers to trust him and entertain his beautifully crafted songs of deception. Once we acquiesce to his enticements, he unleashes his destructiveness upon those who foolishly fall under the spell of his salacious promises.

Satan approaches us in many ways, but he will never knock on the front door of our hearts proudly wearing a name tag on his chest. The old serpent will never politely invite us to ruin our marriages, get addicted, get fired, get arrested, or destroy our testimonies by caving to his carefully crafted temptations. Satan's tactics are substantially more subtle than that, making them all the more deadly. Living soberly and vigilantly is indispensable to our spiritual survival because our enemy, the roaring lion, the cunning dragon, and the father of all lies, will appear as an angel of light and drag us into the depths of sin and destruction. Employing his deceptively sweet melodies, the devil drowns us underneath the pummeling waves of temptation.

Races and Warfare

A picture really is worth a thousand words. In the New Testament, the Christian life is compared to running a race.

When I imagine races, I picture misery. I love lifting weights, but running? Not so much. I've done a few 5Ks, but that's my limit. Some of my good friends enjoy running marathons; I even know two guys who participate in ultramarathons. No thanks, I'll definitely skip those. To run a one-hundred-mile race takes endurance, patience, and perseverance—along with a little insanity, if you ask me. Nonetheless, participating in a race beautifully paints the picture of a believer who shares the characteristics of a good runner. Following Jesus in this twisted and crooked generation certainly requires a great deal of endurance, patience, and perseverance.

As we are learning, the Christian life is also compared to warfare. Combat imagery is used in 1 Timothy 6:12, where Paul tells his protégé, Timothy, to "Fight the good fight of the faith." Fighting the good fight of faith requires Christians to stand in the power of God while being firmly anchored in God's word. While fighting the good fight, we must remain steadfast, always abounding in the work of the Lord so we don't allow temptation to lead us into sin (see 1 Corinthians 15:58).

My father-in-law served in the United States Navy during the Vietnam War. My father served in the Air Force. My brother, Mark, served in the Marine Corps and was deployed to Beirut in the 1980s. Because of my father's and brother's service, I considered enlisting in the military. I actually came within a few hours of joining the Navy. Due to a health issue, which I'll describe later, I never had the opportunity to serve. By God's grace, I have never been in a combat zone like my brother and many of my friends. I have never heard all the details concerning some of the horrifying combat experiences they endured, and I'll never ask them to share. What I do know is that what they experienced in combat was traumatic, and it deeply scarred their souls.

The emotional trauma of warfare traumatizes people deeply because such violence is against human reasoning. Physical war between nations is the epitome of sin. It's violent and bloody and leaves nations in ruin. In every war, people created in the image of God suffer and die. Unfortunately, that's what makes Paul's usage of warfare imagery so effective.

Picturing the conflict between the forces of evil and righteousness as a war helps believers understand what is at stake and the level of sacrifice necessary to mount a counteroffensive to resist Satan's malicious attacks. In the geopolitical world, there are wars that must be fought, as described in the Christian just war theory. Evil, as illustrated by wicked men such as Adolph Hitler, must be militarily confronted in order to protect citizens from the horrors of unrestrained cruelty. In the spiritual realm, Satan is on the warpath, desperately trying to take every inch of ground he possibly can. Beginning with Adam and Eve, he has assaulted God's character, schemed, lied, and manipulated God's truth in order to win people to his cause. He's after the hearts of people, and Christians must not stand idly by and watch him destroy lives. The spiritual battle is one worth fighting. There should not be one single Christian hiding in a bunker, refusing to stand and fight against the devil. If you have been passively letting every other Christian charge on the spiritual battlefield while you have been tucked away well behind the front lines, it's time to stand up straight. Stiffen your spine and prepare to fight.

In Paul's second book to Timothy, he mixes the metaphors of race and war when he writes, "I have fought the good fight, I have finished the race, I have kept the faith" (2 Timothy 4:7). God's will for our lives is that we would display the same level of faithfulness throughout our lives. In light of the spiritual warfare raging between God and the forces of evil, we must be combat-ready and stay clear of spiritual danger zones.

Spiritual Danger Zones

Before diving into Ephesians 6:12, I want to offer an urgent warning. You're a few chapters into this book and maybe you're confused. Maybe all of the discussion about spiritual exhaustion and warfare has you scratching your head wondering what you're missing. If you examine your life right now and you're not experiencing spiritual warfare, you may have an even bigger problem on your hands. There are three possible causes for the lack of spiritual struggle in your life, and each of them can lead us headlong into one of the following spiritual danger zones.

Complacency is the first spiritual danger zone Christians often wander into. According to dictionary.com, complacency is a "feeling of quiet pleasure or security, often while unaware of some potential danger or defect." When complacency sets in, believers often develop a sense of overconfident smugness or uncritical satisfaction with themselves. Spiritually complacent people stop taking initiative in their relationship with Christ and quickly become disengaged. They quit biblically assessing their hearts and fail to invest the necessary time developing a closer relationship with the Lord and with the body of Christ. Detached Christians stop focusing on obedience to Christ, typically to the point where they begin following their own selfish desires.

When believers become complacent, they grow spiritually blind and indifferent to the needs of others. Complacent Christians often lose hope. When believers become indifferent to following Jesus, there is no reason for Satan to launch an assault against them. The old serpent focuses his attention on soldiers actively engaged in the battle, not on deserters who have fled the fight.

Second, you may be free of spiritual opposition because you're lost in the danger zone of hypocrisy. The word *hypocrite* occurs multiple times in the teachings of Jesus. Matthew 6 and 23 are the two best examples of Jesus's usage of the word. The Greek word translated as *hypocrite* is *hupokrites*. In Greek, the word was used to describe an actor performing on the stage.

Like a stage actor, a spiritual hypocrite is a person pretending to be something they have no intention of ever being. Judas Iscariot—identified in Scripture as the betrayer—is arguably the most notorious pretender in human history. For years, Judas walked by Jesus's side only to sell him out for thirty pieces of silver. He pretended to be a loyal follower of the Lord, but in reality he was unbelieving and selfish. To this day, Judas's name is synonymous with betrayal. As Spurgeon warned, "Better be sneered at as a Puritan than be despised as a hypocrite."[25]

Admittedly, we are all hypocritical sometimes as we masquerade about in our false piety and self-glory. All sinners are occasionally guilty of saying one thing and doing another. The difference is a true hypocrite is one who puts on a show and has no intention of developing a genuine relationship with Jesus or with his people. The Pharisees, for example, were more interested in power, respect, and influence than with pleasing and honoring God through humble obedience. True hypocrites parade around wearing their superficial religiosity pretending to be someone they have no desire of ever becoming.

A hypocritical actor will never attract Satan's attention. There's no need to bother tempting individuals with evil who are disingenuous in their claim of being a committed follower of Christ. The great American preacher and theologian Jonathan Edwards eloquently observes, "A hypocrite may retain his hope without opposition as long as he lives, the devil never disturbing it nor attempting to disturb it. But there is perhaps no true Christian but what has his hope assaulted by him."[26] If Satan egregiously assaulted God's Son, who are we to assume that we'll be spared such an attack?

---

25 Spurgeon, 485.
26 Jonathan Edwards, *The Religious Affections* (Carlisle, PA: The Banner of Truth Trust, 2007), 101.

Because Jesus faced the beguiling schemes of the devil, all Christians should expect to experience the same.

Third, you may have unknowingly stepped into the danger zone of a seared conscience. If your conscience has lost its acuteness, it's unsurprising that you're not experiencing spiritual opposition. It's difficult to imagine someone with a completely seared conscience bothering to read a book like this one. But it may be that the sensitivity of your conscience is waning. If so, you need to recalibrate your conscience based on scriptural commandments before you become even more desensitized to the truth.

We all have a conscience, but we are never told by God to allow it to serve as our ultimate guide. Even though "let your conscience be your guide" is a popular axiom in society, Scripture must be our infallible standard. Conscience can be defined as, "A person's inner awareness of conforming to the will of God or departing from it, resulting in either a sense of approval or condemnation."[27] The conscience was given as a warning mechanism to guard us from spiritually and morally collapsing. While no one's conscience is perfectly in line with Scripture, it's essential in protecting us from living outside the protective boundaries God has established.

In 1 Timothy 4:1–2, Paul writes, "In later times some will depart from the faith by devoting themselves to deceitful spirits and teachings of demons, through the insincerity [from *hupokrisis*] of liars whose consciences are seared." There

---

27 Ronald F. Youngblood, ed., *Nelson's New Illustrated Bible Dictionary* (Nashville, TN: Thomas Nelson Publishing, 1995), 295.

are two hazards in these verses, and they fit hand in glove. The first is false teachers who spread deceit. The second is a seared conscience that follows the acceptance of lies. Authors Andrew Naselli and J. D. Crowley explain, "We make conscience *insensitive* by developing a habit of ignoring its voice of warning so that the voice gets weaker and weaker and finally disappears."[28] Because our conscience can be dulled or seared, we cannot allow it to be the ultimate determinant of what's right and what's wrong. The conscience is an important warning system, but God's unchanging word is our ultimate authority.

If you find yourself in one of these three categories, the Lord will send trials into your life for correction and recalibration. Hebrews 12:6–11 reminds us that God chastens those he loves. Like a caring father correcting his sons and daughters, God corrects his children. If you're living in one of these three danger zones, I urge you to repent of your sin, seek the Lord's forgiveness, and find someone to disciple you.

The Participants in Spiritual Warfare

In my estimation, Ephesians 6:12 is the key verse of the armor of God passage. Here's why: the text's overriding argument is preparation to stand against the schemes of the devil. In order to resist the allurements of the evil one, Christians must adorn themselves in God's armor and prepare themselves to fight against evil. In verse 12, Paul provides the reason

---

28 Andrew David Naselli and J. D. Crowley, *Conscience* (Wheaton, IL: Crossway, 2016), 29.

for this crucial warning. The word *for* that begins the verse can actually be translated as *because*. Paul doesn't command believers to stand against the wiles of the devil without offering an explanation of why it's necessary. The reason he offers is sobering counsel that should cause us to pay close attention to what he has to say in the following verses.

People are more than meets the eye; we are not merely physical beings made of flesh and blood. Humans are primarily spiritual beings. Unlike the rest of creation, humankind is created in the image of God (see Genesis 1:26–27). As God's image-bearers, we have souls that will spend eternity somewhere. As we'll soon discover in Ephesians 6:12, we must see beyond what we can examine with our senses and recognize that there are spiritual forces at work behind what our eyes can see and our hands can touch.

I grew up during the height of the Cold War. To this day, I vividly remember the cover of the March 29, 1982 edition of *Time* magazine. The eerie face in the red mushroom cloud haunted me as a kid. I even remember the headline: "Thinking the Unthinkable—Rising Fears About Nuclear War." Horrifyingly, this sounds like an appropriate headline for today. As an eleven-year-old boy, I could imagine the physical ramifications of a nuclear war. Movies and television shows of the day depicted what the world would be like following a nuclear exchange, and it was one I feared—still do, if I'm honest.

Unlike the terrors of physical warfare, the horrors of spiritual warfare are much harder to visualize. It's easy to forget that in every heart of every person, there is a spiritual battle taking place, and there are millions of people suffering as a result. In our marriages, there is spiritual opposition trying to destroy our families. In our churches, there are spiritual battles taking place that can produce devastating consequences. In our culture wars, there are spiritual forces driving the fight between those who stand for biblical truth and morality and those who do not. When all we see is flesh and blood, we forget that our ultimate fight is not with people, it's against the evil spiritual forces at work in the world.

In Ephesians 6:12, Paul warns us that "we do not wrestle against flesh and blood!" Paul's usage of *palay*, the word translated as *wrestle*, portrays hand-to-hand combat. In this case, we are engaged in hand-to-hand combat with spiritual forces. We do not fight this spiritual battle against evil with sniper rifles, drones, or guided missiles from an offshore ship or the safety of a military compound. This is hand-to-hand combat fought at close range where you can smell the enemy's sweat. Hear your opponent's groans. Taste one another's blood. In hand-to-hand combat, soldiers get punched, kicked, scratched, head-butted, and even bit. It's a no-holds-barred type of fight for the spiritual well-being of your soul.

Not only is this spiritual battle fought at close range, we are also confronting a menacing opponent. According to Paul's description, the spiritual forces we face are exceedingly powerful and must never be underestimated. Think David versus Goliath times a million. This spiritual struggle isn't an ordinary street fight. It's a battle against rulers, against the authorities, against the cosmic powers lurking over this present darkness (i.e., dark sinful world), and against the diabolical spiritual forces of evil. We are in the fight of the ages.

Even though the list above may imply it, I don't personally believe Paul is presenting a spiritual caste system in which Satan's henchmen are ranked. We must all agree, however, that the forces of evil are a formidable enemy capable of catastrophic spiritual destruction. Note the groups of evil forces participating in this spiritual battle:

1. Rulers and authorities (see also Ephesians 1:20–21; Ephesians 3:8–10)—created and defeated; therefore, limited in power and influence.

    - Colossians 1:16 "For by him all things were created, in heaven and on earth, visible and invisible, whether thrones or dominions or rulers or authorities—all things were created through him and for him."
    - Colossians 2:15 "He disarmed the rulers and authorities and put them to open shame, by triumphing over them in him."
    - 1 Peter 3:21–22 "Through the resurrection of Jesus Christ, who has gone into heaven and is at the right hand of God, with angels, authorities, and powers having been subjected to him."

2. Cosmic powers (only occurs here in the New Testament) and spiritual forces—part of this present darkness and evil.
   - Colossians 1:12–14 "Giving thanks to the Father, who has qualified you to share in the inheritance of the saints in light. He has delivered us from the domain of darkness and transferred us to the kingdom of his beloved Son, in whom we have redemption, the forgiveness of sins."
   - Acts 26:18 "To open their eyes, so that they may turn from darkness to light and from the power of Satan to God, that they may receive forgiveness of sins and a place among those who are sanctified by faith in me" (i.e., God).
   - Ephesians 5:8 "For at one time you were darkness, but now you are light in the Lord. Walk as children of light."

Given the spiritual and evil nature of our enemy, we cannot fight the battle trusting in our strength and limited resources alone. As humans, we are not cosmic powers; we're nothing but ordinary, fallen, finite, flawed mortals who are merely flesh and blood, incapable of defending ourselves against Satan and his legions. We need God's armor to resist these demonic forces. By no means does Paul's argument negate the role of wicked people (i.e., flesh and blood) in this evil age. Sinful people seeking to undermine God and his word are certainly involved in the carnality dominating the culture. Because we are morally culpable for our decisions, we are liable for our choices. Blaming Satan for our volitional sinful decisions is not acceptable and will never produce true repentance. Human responsibility and accountability, however, do not diminish the reality of satanic influences in the world.

Concerning the nature of spiritual warfare, Paul writes to the church at Corinth, "For though we walk in the flesh, we are not waging war according to the flesh. For the weapons of our warfare are not of the flesh but have divine power to destroy strongholds" (2 Corinthians 10:3–4). In the following chapter, he adds, "For such men are false apostles, deceitful workmen, disguising themselves as apostles of Christ. And no wonder, for even Satan disguises himself as an angel of light. So it is no surprise if his servants, also, disguise themselves as servants of righteousness" (2 Corinthians 11:13–15). In this world, we will be regularly confronted with human cunningness, craftiness, and deceitfulness that stand in opposition to the gospel (see Ephesians 4:11–14). Satan and his forces are at play in this age, but so are wicked people following in his footsteps. When we live each day only viewing the world through our physical eyes, we are missing the violent spiritual struggle taking place between those who love God and those who do not. In order to wrestle against the forces of evil, we must be dressed in the whole armor of God and fully equipped with truth so we are combat-ready.

Takeaways

Many believers seem oblivious to the spiritual battle Paul describes in the sixth chapter of Ephesians, so they are ill-prepared for the fight. Only God's armor is sufficiently strong enough to help us stand against the schemes of Satan and his henchmen. In order to digest the nature of this battle, we need to begin by understanding the word translated as *wrestle*.

The word Paul uses to describe this spiritual struggle is not found elsewhere in the New Testament. It was, however, commonly used outside of Scripture to describe the sport of wrestling. *Wrestle* is an English translation of the Greek word *palay*, meaning "to wrestle." Easy enough. Specifically, the word was used to portray a contest between two individuals in which each contestant endeavors to throw the other on the ground. The match is decided when the victor is able to hold his opponent down with his hand upon his neck. Sounds pretty violent to me.

In seventh grade, I tried wrestling. I definitely liked the idea of slamming people on the ground, so it sounded fun. As it turned out, wrestling was plain awful. I hated everything about it. Rolling around on a mat with my nose stuck in some middle school boy's armpit, or worse, was plain gross. If there's one thing I learned during my failed attempt at wrestling, it's this: the sport requires a lot of hard work. I vividly remember one particular practice. It was the day before Thanksgiving, and the coach was pushing us harder than ever before. We were running in place on the mat and doing burpees for what seemed like an hour. My heart was pounding, sweat was stinging my eyes, and I felt like I was about to collapse. That was the moment I knew that I didn't want to wrestle anymore. I finished practice that horrible afternoon and went home for the Thanksgiving holiday. I never went back.

Wrestling against spiritual beings is a whole different ball game; it's a battle in which I can't simply turn in my equipment and go home feeling sorry for myself. Like staying physically in shape, staying spiritually fit requires a lot of hard work. The exhaustion that comes from spiritual warfare can leave us feeling like packing up and handing in our suit of armor, then heading home for a spiritual holiday that quickly becomes a permanent vacation. Before you quit the fight and turn your back on following Jesus, consider the following three takeaways.

1. If you're questioning why you're not exerting any significant energy wrestling against the forces of evil, take a careful inventory of your heart. Find out if you're aimlessly wandering around in one of the danger zones discussed earlier. If you need help, ask a spiritually mature friend or pastor to guide your assessment. Consider the signs of each of the three danger zones and make certain that you're not stuck in one.

Signs of spiritual complacency would include:

- You have developed a false sense of security.
- You are unaware of or indifferent to spiritual dangers in your life.
- You have a spiritual deficiency that you are either refusing to see or are blind to.
- You have developed a sense of spiritual smugness that is keeping you from an honest evaluation of your relationship with Christ.
- You have stopped taking initiative to grow spiritually (e.g., no longer praying or reading Scripture).
- You are disengaged from the body of Christ (e.g., no longer attending or serving in a local church).
- You no longer invest time in your relationship with the Lord or with other Christians.

Signs of hypocrisy from the religious leaders seen in Matthew 6 and 23 would include:

- You don't practice what you preach.
- You perform outward religious acts to be seen by men.
- You enjoy occupying positions of honor.
- You focus on minor details while rejecting the most important commandments.
- You have cleaned up your outward appearance to the neglect of developing an inner character that resembles Jesus.

Signs of a seared or waning conscience would include:

- You are engaged in blatantly sinful activities with no sense of guilt or remorse over your choices.
- You are allowing your weakened conscience to guide your decisions.
- You no longer consider God's unchanging word as the ultimate authority in your life.
- You are rejecting godly counsel from those who love you.
- You are tolerating sin in your life that you once found repulsive.

2. Recognize that while Satan and his henchmen comprise a defeated army, they are not to be underestimated. Even defeated armies don't always surrender and willingly sign a peace treaty. They often fight as long as they can to continue inflicting damage upon their enemies. It's the "if I'm going down, I'm taking everyone else with me" mentality. The gates of hell cannot prevail against the kingdom of God, but Satan will not admit or accept defeat easily. Satan's goal is to strip God of the glory due his name while demanding that the praise and admiration the Creator alone deserves be directed at him. During the devil's relentless pursuit of glory, there will be no peace treaty signed in this age; therefore, we must be prepared for the battle as it continues to rage.

Peter likened Satan to a roaring lion seeking whom he may devour (see 1 Peter 5:8). So we don't fall prey to the devil's tactics, Peter commands us to be spiritually wise and vigilant. He also commands believers to resist the devil in immovable faith (see 1 Peter 5:9). James promises that if we steadfastly resist the devil, he will flee from us (see James 4:7). That's why we must live vigilantly, stand firm in immovable faith, and resist the devil. He will flee from you, but not without a fight.

3. Fighting the good fight of faith requires Christians to stand in the power of God. Trying to rely on our own strength is what comes naturally, but when wrestling against the rulers, authorities, cosmic powers, and forces of evil influencing this present age, we are woefully outmanned and outgunned. We need God's help to win this spiritual struggle. As Jesus taught in John 15:5, "Apart from me you can do nothing." Certainly, the nothing Jesus had in mind includes fighting the good fight of faith against the forces of evil. In order to stand strong against the schemes of the devil, you must be combat-ready.

In the next chapter, we will begin putting on our armor. As we consider each piece, we can develop a more comprehensive plan for wrestling with the devil.

Oh, by the way, the person who hit me in the opening story was a young woman who was driving to work. She fell asleep at the wheel! I'll tell you this much: she was wide awake after she hit me.

Key Point: Knowing that the forces of evil are formidable foes, Christians must refuse to be passive and prepare ourselves to wrestle against Satan and his minions.

For Further Consideration

1. How do the following verses relate to spiritual warfare?

    Colossians 2:13–15
    1 Corinthians 9:24–25
    2 Corinthians 2:11
    2 Corinthians 10:3–5
    Ephesians 1:20–21
    Ephesians 2:1–3
    Ephesians 3:8–10
    Ephesians 4:25–29
    1 Thessalonians 2:18
    1 Timothy 6:12
    2 Timothy 4:7
    Hebrews 12:1–2
    James 4:7
    Revelation 20:1–3

2. How well are you running the race and fighting the good fight of faith?
3. How does understanding the power of the enemy influence your approach to spiritual warfare?
4. Of the three danger zones mentioned in this chapter, which one(s) are you struggling with? What steps can you take to escape the danger zone?

Strategy Five
Put On the Armor of God

Preliminary Observations Regarding God's Armor

Therefore take up the whole armor of God, that you may be able to withstand in the evil day, and having done all, to stand firm.

Ephesians 6:13

Up to this point, we have discussed four important strategies that will equip us to stand against the evil forces influencing this world. While the first four tactics are necessary, they are not enough. We also need to implement the fifth strategy, which is putting on and taking up the whole armor of God. Without the protection provided by the armor of God, we are dangerously vulnerable on the spiritual battlefield. Before addressing God's armor in detail, I would like to make six preliminary observations regarding the armor of God found in Ephesians 6:13. These introductory remarks will prepare you for future content. As we prepare to address the particular pieces of armor, keep in mind that God is the one who ultimately provides the protection, strength, and power necessary for fruitful Christian service.

The first preliminary observation is a simple reminder concerning the Greek word *enduo* from Ephesians 6:11. It means to "put on" or "to sink into as with clothing." We will see this word once again in verse 14, which we'll cover in the next section.

Second, because God's enemies are spiritual in nature, we must be spiritually equipped to withstand their ferocious attacks. In order to resist the old serpent's schemes, we must also *take up* the armor of God. *Take up* is a translation of the Greek word *analambano*, meaning "to take up an object in order to use it." Whenever we pick up God's armor, we are expected to put it to use. The pieces of God's armor are not merely decorative; they are specifically designed for spiritual warfare. Putting on and taking up God's armor with the intention of using it empowers us to resist evil.

Third, putting on the whole armor of God allows us to stand firm against the forces of evil. The Greek word *histemi*, meaning "to cause a person to keep his place" or "to stand ready" is used in verses 11, 13, and 14. This word describes someone who does not hesitate and does not waver when the time comes to fight. Like the apostles and many other early Christians who stood firm on the gospel to the point

Preliminary Observations Regarding God's Armor

they were martyred for their faith, our resolve cannot waver. Rather than retreating from the fight, we must stand firm and use God's armor to fend off the forces of evil.

Fourth, the day of evil describes the age leading up to Christ's return in general, as well as serving as a reference to critical times in which Satan's schemes will be intensified. In Ephesians 5:15–16, Paul writes, "Look carefully then how you walk, not as unwise but as wise, making the best use of the time, because the days are evil." Today is evil, but there is coming a time in which the assault against God's people will be at its worst. Regardless of exactly how God's plan for the world unfolds, we must be armed and ready to stand against the devil's cunning plots. Wearing the whole armor of God offers much-needed protection from Satan and his forces.

Fifth, the first three pieces of armor—belt, breastplate (i.e., shirt), and shoes—are clothing. The second set of three—shield, helmet, and sword—are armaments that are to be taken up for the purpose of warfare. It's been argued that the sword is the only offensive armament mentioned. That's true to some degree. But I believe both verbs Paul uses to introduce the armor (*put on* the whole armor of God and *take up* the whole armor of God) apply to all six pieces of armor. *Put on* would indicate defensive actions whereas *take up* would be indicative of offensive movements. According to Paul's usage of these two verbs, we are called to play both offense *and* defense. We have been drafted into a spiritual battle, called to serve Christ with courage, boldness, compassion, and dignity. Attacks from Christ's bloodthirsty enemies will come from all directions, so keep your eyes open and your armor strapped on.

Sixth, what Christians are asked to *put on* and *take up* are immaterial; truth, righteousness, readiness, faith, salvation, and the word of God are all spiritual in nature. The labor Paul calls us to perform isn't accomplished with our hands. Spiritual warfare isn't waged using physical objects. The battle we are called to fight is fought with our minds, hearts, will, and reason. You can't go into your closet and pull out a pair of truth or righteousness or faith. These immaterial pieces of armor are essential for our spiritual well-being, and it all begins with God's belt of truth.

Belt: Believe the Truth

Stand therefore, having fastened on the belt of truth.
Ephesians 6:14

Currently, we are living in an age of confusion where people believe they possess the authority to define truth however they see fit. Despite the increasing rancor over the offensive idea of objective truth, absolute truth does exist. It always has. It always will. In order for something to be true, there must be an objective standard by which accuracy is measured. When the objective standard is ignored, people are left to determine their own definition of what is right and what is wrong. Because our Creator is a God of order, whenever we attempt to manage the world on our own, chaos and disorder always follow.

Our depravity is the reason we prefer a standard of truth that fits our personal lifestyle and approves of whatever behaviors we want to practice. Theologian Norman Geisler and apologist Frank Turek warn, "False ideas about truth lead to false ideas about life. In many cases, these false ideas give apparent justification for what is really immoral behavior.

For if you can kill the concept of truth, then you can kill the concept of any true religion or any true morality."[29] Kill the truth; that's exactly what some in our culture long to accomplish. Put the truth to death and deny the existence of God, then you can live however you choose without fear of consequences or divine accountability. Our insatiable desire to be our own god makes the idea of objective truth repulsive. Those who advocate for the concept of divinely ordained authoritative truth are categorized as hateful, outdated, or fools unworthy of having a seat at the cultural round table of knowledge.

Personally, I find the objective truth that I'm five foot eleven and a fit 180 pounds abhorrent. Based on my ideal truth, I'm six foot two, 225 pounds of pure muscle; I can bench-press 400 pounds, deadlift 600, squat 500, and run the forty in under five seconds. Even when I was young and at the peak of my athleticism, I could never have reached those numbers. The only way, and I mean *the only way*, I will ever reach this ideal is to change the scale on which my physical attributes and performance are measured. That's how we prefer to live. If we don't like God's absolute truth as recorded in Scripture, we bend it to fit our own version of truth.

Objective truth becomes particularly intolerable when applied to salvation and morality. People like choices, and they demand the right to define truth by their own dictionary.

---

[29] Norman L. Geisler and Frank Turek, *I Don't Have Enough Faith to Be an Atheist* (Wheaton, IL: Crossway, 2004), 40.

No matter how ardently people deny the idea of objective truth, however, it still exists. Truth has been revealed in the Bible. According to Scripture, there is only one way to heaven, not many. According to Scripture, what is right and what is wrong is defined by God, not humanity. Because fallen people prefer autonomy over submission, scores of people are actively and creatively working hard to deny God's unchanging truth. People can deny God's commandments all they want, but they will be no less true and no less binding.

Truth and Lies

Given what's at stake, Satan's vehement opposition of God and his absolute truth isn't surprising. The father of lies wants nothing to do with truth, and he crafts his cunning schemes to keep people from believing God's eternal word. Jesus's words in John 8:44 are startling and worth noting. To his opponents, he said, "You are of your father the devil, and your will is to do your father's desires. He was a murderer from the beginning, and does not stand in the truth, because there is no truth in him. When he lies, he speaks out of his own character, for he is a liar and the father of lies." Because lies and deception define Satan's iniquitous character, he has no choice but to lie and deceive. Lying is the great deceiver's native tongue, and like most Americans, he isn't bilingual.

Like all good liars, Satan seasons his lies with just enough truth to make them palatable, otherwise we would never believe them. He deviously uses his intricate dishonesties to deceive us, to convince us that we deserve what he's offering, and to draw us away from God's life-giving, unadulterated truth. The devil is also described as a murderer who is bent on causing as much chaos and destruction as he can. Whether he enmeshes the world in anarchy or despotism is of little consequence in his mind. As long as he sees as much of the world burn as possible, he's amused. Based on Jesus's description, the devil is not your friend, nor does he have your best interest in mind. He is a masterful manipulator and a mass murderer; he is God's enemy, and he is ours too.

As the great deceiver, Satan's unholy character drives him to manipulate, swindle, and lie. It's who he is. In his destitute state of wickedness, Satan refuses to glorify God and seeks to deceptively distract people from recognizing God's infinite righteousness and goodness. The devil's incessant lying weaves a web of deception that lures unprepared individuals into his fraudulent and devious schemes. Notice the words of Revelation 12:9, "And the great dragon was thrown down, that ancient serpent, who is called the devil and Satan, the deceiver of the whole world—he was thrown down to the earth, and his angels were thrown down with him." As the father of lies, god of this world, the great dragon, and the atrocious deceiver, the ancient serpent poses a clear and present danger to humanity. Spiritual blindness is one of the most deadly spiritual dangers we face. Ever since the Garden of Eden, mankind has been corrupted by the sinister serpent's breath, making us prone to denying, ignoring, forgetting, or neglecting God.

Belt: Believe the Truth

According to 2 Corinthians 4:4, Satan is "The god of this world [who] has blinded the minds of the unbelievers, to keep them from seeing the light of the gospel of the glory of Christ." Satan's deceptive schemes have blinded those who categorically reject God and his word, leaving them in danger of an eternity separated from God. Blinding people to the truth of the gospel is one of Satan's most deadly maneuvers, which helps explain the prevalence of biblical illiteracy. If the god of this world actively shields unbelievers from the truth, it's foolish to expect that those who zealously serve his archenemy will be spared from hostile spiritual assaults intended to derail our commitment to Christ. That's why followers of Jesus must be armed and ready to wrestle against the great dragon and those who follow him.

In the opening phrase of Philippians 4:8, Paul commands Christians to consistently think on what is true. It's impossible to dwell on what's true if we can't define truth. We would be hard pressed to find a more fitting definition of truth than the one offered by John MacArthur, who writes, "*Truth is that which is consistent with the mind, will, character, glory, and being of God.* Even more to the point: *truth is the self-expression of God.*"[30] Perfectly said. In the Bible, we find God's self-expressed truth that is based on his absolute holiness.

Speaking to a group of Jews who believed in him, Jesus said, "If you abide in my word, you are truly my disciples, and you will know the truth, and the truth will set you free"

---

30 John MacArthur, *The Truth War* (Nashville, TN: Thomas Nelson Publishing, 2007), 2.

(John 8:31–32). To the Jews standing in opposition to him, he said, "You cannot bear to hear my word" (John 8:43). Believers abide in God's truth; unbelievers find God's truth unbearable. Later, Jesus prayed to the Father, "Sanctify them in the truth; your word is truth" (John 17:17). Based on Jesus's divine prayer, along with MacArthur's insightful definition, we're left with but one conclusion: God defines truth; people do not. True disciples of Jesus find comfort and hope in God's truth and are set free from the penalty and bondage of sin. Those who reject God consider the truth of his word intolerable and will suffer the consequences of their rejection.

Our divine Creator, who is above all of creation, retains every right to define how the world should work and the boundaries in which people must live. God alone possesses the authority to delineate what is right and what is wrong. This is why so many people today reject the idea of an omnipotent Creator: If there is a Creator, the world is the result of intelligent design. If there is intelligent design it means the Creator crafted the world with a distinct and holy purpose. If there is a perfect plan behind creation, then the world is bound by a Creator-defined objective and morality. And if there are absolute definitions of purpose and right and wrong, then there must be accountability and justice for those living in creation.

From passages like Joshua 4:24, we learn that God's divine and miraculous acts are performed "so that all the peoples of the earth may know that the hand of the Lord is mighty, that you may fear the LORD your God forever." What an incredible truth! God performs marvelous deeds so the entire world knows that he is mighty and will honor his name with reverential awe. In a futile attempt to live outside of any accountability to the Creator, and to escape his justice, much of humanity chooses to place their faith and trust in an evolutionary process that is based on randomness, blind chance, and mathematical improbabilities. The reason the theory of evolution is appealing is because it allows people to deny God's existence so they can live on their own terms and for their own glory.

During the Exodus generation, God provided Israel with the Mosaic Law. In the preamble to the law, we find the Ten Commandments (see Exodus 20:1–17; Deuteronomy 5:1–21). These foundational commandments have served as a vital building block of civilization since God spoke them to Moses on Mount Sinai. My goal isn't to present a theological treatise on how the Old Testament Law fits into the life of the New Testament Christian, but a brief explanation is in order.

When Jesus died on the cross, he completely fulfilled the Old Testament Law. Because Jesus's sacrifice satisfied God's wrath and fulfilled the law, the church is not required to adhere to the laundry list of laws and regulations found in books like Leviticus. This is not to say, however, that books like Leviticus don't have a divine purpose for New Covenant believers. Since all Scripture is given by God's inspiration and is profitable for spiritual growth, we cannot ignore any portion of the Bible (see 2 Timothy 3:16–17). But it's essential that we keep each text in its context and understand where it fits in the unfolding of God's progressive revelation to humanity.

While we're no longer required to sacrifice animals and keep the other laws found in the Mosaic Law, all of the Old Testament is instructive and authoritative for Christians today. For instance, the main point of Leviticus for the church is that God is absolutely holy and we are not. Regarding the book of Leviticus, Old Testament professor Allen Ross writes, "The idea of the holiness of God is understood from the outset by God's prohibiting from his presence every sinful and diseased person or thing—they were simply incompatible with the holy Lord God."[31] As fallen sinners, we are also incompatible with God. That may sting your ego, but it's the truth. Apart from God's mercy, grace, and love, we are hopelessly lost. According to God's perfect plan of redemption, Jesus took the penalty of our sin upon himself so that we might enjoy justification through him, and only through him.

Like Old Covenant believers, we're incapable of perfectly fulfilling the law. Scripture teaches that if we violate the law in even one point, we're considered guilty of it all (see James 2:10). The Mosaic Law also pointed forward to the coming Messiah, the one who would perfectly satisfy the lofty demands of the law on our behalf. Throughout books like Leviticus and Numbers, we repeatedly see the phrase

---

31　Allen P. Ross, *Holiness to the Lord* (Grand Rapids, MI: Baker Academic, 2002), 45.

without blemish regarding the animals that were to be offered as sacrifices. No animal is perfectly blemish-free. That's one of the reasons the Old Testament sacrifices could never atone for our sins. The imperfect sacrifices prescribed under the Mosaic Law pointed to the perfect Lamb of God who would come and atone for our transgressions. Only the Lord Jesus Christ, the sinless and spotless Lamb of God, was the sufficient sacrifice given by the Father to fulfill the Old Testament Law. Because of the Messiah's perfect and atoning sacrifice on the cross, the church is not required to sacrifice animals or keep the hundreds of other laws given to Old Testament Israel.

The Ten Commandments

Listing all the laws and regulations included in the Mosaic Law from memory is a tall task. Nonetheless, most Christians can name many, if not all, of the Ten Commandments, which have served as the basic morality for people since the days of Moses. The reason every culture recognizes at least a portion of these commandments is because humanity, being created in God's image, possesses a conscience that allows us to have a general sense of what is right and what is wrong. This rudimentary sense of morality is given to people as a part of God's common grace, and explains why so many non-Christians are still morally upright individuals who believe that disrespecting parents, murder, adultery, stealing, lying, and—arguably to a lesser degree—covetousness are wrong. To be clear, God's common grace and the general sense of what is righteous and what is unrighteous do not save anyone from their sin. Living a life of impeccable moral integrity cannot redeem anyone, only faith in Christ can accomplish that miracle.

As the spotless Lamb of God, sacrificed on the cross of Calvary, Jesus fulfilled the entirety of the Old Testament Law. The death, burial, and resurrection of Christ explains why the New Testament church doesn't sacrifice animals, strictly obey all of the purity laws, and adhere to the detailed ritualistic practices as commanded to Israel in the Mosaic Law. When it comes to the Ten Commandments portion of the Mosaic Law, it's essential to note that Jesus restated nine of the ten during his earthly ministry, and they are reaffirmed by the New Testament writers.

Only the commandment concerning the Sabbath was not reinstituted by Christ; therefore, it's no longer binding for the New Testament church. In Ezekiel 20:12, we learn that the Old Testament Sabbath was given in the Mosaic Law as a sign of the unique covenant God had with the nation of Israel (see also Genesis 31:13–17). As Christians living under the New Covenant, we are no longer bound to the strict Old Testament Sabbath laws as outlined in the Pentateuch. Jesus, whose earthly ministry took place under the law, adhered to the Sabbath laws but also challenged the religious elites' abuses of the Sabbath. As members of Christ's church, which was inaugurated in Acts 2, we are responsible to regard the principle of work and rest as presented in the New Testament. We are not, however, bound to the Sabbath laws as described in the Mosaic Law because Christ fulfilled all of the law and never reinstated the Sabbath for the church age.

During his earthly ministry, Jesus internalized the Ten Commandments and clarified the expectations of them. We are certainly not free from the moral commandments found in the Ten Commandments because Jesus clearly reinstituted them. While the church is no longer bound to the Mosaic Law, we are responsible for obeying what Paul calls the *law of Christ* in Galatians 6:2. External obedience to a list of rules has never been sufficient for redemption. Salvation has always been the result of genuine faith in God as illustrated by Abram, later renamed Abraham, in Genesis 15:6. In Romans 4:1–3, Paul makes it clear that Abraham was deemed righteous long before the Law of Moses. Abraham was not justified by works; he believed God by faith and "it was counted to him as righteousness." Salvation, therefore, is a gift given to repentant sinners by faith.

According to the teachings of Jesus in Matthew 5, being angry with someone without cause is akin to murder. Lusting after someone in our hearts makes us guilty of adultery. Theologian Dwight Pentecost observes, "To refrain from the physical act did not fulfill the spiritual demands of the law, for the law demanded not only abstinence from a physical act but from the lustful desire that would produce the act."[32] Jesus's point is sufficiently clear: the external adherence to a list of laws and regulations is insufficient. In the case of

---

32 J. Dwight Pentecost, *The Words and Works of Jesus Christ* (Grand Rapids, MI: Zondervan Publishing House, 1981), 179.

adultery, God demands purity in thought as well as abstaining from the physical sexual act. Those who lust after another in their heart have already committed adultery; therefore, they stand guilty before God. No matter how hard we try, none of us will ever be holy enough to earn salvation.

Because no one can perfectly keep the requirements of the law in thought or deed, Jesus had to die on Calvary's cross to satisfy God's righteous wrath toward sin. As the author of Hebrews writes, "Without the shedding of blood there is no forgiveness of sins" (Hebrews 9:22). The blood of goats, rams, and lambs shed under the Old Testament Law could not atone for the sins of humanity. Only the blood of Jesus can atone for our sins and make redemption possible.

The New Testament church is called to preach the whole counsel of God. The authority of the gospel message, however, does not originate with us. As K. Scott Oliphint, professor at Westminster Theological Seminary, writes, "Since our message comes with God's own authority—since, that is, we come as his representatives, armed with the truth of God as our belt (Ephesians 6:14)—it carries the power and dominion and authority of God himself with it. When we speak the truth, we speak his truth. Our message is not something that we have invented; it is not something that we have thought up. It is something that we have been given. It carries the authority of its infallible source."[33] As we minister to our culture, we must keep these wise words in mind.

---

33 K. Scott Oliphint, *The Battle Belongs to the Lord* (Phillipsburg, NJ: P&R Publishing, 2003), 75.

God's authoritative truth—not our opinions, sentiments, or feelings—is what changes lives. When we proclaim truth, we must make it clear that the authority of our words resides in God rather than us.

God's Belt of Truth

When it comes to the armor of God, we often see the familiar picture of a Roman soldier as an illustration of Paul's imagery. By no means is that an inappropriate parallel to make; after all, Paul was imprisoned in Rome during the time he wrote his letter to the church at Ephesus. He was surrounded by soldiers, and likely chained to one. The citizens of Ephesus were obviously equally familiar with Roman soldiers. However insightful this comparison may be, I would suggest, as previously mentioned, that Paul is primarily drawing his imagery from the Old Testament.

Undoubtedly, we want to be careful to not overinterpret these parallels or read into them more than is interpretively honest. Nevertheless, I find there is sufficient reason to believe that Paul has Old Testament imagery in mind. Admittedly, some of the parallels are clearer than others; therefore, we must approach these verses with humility.

Isaiah 11:5 offers a clear parallel to the belt of truth found in Ephesians 6. The prophet Isaiah writes, "Righteousness shall be the belt of his waist, and faithfulness the belt of his loins." In the English translation, it's easy to miss the parallel imagery of God's belt because the idea of truth is seemingly absent. Upon closer inspection, however, we find that the word *faithfulness* is translated from the Hebrew word *emuwnah,* meaning "fidelity or truth." In Isaiah 11:5, righteous truth is God's belt.

In the Septuagint, which is the Greek translation of the Old Testament, *faithfulness* in Isaiah 11:5 is translated as *aletheia.* Paul uses the same Greek term in Ephesians 6:14 to present the belt of *aletheia.* The term a*letheia* means "that which is objectively true in any matter under consideration." Think of aletheia this way: Paul is describing what is objectively true in all matters pertaining to God, and the responsibilities of humankind in moral and religious affairs. *Aletheia* is used in other key New Testament texts; examples are included in the review questions at the end of this chapter for your consideration.

For now, consider one example of another passage in which Paul uses *aletheia.* It's found in Ephesians 4:24–25, where Paul writes, "Put on the new self, created after the likeness of God in true [aletheia] righteousness and holiness. Therefore, having put away falsehood, let each one of you speak the truth [aletheia] with his neighbor." From these verses, we learn that Christians are to live truth-centered lives built around God's objective truth, which is equally true for all people in all places for all time. As followers of Jesus, we are called to practice true righteousness while lovingly proclaiming God's truth to our neighbors.

In Isaiah 11, we see that the belt of truth is an essential part of the divine warrior's arsenal. Sinking into and taking up the belt of truth is equally important to Christians.

The belt of truth is what holds our uniform together and keeps our limbs free so we can effectively fight. God's truth undergirds everything we do. Without the belt of truth, we would be misguided and unprepared to face the unrelenting schemes of Satan.

It's difficult to stand and wrestle an opponent when one of your hands is preoccupied holding up your pants. I'm a super competitive person. There are many things in this world I don't do well; losing happens to be one of them. One morning at the gym, I was challenged to a jump rope competition. Naturally, I accepted the challenge. I was hanging in there relatively well until my shorts began slipping off my waist. Each time my feet hit the floor, I could feel my shorts sliding downward. Because I couldn't jump and keep my shorts from falling to my ankles at the same time, I had one of two choices: I could keep going and let my shorts drop to the floor or give up the fight. For obvious reasons, I had to swallow my pride and admit defeat.

This is why the belt worn by Roman soldiers was the central piece of their armor. The soldier's belt connected to the other pieces of armor through loops or buckles or clamps. It was the belt that held everything else in place. Likewise, it's God's truth that anchors Christians in the faith and secures the other pieces of armor so we are prepared to wrestle against the forces of evil. Without the belt of truth, we would have no choice but to surrender and accept defeat.

In our crooked culture, it's not palatable for most people to accept the idea that God created them and has the absolute authority to set boundaries for their lives. God's truth is the perfect standard by which all matters of life are measured. There should be no confusion about what is true because God has written the truth in Scripture for us to read, know, study, apply, and teach. But because of the pervasiveness of sin, truth is regularly ignored, distorted, or misused.

At the end of the day, what people think or wish to be true doesn't really matter. What matters is the truth as defined by God in his word. The objective truth that is based on his character and will is what we are called to obey. In order to lovingly confront the ungodly philosophies of the world, we must gird ourselves with the belt of truth. Otherwise, we will be fighting a losing battle with at least one hand tied behind our backs. Without God's belt of truth, we have no chance of standing firm in this fight.

But as with all belts, the belt of truth is not effective if it isn't properly secured. That's why Paul instructs Christians to fasten the belt around their waist so it stays firmly in place. For most of my life, I grew up hearing the King James Version of the Bible preached. I love how the KJV translators capture this aspect of the verse. Some of the words are a bit archaic, but the high regard for the English language creates a poetic image that, in my opinion, hammers down the intended urgency. In the KJV, Ephesians 6:14 reads, "Having your loins girt about with truth." The belt of truth does no good if it's hanging in your closet; it must be tightly secured around your loins so you are prepared to stand, fight, and wrestle.

Belt: Believe the Truth

At the age of twenty, our oldest son, Jonathan, became interested in skydiving. On the day of his first tandem jump, my wife and I went to watch. After signing all the necessary if-you-die-it's-not-our-fault-or-responsibility paperwork, Jonathan was paired with a man who had over ten thousand jumps in his logbook. When it came time for Jonathan's jump, he was harnessed up and loaded on the plane. Before jumping from the plane, Jonathan's instructor fastened his harness to Jonathan's. Michelle and I found great comfort knowing that Jonathan was fastened to an experienced skydiver. Some fifteen minutes after takeoff, we saw our son floating safely to the ground harnessed to a well-trained instructor. Like Jonathan being fastened to someone who could get him safely to the ground, Christians need the belt of God's truth securely fastened around our waist so we are adequately protected against the wiles of the devil.

I would like to share an important verse of Scripture found in John 14:6. In this text, Jesus said, "I am the way, the truth [aletheia], and the life: no man cometh unto the Father, but by me." Jesus, as God's divine Son, unapologetically claimed to be the only way to heaven. As the Son of God, Jesus shared the Father's divine essence and authority. As David proclaims in Psalm 103:3, the Lord is the only one who can forgive iniquity. Because Jesus shares the Father's divine nature, he also shares the Father's authority. God alone can forgive sins, and he does so through the blood of his Son, which was shed on the cross for us.

Takeaways

The primary battle between God and Satan is God's truth verses Satan's lies, underscoring the importance of God's belt of truth. Applying the two verbs Paul uses when discussing the armor of God, we must *put on* the truth as clothing so we will be protected from the deceptive philosophies dominating this wicked age. We must also *take up* truth as an armament so we can offensively fight against the lies and deception of Satan. With these two verbs in mind, let's consider four takeaways concerning God's everlasting truth.

1. The truth convicts people of their sinfulness. Too often, we erroneously believe that it's our airtight arguments that convict people of their sin. In reality, only exposure to God's truth can open spiritually blind eyes. God uses his perfect and eternal word to convict people of their sin through the working of the Holy Spirit. Our job isn't to convict people, it's to faithfully share the truth in love and allow God to do the convicting.

2. The truth saves people from their sins. Some Christians mistakenly believe that it's loving to refrain from sharing the truth with others. Mature Christians never enjoy offending people. We must remember, however, that it's unloving to withhold what Scripture teaches about sin, the world, Satan, and redemption. To our shame, Christians are often offensive in how they present God's truth. Being rude and unkind when sharing the gospel is never acceptable. In the

name of Christ, some believers are demeaning and condescending when proclaiming God's truth. Being harsh, mean-spirited, and demeaning is always the wrong approach. Faithfully and boldly proclaim the gospel, but do so with a compassionate and loving heart.

3. The truth determines what is morally right and wrong. Sin is so egregiously deceptive, people will come up with all kinds of creative excuses and hermeneutical gymnastics to manipulate Scripture to say whatever they desperately wish the Bible taught. Admittedly, there are passages of Scripture that are challenging to understand, and the Bible certainly contains verses that godly people disagree over. But let's be honest; concerning the moral issues that our world is currently fighting over, God's word is clear. There is little confusion over the moral boundaries God has lovingly placed on us. In our culture's quest for autonomy and the right to define sin using their own lexicon, society is working hard to erase these boundaries and redraw the lines between what is moral and what is immoral. As Christians, we must stand against the cunning nature of evil and defend the boundaries God has definitively revealed in his word.

4. The truth sets people free from sin. Under the influence of Satan's lies and deception, our world is convinced that freedom only comes from living an

autonomous life where the only restrictions are the ones individuals determine for themselves. But as Paul teaches in the book of Romans, those trapped in the clutches of sin are actually slaves to their sin (see Romans 6:12–23). According to Jesus in John 8:31–32, freedom is found in obeying God's truth. Jesus said, "If you abide in my word, you are truly my disciples, and you will know the truth, and the truth will set you free." Outside of Christ, mankind is spiritually dead and enslaved to their sinful nature (see Ephesians 2:1–9). Because of the life-destroying nature of immorality and the slavery it produces, the most loving and compassionate action is to share scriptural truth to those living apart from God. Through the life-changing power of the gospel, individuals can break free from the chains of sin and no longer live as hostages to their fleshly desires.

God's truth, as recorded in Scripture, is what empowers us to effectively wrestle against the forces of evil. Wearing God's belt of truth will leave us prepared to stand against the schemes of the enemy. In the Bible, God has provided the necessary instruction needed to please and obey him. Our responsibility is to secure God's belt of truth around our waist and stand prepared to resist Satan's schemes. Once our belt is secure, we must put on and take up the next piece of armor: God's breastplate of righteousness.

Key Point: Putting on and taking up the belt of truth prepares Christians to stand against the lies and deception of Satan.

For Further Consideration

1. Does your definition of truth coincide with the clear commandments and teachings found in Scripture?
2. Note Paul's usage of the Greek word *aletheia* (truth) in the following verses:

   1 Corinthians 13:4–6
   Ephesians 1:13
   Ephesians 4:21
   Philippians 4:8
3. Read and explain John 8:56–59.
4. How does wearing the truth protect you from the temptations of this world?
5. How does taking up the truth prepare you to withstand the unbiblical ideologies of the culture?
6. Describe why God has the authority to decide what is morally right and wrong.
7. Why do most people prefer to determine their own code of ethics instead of obeying God's definition of morality?

Breastplate: Practice Righteousness

Having put on the breastplate of righteousness.
Ephesians 6:14

When considering the topic of righteousness, one of the clearest accounts in the Bible is found in Luke 18:9–14. In this passage, Jesus tells a parable aimed at those who were "trusting in themselves that they were righteous" (v. 9). As a result of their self-righteousness and quest for self-glory, these individuals were treating people contemptuously. In the parable, Jesus describes two men who went to the temple to pray. One of these men was a Pharisee—a man who was well versed in religious matters and rule keeping. In the opinion of those in Jesus's audience, the Pharisee would have been highly regarded. The second man is a tax collector. Jesus's listeners would have shared a negative reaction to this person. Tax collectors were corrupt and part of the Roman government, making them unpopular, even despised.

In the parable, the Pharisee is standing by himself, praying his self-congratulatory prayer. His prayer is filled with self-righteousness as he basks in his own glory. He was a deeply religious man who knew how to use his false piety to impress people. In his prayer, the Pharisee's self-centered religiosity is seen in his prideful comparison to others. In verse 11, he prayed, "God, I thank you that I am not like other men, extortioners, unjust, adulterers, or even like this tax collector." Once the pious Pharisee established his greatness, he turned his attention to his works of righteousness. In verse 12, he arrogantly proclaimed, "I fast twice a week; I give tithes of all that I get." Did you catch the key word in the second section of the Pharisee's prayer? It's the word we all use more often than we should: I.

Throughout the gospels, the Pharisees were well known as individuals who excelled at observing the law, making them a perfect illustration of those who imagine themselves to be righteous through their own efforts. In Jesus's parable, the Pharisee's hypocrisy was at great odds with God's assessment of his spiritual condition. This Pharisee would have been wise to remember that "every way of a man is right in his own eyes, but the LORD weighs the heart" (Proverbs 21:2).

While the Pharisee waxes eloquent, the despised tax collector is standing far off, broken by the weight of his sin. Humbled before God, he refused to lift his eyes toward heaven. In true repentance, the tax collector beat his breast, crying, "God, be merciful to me, a sinner" (v. 13). There is no hint of self-righteousness in the tax collector's heart. All we see is a broken and contrite spirit. According to Jesus, the genuinely repentant tax collector went home that day justified. The self-righteous Pharisee, however, returned to his house spiritually lost and lacking a relationship with God.

Don't miss the importance of this dichotomy. The Pharisee was culturally accepted but blinded by pride and self-righteousness. His religion was in vain, leaving him outside of God's family. Shockingly, it was the despised tax collector who was justified. Because his heart was filled with genuine repentance, he became the recipient of God's grace and mercy, placing him inside God's family. In God's economy, social status doesn't earn your way to heaven. Celebrity is superficial. It may impress people, but God is more concerned with pure hearts than with how many followers we have on social media.

A Biblical Understanding of Justification

Justified is an important term in Jesus's parable. It's translated from the Greek word *dikaioo*, meaning "to pronounce one to be righteous." The Pharisee tried to produce righteousness through his own religious efforts, and he came up woefully short. Recognizing the depths of his depravity, the tax collector contritely admitted his sin, humbly repented, and placed his faith in the only one who could justify him. In his mercy, God pronounced him to be righteous, making him justified.

At the end of every wedding, I say something to the effect of "I now pronounce you man and wife." According to the state of North Carolina, I have the authority to perform weddings and declare a couple legally married. But I have absolutely no power to declare someone righteous. Only the Lord Jesus Christ has that kind of power. In Romans 5:1, Paul writes, "Therefore, since we have been justified by faith, we have peace with God through our Lord Jesus Christ." God's peace is current, but more importantly, it's eternal. The only means through which God's peace can be enjoyed is through justification by faith in Christ.

Jesus's warning in Matthew 23:12 and Luke 18 is abundantly clear: those who exalt themselves will be humbled by God's judgment. Meanwhile, people who humble themselves and repent of their sins will be exalted and experience the joy of a personal relationship with our Heavenly Father.

Righteous Lot

Before considering the particulars of God's breastplate of righteousness, I want to briefly examine the biblical character known as Lot. Lot is infamous for his despicable actions in the nineteenth chapter of Genesis where the Bible records the destruction of Sodom and Gomorrah. While Lot is unknowingly hosting two angels, his home is belligerently surrounded by the men of Sodom. The rancorous crowd asked Lot to grant them access to his guests. While the Bible tells the reader Lot's guests were angels, neither Lot nor the men of the city were aware of their true identity. Believing the angels to be men, the men of Sodom expressed their desire to have sexual relations with them. In an attempt to protect his guests, Lot offers his virgin daughters to the crowd instead. Thankfully, the angels protected Lot's daughters from defilement. Because of God's grace, Lot and his family escaped Sodom before its destruction. Sadly, Lot's wife disobediently looked back at the city on their way out, and God took her life as a result.

Despite Lot's blatant failure, it will probably surprise you to know that in 2 Peter 2:7, Peter labels Lot as righteous. From reading the accounts of Lot's life, he appears spiritually weak and compromised—a far cry from blamelessly righteous. Sure, he was hospitable to strangers and did some other nice things, but he was miles away from being perfectly righteous.

As someone who grew up believing Christians can lose their salvation, I find Peter's description of Lot profoundly comforting. While Lot was hospitable to the two angels and seemed distressed by the city's iniquity, he was willing to offer his daughters to satisfy the sexual desires of the lustful men surrounding his home. As the father of a daughter, I find Lot's suggestion horrific and unimaginable. Despite the depths of his sinfulness, he had repented of his sin, placed his faith in God, and enjoyed a personal relationship with the Lord. Outwardly, Lot was a man who made several troubling decisions, but he still maintained a basic orientation toward his Creator. According to Peter, Lot was deemed righteous and had been justified by God through faith. Although his faith was imperfect, God redeemed him. Because God mercifully justifies everyone who repents, no matter how flagrant their sin, Lot was declared righteous. Like Abraham in Genesis 15:6, Lot was justified by his personal faith in God.

The Breastplate of Righteousness

To be genuinely truth-centered, we must not only know the truth, we must also understand it, believe it, and apply it. Because we're wrestling against the rulers, authorities, and the cosmic powers over this present darkness, we need God's strength. We fight this spiritual battle by resisting temptation, saturating our minds and hearts with God's truth, and adorning ourselves in God's armor. The belt of truth is where the armor begins, but the second piece is equally important. God's breastplate of righteousness is given to protect our hearts against the schemes of the devil.

Thousands of years ago, the prophet Isaiah cautioned against celebrating and affirming what God defines as evil. Isaiah warned, "Woe to those who call evil good and good evil, who put darkness for light and light for darkness" (Isaiah 5:20). Today's culture is brazenly violating Isaiah's warning as we promote and celebrate sinful activities. Responsible for lovingly sharing the gospel in an increasingly wicked and hostile society, we need God's strength and protection. Psalm 91:4 reminds us that under God's wings, we "will find refuge; his faithfulness is a shield and buckler." God's faithfulness provides ultimate protection in this evil age. But as we wrestle against Satan and his forces, we must put on and take up God's breastplate of righteousness.

In Isaiah 59:17, the prophet uses imagery that parallels Paul's in the book of Ephesians. The text reads, "He put on righteousness as a breastplate, and a helmet of salvation on his head; he put on garments of vengeance for clothing, and wrapped himself in zeal as a cloak." Paul's language mirrors the prophet's description of the divine warrior's armor, reminding us of the security found in wearing the whole armor of God.

Our Hearts

A Roman soldier's breastplate covered him from the bottom of his neck to his upper thigh. The purpose of the breastplate was to protect vital organs such as the heart and lungs. No Roman soldier would ever consider going into battle without his breastplate. Likewise, God's breastplate of righteousness protects our hearts from the devil's schemes and flaming arrows.

In the Bible, the heart is considered to be the seat of all of our thoughts, words, and actions. It's our inner self that drives our outward behavior. As Jesus said in Luke 6:45, "The good person out of the good treasure of his heart produces good, and the evil person out of his evil treasure produces evil, for out of the abundance of the heart his mouth speaks." Our hearts require divine protection because they determine the decisions we make, the thoughts we dwell upon, and the overall direction of our lives. This is the reason Proverbs 4:23 warns us to guard our hearts with all diligence.

If our hearts are left unprotected and vulnerable to attack, we're prone to falling prey to the devil's schemes. Throughout Scripture, the heart is pictured as the most important spiritual organ. Securely protected by the righteousness of Christ, we are prepared to withstand Satan's cunning attempts to place our souls under siege. As we resist the enemy on a daily basis, our lives become marked by the pursuit of righteousness through obedience to God's commandments.

A Biblical Understanding of Righteousness

It's imperative that we understand Paul's usage of the word *righteousness*. The Greek word used in Ephesians 6:14 is *dikaiosune*. It's a rather general term that can be defined as "integrity, virtue, purity of life." What I find interesting is that even unbelievers expect Christians to display a certain level of virtue and righteousness. The question for us to consider is, what type of righteousness is Paul referencing? To better understand Paul's teaching, let's consider three types of righteousness: self-righteousness, imputed righteousness, and practical righteousness.

The first type of righteousness is clearly not what Paul has in mind. Obviously, the apostle is not referencing self-righteousness, which is the most common form of righteousness the world displays. As previously discussed, self-righteousness is one of the most dangerous sins imaginable. Sadly, this is the breastplate many people wear. Those spiritually blinded by self-righteousness quickly become overconfident in their own spiritual abilities and religious acts. Rarely do the self-righteous sense the need to seek the Lord's forgiveness and strength. Due to their inflated ego, self-righteous individuals also often lower their guard, making them prime targets of Satan's attacks.

As Proverbs 30:12 says, "There are those who are clean in their own eyes but are not washed of their filth." The lens through which we generally see ourselves is rose colored and filled with sparkles, hearts, and thumbs-up emojis. Like walking through a house of mirrors, how we see ourselves is usually a distortion of the truth. For better or worse, we are incapable of seeing ourselves with perfect accuracy. Self-righteousness does not promote high morals and outward acts of service for the glory of God. Pharisaical individuals perform religious and righteous actions for self-glory with little or no concern for what actually pleases God.

The second type of righteousness is imputed righteousness, which is Christ's righteousness credited to repentant sinners at the moment of their justification. According to theologian Augustus Strong's definition, justification is God's declarative act in which he proclaims the repentant sinner to be "no longer exposed to the penalty of the law, but to be restored to his [God's] favor."[34] God doesn't accept us because we work hard, try our best, or our good deeds outweigh our bad ones; he welcomes us into his presence because of what Jesus accomplished on the cross. Jesus's righteousness is reckoned to our account, allowing us to have fellowship with the Father.

---

34 Augustus H. Strong, *Systematic Theology* (Valley Forge, PA: Judson Press, 1996), 849.

Imputed righteousness is what allows egregious sinners like Lot to be called righteous. In our own merit, we have no righteousness. That's what makes the imputed righteousness of Christ taste so sweet to a parched and thirsty soul. The undeserved righteousness bestowed upon us through Christ's sacrifice on the cross is ample reason to praise God for his grace. In 2 Corinthians 5:21, Paul explains imputed righteousness this way: "For our sake he made him to be sin who knew no sin, so that in him we might become the righteousness of God." When sinners place their faith in Jesus, they are instantaneously forgiven of their sins and brought into a legal union with God.

While there is sweet truth in the doctrine of imputed righteousness, I do not believe this is Paul's meaning in Ephesians 6:14. Paul is writing to Christians who have already received Christ's righteousness through faith. Because this righteousness is solely dependent on the work of God, there is no reason for Christians to be commanded to put on imputed righteousness. We cannot put on what God has already put on for us. Imputed righteousness keeps us from hell and secures our place in heaven, but it doesn't inherently keep us free from the schemes of the devil.

In Ephesians 6:14, Paul appears to be referencing practical righteousness. He is calling us to put on and take up the volitional act of choosing obedience to God's commandments while standing against the forces of evil. Imputed righteousness happens at a moment in time. Practical righteousness takes place on a daily basis and will continue until we see Jesus face-to-face. In theology, the arduous process of becoming more like Jesus (i.e., practical righteousness) through consistent obedience to God's word is called sanctification.

A Biblical Understanding of Sanctification

Jesus's sacrifice on the cross was a decisive blow to Satan's kingdom. The victory over the forces of evil, sin, and death secured by the Lamb of God is one we never could have achieved through our own righteous deeds. Our imputed righteousness was purchased through the blood of Christ. His robes of righteousness have replaced our filthy rags of sin and provided eternal hope to all who accept the gospel. But even those who have placed their faith in Jesus are not sinless. As the great reformer John Calvin observed, "There remains in a regenerate man a smoldering cinder of evil, from which desires continually leap forth to allure and spur him to commit sin."[35] While we're robed in Christ's righteousness, our sin nature still remains. That is the reason we must consciously choose to forgo our fleshly desires and consistently obey God's commandments.

While saved from the penalty of our sin, we must never recklessly presume upon God's imputed righteousness and believe that our outward actions are of no consequence. Our justification is not an excuse to continue living in the works of the flesh (see Romans 6). Abusing our justification as a

---

35 John Calvin, *Institutes of the Christian Religion* (Louisville, KY: Westminster John Knox Press), 602.

pretext to continue violating God's commandments is an act of blatant insubordination. In the heart of every genuine Christian, there must reside a love for God that nurtures a consistent and growing level of obedience to the Lord. One summer, I was in vacation Bible school with a little boy who espoused the idea that you could sin all day long, as much as you wanted to, as long as you prayed before bedtime and asked God to forgive you for everything you did that day. This little self-serving ritual was the boy's license to sin.

God *will* forgive a genuinely repentant sinner, no matter what they have done. That is a true statement. But even at ten years old, I knew this kid's cheap grace philosophy was dead wrong. Now as a pastor, I'm sometimes concerned that too many Christians think the way this boy did: sin it up all day and pray at night. Get your dose of cheap grace, and you're all good to sin to the hilt the following day. I adamantly agree with the Apostle Paul on this one: "Are we to continue in sin that grace may abound? By no means!" (Romans 6:1–2). Or as the KJV puts it, "God forbid!" that we would ever take advantage of God's amazing grace in such a reckless manner.

Works of righteousness that flow from a heart that sincerely loves God should be the norm of every Christian. In Matthew 5:6, Jesus said, "Blessed are those who hunger and thirst for righteousness, for they shall be satisfied." Every follower of Jesus, no matter how old or young, should possess an insatiable hunger and thirst for righteousness. Pursuing Christlikeness will change the way we live before the fallen world and will allow us to serve as light in the prevailing darkness. Concerning the relentless pursuit of holiness, Luther writes, "In order to attain it one must have great earnestness, a yearning eagerness and incessant diligence: that where there is a lack of this hunger and thirst, all will amount to nothing."[36]

When we lack passion for something, we will not remain faithful for long. Newcomers to my gym always start with fire in their bellies, but their commitment often quickly fizzles in a few short weeks and they disappear. Too often, Christians follow the same pattern. If we allow our passion for the gospel and righteousness to fade, our level of obedience to God will quickly decline, and our ability to serve as salt and light in this world will also dwindle.

When we sincerely love God, his commandments are never burdensome (see 1 John 5:3). It's a privilege and joy to serve Christ. May we never allow our passion for obedience and righteousness to deteriorate because we are too consumed with what we can get away with or with doing the least amount necessary to still be considered a faithful follower of Jesus. May it never be!

Sanctification is the progressive process of spiritual growth that develops over a lifetime. This side of heaven, no one achieves sinless perfection. Pastor and biblical scholar Paul Enns explains it this way: "Although the believer's positional sanctification is secure, his experiential sanctification may

---

36 Martin Luther, *Commentary on the Sermon on the Mount* (Bellingham, WA: Lexham Press, 2017), 26.

fluctuate because it relates to his daily life and experience."[37] While our ultimate glorification will have to wait until we enter God's presence, we are expected to put on God's breastplate of righteousness to mature in our faith.

Ephesians 6:14 is a call to arms. Paul commands followers of Christ to apply our imputed righteousness to our daily decisions. Wearing the breastplate of righteousness means there ought to be consistent outward expressions of the internal reality of our imputed righteousness. In Romans 6:13, Paul writes, "Do not present your members to sin as instruments for unrighteousness, but present yourselves to God as those who have been brought from death to life, and your members to God as instruments for righteousness." Interestingly, the Greek word Paul used for *instrument* is *hoplon*, meaning "any tool" or "arms used in warfare." Believers are to use our acts of righteousness during this time of spiritual warfare to stand obediently to the gospel. During this wicked age, we need God's breastplate of righteousness to protect us from the vicious schemes of the enemy.

Takeaways

According to James 2:26, faith without works is dead. Our works of righteousness cannot save us from sin; only faith in Christ can justify us. This does not mean, however, that followers of Christ are free from the responsibility of putting their faith into action. In Titus 2:14, Paul says that Christ

---

[37] Paul Enns, *The Moody Handbook of Theology* (Chicago, IL: Moody Publishers, 2008), 341.

"gave himself for us to redeem us from all lawlessness and to purify for himself a people for his own possession who are zealous for good works." Redemption should produce a zealousness in the heart of every Christian that seeks opportunity to perform good works for the sake of the gospel.

Serving others in the name of Jesus is an important reason our Heavenly Father keeps us in this fallen world. As John Piper writes, "The achievement and aim of the cross is not just final perfection, but measures of holiness in this life that confirm election (2 Peter 1:10), show life (1 John 3:14), and glorify Christ (2 Thessalonians 1:11–12)."[38] The visible fruits we bear give indication of the genuineness of our faith. God uses our zealous works of righteousness to call people to himself. As Jesus said in Matthew 7:20, "You will recognize them by their fruits." What outwardly distinguishes Christians from unbelievers is their visible and measurable fruit. When the Holy Spirit resides in us, he will change our hearts so we can produce gospel fruit.

Hungering and thirsting after righteousness should motivate every Christian to serve others and consistently be salt and light in the world. Whenever we pursue righteousness and zealously serve God, Satan will always stand in ardent opposition to our efforts. Attempting to keep Christians' practical righteousness at bay, Satan uses a multifaceted battle plan to keep us sitting safely on the sidelines. I can't cover all of Satan's conniving tactics here, but I will mention three common temptations that he uses to deter us from the battle.

---

38 John Piper, *Providence* (Wheaton, IL: Crossway, 2020), 629.

Breastplate: Practice Righteousness

1. Satan and his forces tempt us with self-condemnation. This is arguably the most spiritually exhausting trap Christians fall into. Whenever we become physically or emotionally drained, we are highly susceptible to the cunning schemes of the enemy. When spiritual exhaustion takes over, temptations that are typically avoided are like boulders falling on our heads. Living under the crushing lies of self-condemnation makes us vulnerable to a variety of sins. One of the accuser's favorite strategies is to convince discouraged Christians that they're unloved and unwanted by God and others. When we're discouraged, or involved in sin, Satan sees a golden opportunity to convince us that God could never love someone like us. Believing God's love is absent from our lives, we quickly fall into discouragement, typically leading us to sinful choices.

   Tempting Christians to believe they are all alone in their iniquity is a destructive and effective strategy. This soul-crushing untruth leaves us overcome by shame, discouragement, and despair. When we fall prey to the temptation of self-condemnation, we're tempted to isolate ourselves, compounding the problem even more. When we feel unworthy or incapable of righteous choices, Satan doubles down and throws more condemnation on the fire.

   When tempted to believe the lie of self-condemnation, remember that Christ's imputed righteousness defends you against the schemes of the devil. Because we are secure in Christ, we can choose to believe a biblical perspective of ourselves and not allow our feelings of inadequacy to draw us away from God. Put on and take up the breastplate of righteousness and stand confident in knowing that you have been adopted into God's family.

2. Satan tempts us with self-righteousness. As previously mentioned, this is a common and intoxicating temptation. There's an obvious reason the Bible includes so many verses that address pride. Arrogance and the enticement of self-glory reside in all of us. When reading passages about the self-righteous Pharisees, it's easy to believe we're not like them. Unfortunately, we're a lot more like them than we want to admit. Self-righteousness can take many forms. But common symptoms include a judgmental attitude, condescension, self-sufficiency, selfishness, an attitude of superiority, callousness to the needs of others, excuses for sinful decisions, and outward religious activities that are carried out for the praise of people rather than for God's glory. The father of lies convinces us that we are righteous and sufficient in our own strength and knowledge. To combat this propaganda, we must put on and take up the breastplate of God's righteousness and stand humbly before him.

3. Satan particularly loves tempting us with self-indulgence. Because we're naturally drawn to comfort,

convenience, and pleasure, the old serpent has to expend little energy luring us away from righteous living when it comes to the temptation of self-indulgence. Rather than living righteously, we regularly cave to Satan's enticing plan to seduce us with sexual immorality, slothfulness, greed, envy, hatred, addiction, gluttony, covetousness, and any other vice he can employ to render us ineffectual. This is the reason Peter orders, "Abstain from the passions of the flesh, which wage war against your soul" (1 Peter 2:11). We all possess lingering self-indulgent desires, and Satan enjoys using them against us.

Whenever we become enamored with and immersed in the world, we will not be interested or concerned with living righteously. As Spurgeon poetically prayed, "My soul, never laugh at sin's fooleries, lest thou come to smile at sin itself. It is thine enemy, and thy Lord's enemy—view it with detestation, for so only canst thou evidence the possession of holiness, without which no man can see the Lord."[39] When Christians tolerate, laugh at, participate in, and promote what God hates, we place ourselves squarely in the enemy's camp. If Satan can convince us to endorse or ignore what evil is doing in the world, we are rendered ineffectual for gospel ministry.

Given the evil nature of Satan's enticements, we must stay alert and ready to withstand his schemes. Rather than

---

39 Spurgeon, 615.

granting the forces of evil access to our hearts, we must guard them with God's breastplate of righteousness. As Jeremiah Burroughs urges, "Oh, all you who love God, hate sin! Let your hearts be set against sin because it is so much against God."[40] The breastplate of righteousness protects us from falling prey to the salacious invitation of sin and idolatry. It's better to live righteously than enjoy the temporal pleasures of sin for a season; therefore, because Satan would love to put one of his flaming arrows through your heart, you must adorn yourself in God's breastplate of righteousness. Failing to do so will leave you at risk of forfeiting the privilege of serving as salt and light in the name of Christ, and place you on the road to terrible consequences.

With the breastplate of righteousness securely protecting our hearts against Satan's attacks, we must now turn our attention to our feet.

Key Point: Wearing the breastplate of righteousness protects our hearts from Satan's attacks and allows us to perform works of righteousness for God's glory.

For Further Consideration

1. What truths do these verses communicate regarding our sin nature?

    James 2:10

    Romans 6:23

---

[40] Jeremiah Burroughs, *The Evil of Evils* (Grand Rapids, MI: Soli Deo Gloria Publications, 1992), 77.

Breastplate: Practice Righteousness

Isaiah 64:6–7

Isaiah 53:5

2. What truths do these verses communicate regarding our redemption?

Romans 6

2 Corinthians 5:21

Philippians 3

3. Read Colossians 3:12–14. Make a list of what Christians are called to put on and describe each one.

4. Which of the three common schemes of the devil are you prone to following?

Self-condemnation

Self-righteousness

Self-indulgence

5. Make a list of Bible verses that address your particular area of struggle, and journal ways these truths can assist you in the battle against the devil and his evil forces.

Shoes: Lace Up Readiness

As shoes for your feet, having put on the readiness given by the gospel of peace.

Ephesians 6:15

Okay, time for a confession. I have more brand loyalty than I care to admit. I'll take Skippy peanut butter over all the competition. Costco over Sam's. Toyota hands down. Local coffee before Starbucks. I'm not much of a soda drinker, but I'll take Pepsi over Coke. My deepest brand loyalty, however, belongs to Nike. I fell in love with everything Nike in the sixth grade. Kids were coming to school wearing bright-white shoes with a black swoosh on the side, and it was love at first sight. Up until then, I was a Converse guy. But Nike stole my affection in an instant and has held it for a long time.

In today's economy, shoes are a multimillion-dollar industry. Thanks to loyal customers like me, in its June 2022 fiscal report, Nike posted a revenue of $46.7 billion.[41]

---

[41] Peter Verry, "Phil Knight and Warren Buffett Are the Top Sneaker Players on the Forbes 400 Wealthiest People in the U.S. List," accessed October 24, 2022, https://finance.yahoo.com/news/phil-knight-warren-buffett-top-162231271.html#:~:text=In%20June%20of%20this%20year,of%20 5%25%20to%20%2446.7%20billion.

Think about our footwear choices for a moment; we have dress shoes, casual shoes, shoes for the beach, for golf, bowling, tennis, baseball, football, biking, weightlifting, rock climbing, hiking, and practically any other activity you can imagine. Oftentimes, shoes are as much of a fashion statement as they are for protection. There may very well be shoes on the market that would fit my feet better and provide better support, but I don't bother looking. Why? Because I like the way Nike sneakers look. I guess years of habitual brand loyalty are hard to overcome.

For soldiers, however, shoe choice isn't a matter of vanity or style. What soldiers wear on their feet is an important and practical part of their uniform. A soldier's shoes, especially in ancient times, were a matter of life and death. Suitable footwear enables a soldier to complete long marches over hot, dusty, or muddy roads at rapid rates of speed while facing all types of inclement weather. The soldier who develops injured, swollen, or blistered feet cannot fight well, making them susceptible to the enemy's army. Even the smallest blister can make it too painful to walk comfortably.

Shoes of Readiness

Roman soldier shoes were studded with sharp pieces of metal, similar to the cleats athletes wear today. Among today's elite athletes, different types of cleats are worn for various field surfaces. The studs on the Roman's shoes provided much-needed traction as the soldiers climbed, advanced on their target, and fought in hand-to-hand combat. Shoes with slick bottoms or worn soles made it difficult to maneuver on the battlefield. Proper footwear matters.

Choosing the wrong shoes can leave us incapacitated or in pain. For followers of Jesus, the gospel provides the solid footing we need in our personal lives and supplies the necessary traction required to progress forward on the spiritual battlefield. Gospel shoes prepare us to withstand the devil's offensives while proclaiming God's word to the world. As we wrestle against the rulers, authorities, and the cosmic powers over this present age of darkness, God's shoes enable us to stand our ground without slipping or falling.

Christians must adorn themselves with the belt of truth and the breastplate of righteousness, but we cannot overlook our feet. If our feet are not properly protected, we will slip, stumble, and eventually fall. In a wrestling match, the one who gets his rival on the ground first has a huge competitive advantage. If Satan can slam us on the mat, he'll pounce before we can get up. Our shoes help us maintain the balance, strength, and position needed to stay on our feet.

In Ephesians 6:15, Paul calls Christians to put on the readiness that is given by the gospel. *Readiness* is a translation of the Greek word *hetoimasia*. This word can be defined as "the condition of a person being prepared and in a state of readiness." We are all well aware of the cultural hostility toward absolute truth. In order for the church to faithfully advance with the gospel of Jesus Christ, those who have been justified by faith in Christ must be ready by putting on and taking up the shoes of the gospel.

Sure Footing

In the book of Isaiah, we find language similar to Paul's words in Ephesians 6:15. Isaiah 52:7 reads, "How beautiful upon the mountains are the feet [correlates to *shoes* in Ephesians 6] of him who brings good news [correlates to *gospel* in Ephesians 6], who publishes peace, who brings good news of happiness, who publishes salvation, who says to Zion, 'Your God reigns.'" This verse is the only other Bible passage where feet, good news, and peace occur together. It's perfectly reasonable to presume that this text was in the forefront of Paul's mind when he penned Ephesians 6:15.

This certainly does not negate passages such as Psalm 18, which includes imagery suitable for a discussion on the importance of God's gospel shoes. In Psalm 18, David writes, "You gave a wide place for my steps under me, and my feet did not slip" (v. 36). Everything David accomplished was because of the Lord's enabling. It was God who made sure David's footing was sure. During the timeframe of Psalm 18, David rested in God's power, enabling him to keep his feet from slipping on the slippery rocks of temptation and idolatry. As New Testament believers, it's the shoes of the gospel of peace that keep us from slipping and falling over the edge.

Two other verses from the Book of Psalms also illustrate the need for proper foot protection. The first is Psalm 25:15, where David writes, "My eyes are ever toward the Lord, for he will pluck my feet out of the net." David's eyes were fixed on his Creator, meaning his faith and trust were set upon him. Understanding that his life was safe and secure in God's power and strength, he patiently waited in the Good Shepherd's care. Whenever David's feet were ensnared by the problems and troubles of the world, he knew God had the ability to deliver him. David's Godward focus protected him from the dangers surrounding him. With his eyes on the Lord, his paths were set straight and his heart protected from evil. Like David, when we are in the wearisome routine of the battle, we must find hope and joy in the glorious security provided by God's immutable faithfulness.

The second example of the need for proper shoes is found in Psalm 37:31. Concerning the righteous, David writes, "The law of his God is in his heart; his steps do not slip." When our feet are firmly planted on the word of God, our footing is secure. God's wondrous truth keeps us from slipping into the temptations of the world and protects our hearts from the snare of idolatry. Under the devil's influence, the wicked will oppose us and do all they can to get us on the ground, stuck in the mire of sin and hatred. The wicked adamantly oppose the righteous with venomous words and accusations, discouraging many Christians from staying faithful to the gospel. Those following the paths of darkness will go to great lengths to trip us and bring us down. But as David says in Psalm 37:13, "The Lord laughs at the wicked, for he sees that his day is coming." Later, in verse 20, we are told that the wicked will perish. Consumed by God's righteous judgment, they will face the deadly consequences of their wickedness. Rather than following the path of evil and immorality, keep your feet planted on the Rock of your salvation, your eyes on him, and obey his divine orders (see Psalm 40 and 62).

Returning to the Isaiah 52:7 passage, we see the importance of heralds (i.e., messengers). In the New Testament, Jesus called the members of his body to serve as faithful witnesses of the gospel to all nations. Remember, Isaiah was written hundreds of years before the Messiah was born in Bethlehem; therefore, the prophet was looking forward to the time when the promised Messiah would come. In the meantime, Isaiah was called to proclaim the good news of God's faithfulness, mercy, grace, and hope of salvation to his culture. On this side of the cross, Christians have a fuller and more complete revelation. The Messiah has already come in his first advent. He died on the cross and rose from the dead three days later. Like the Old Testament prophet, we are called to proclaim two essential truths.

First, Christians are to boldly proclaim the good news of peace (i.e., the gospel), which brings eternal salvation to those who believe. The gospel declares that (1) all of us have sinned against God (see Romans 3:23), (2) those who call upon the name of the Lord with a repentant heart will be saved (see Acts 4:12; Romans 10:13; Ephesians 2:1–10), (3) God faithfully justifies those who believe in Jesus Christ alone as Savior (see Romans 3:24; Romans 5:9), (4) God adopts believers into his family (see Romans 8:15), and (5)

God provides lasting peace to all who believe (see Ephesians 2:13–14). In Romans 10:10–20, Paul passionately describes the importance of believers faithfully preaching the gospel of peace to the world. According to this passage, in conjunction with Isaiah 52:7, even the feet of those who preach the gospel are beautiful.

Second, Christians are to boldly proclaim that God rules and reigns over the world. As we learn throughout Scripture, God is sovereign in the affairs of men. In a world that worships autonomy, the idea of a sovereign, omnipotent, and holy God typically goes down sideways. If God is real, and if he rules supreme over the world, then only a fool would reject him and his commandments. If a culture can categorically dismiss the idea of an all-knowing, all-powerful God who rules and reigns over creation, then people can discard him and feel perfectly at ease with their rejection. Successful spiritual warfare can be waged only when we're trusting in God's sovereign authority while safely adorned in his armor.

Days of Noah

From a human perspective, the world appears to be coming apart at the seams. From the looks of things, evil seems to be winning, Christians are increasingly marginalized, and there is little regard for objective truth. And yet, we learn from the darkest days of Noah's life that God is in control and working his plan even in desperate times. While the world mocked and ridiculed Noah for his apparently unreasonable beliefs,

God was graciously providing humanity with sufficient time to repent of their sin and believe in their Creator.

Day after day, board after board, nail after nail, Noah assembled the ark as a sign of what was to come. As the ark grew in height, the warning of God's pending judgment screamed louder and louder, calling the mockers to believe and be saved. Faithfully, Noah obeyed God. When it came time to load the ark, Noah obediently gathered the animals and prepared for the rains to fall. And what did Noah receive for his intrepid faithfulness and obedience? Ridicule. Mockery. And a heavy dose of cold-hearted rejection.

Ultimately, the people were not rejecting Noah; they were rejecting God and turning their backs on their only hope of salvation. In Noah's day, the ark stood as a beacon of hope for deliverance from the promised flood. But to those who ignored Noah's testimony and warnings, the ark served as a promise of God's pending judgment. When judgment came, only Noah and his family were spared. The months of ridicule were undoubtedly discouraging and difficult to swallow. In the end, however, Noah's faithfulness paid off. Living with eternity in mind keeps our hearts settled in the face of rejection and controversy. When we lose sight of God's sovereign glory and power, fear sets in. When we become fearful, we lose hope and soon slip into sin. Noah's feet were firmly planted on God's promises, and it produced lifesaving obedience, making all the ridicule, mockery, and rejection worth it.

Under the New Covenant, the cross stands as a symbol of the confident hope we have in Jesus. Regrettably, like in the days leading up to the flood, the majority of people are jeering, scorning, and deriding the teachings of Scripture and those who serve as obedient heralds of the gospel. Despite the pervading presence of evil in the world, God remains the sovereign king over all of his creation. To Christians, the cross symbolizes hope. But for those who scorn the truth, the cross is a warning of God's justice and coming judgment upon all who reject the gospel.

Like Noah, we can't make anyone believe in Jesus. We can, however, serve as obedient witnesses and heralds of God's glorious promises of redemption and lasting peace, and his pending judgment on the world—like Noah. To fulfill our God-given responsibility, we need the laces of our gospel shoes tightly tied on our feet so we don't slip and fall as we wrestle against doubters, naysayers, scorners, and accusers. If you're tired of the twisted culture pushing you around, put on your shoes and stand firm on the glorious truths of Scripture.

Set Your Feet

Facing rejection and ridicule is never easy. We can quickly grow spiritually exhausted when it feels like the entire world is standing on our chest. Since the early days of the church, the world has hated those who follow Christ. Jesus taught that because the world reviled him, it would continue to detest those who preach his name (see John 15:18–19; 1

John 3:13). We should actually be more concerned if the world fully accepts us without opposition. If the world fully accepts you, to whom do you actually belong? Jesus taught in John 15:19 that the world loves its own. Wearing gospel shoes makes sure we don't slip into a destructive pattern of worrying about the opinions of other people more than God's.

During my sophomore year of high school, we were playing football against a team well known for its dominating program. On our first offensive play, we came to the line of scrimmage and settled into position. As the offensive center, I was the one responsible for snapping the ball to the quarterback. The laces barely reached the quarterback's hand when the defensive noseguard hit me so hard, I thought my helmet cracked. When the play was over, the monster grabbed my face mask and snarled, "I'm going to kill you" (edited for your spiritual protection). You have to love the game of football.

Kill me, he did not. He did, however, give it his best shot. He beat the living daylights out of me during the game that night, and he punctured my confidence in the process. On one particular play, he hit me with such force, I performed what amounted to a backward somersault and took out our quarterback in the process. It was UGLY. On Monday afternoons, our team watched the game film of the previous Friday's game. I cannot express how deeply I was dreading that Monday film session. If there was ever a play for a blooper reel, it was that one. And I was the star.

When the head coach reached the moment I was not looking forward to, I braced myself for what I knew was coming. The coach paused the film at the end of my tumble and yelled in front of the entire team, "Knolls, that can never happen again!" I wanted to crawl under my chair and never come out. From the crushing silence hovering over the locker room, I think the entire team felt bad for me. Or maybe they were trying not to laugh. Not sure. What the coach said next was what I had been taught on the practice field for months but failed to apply the night I got pummeled. The coach roared, "Your feet have to be set!" After all these years, I have never forgotten that play or the lesson from that humiliating film session.

Like my failure in that football game, if your spiritual feet are not securely planted in the gospel, you're going to get knocked on your tail; you'll be doing backward somersaults and wiping people out in the process. One of my goals during football games was to never have a speck of dirt or a grass stain on the back of my jersey. I wanted the front to be muddy and nasty because that indicated a successful night. But the back of my jersey was always to stay pristine. I assure you, after my sad performance that night, there was plenty of dirt and grass on the back of my white jersey—not my best showing. I was outmatched and beaten on that play because my feet were not planted.

When it comes to spiritual warfare, we're all woefully outmatched. Left to our own strength and resources, the forces of evil will flatten us like cardboard boxes under the tires of a dump truck. Without the power of the gospel and God's shoes tied tightly on our feet, we have no hope of resisting the devil or spiritually flourishing in this evil age. It's imperative that you set your spiritual feet, square your shoulders, and brace yourself for the devil's flaming arrows. In order to withstand the brutality of Satan's spiritual attacks, we need the readiness made available to us through the gospel of peace. In Ephesians 6:15, *peace* is a translation of the Greek word *eirene*, which can be defined as an "exemption from the rage and havoc of war" or "harmony, safety, contentment." In the New Testament, *eirene* is used in reference to the quiet state of one's soul resulting from personal faith in Christ, which the forces of evil can never snatch away from God's children. The eternal peace provided by the gospel is possible even in the midst of the spiritual warfare we are called to fight. Whatever our earthly circumstances may be and no matter how fierce the fight against evil may become, we can confidently rest in God's unfaltering peace.

The Glorious Gospel

I'm concerned that too many Christians perceive the gospel as something they only needed in the past for salvation that has no bearing on their present lives. The gospel is not meant to merely serve as a means to secure an eternity in God's presence. It's misguided to believe that once we have accepted the gospel for justification that we are then free to move on to something deeper, fresher, or hipper. Christians need the gospel each and every day. Paul David Tripp explains that the gospel, "Provides for us, right here, right now, a way of seeing, a means of interpreting, a guide to understanding, and a way of living."[42] The life-changing gospel is given to believers to inform, influence, and motivate every decision made, every church program managed, every sermon preached, and every lesson taught.

Minds can be informed with exposure to information. Motivation can be found in TED talks and podcasts. Hearts can be touched by sentimental movies and sappy love songs. But the soul can only be reborn and transformed through the supernatural power of the gospel. That's why the gospel is as much for the present moment as it was for our past justification or for our future glorification. In order to stand against the schemes of the devil, we must be firmly rooted in the life-giving gospel. Biblical scholar F. F. Bruce writes, "Those who must at all costs stand their ground need to have a secure footing; in the spiritual conflict, this is supplied by the gospel."[43] Even the most spiritually mature Christian needs the gospel each and every day. Without God's truth securing our stance, our feet are on slippery ground, making it inevitable that we'll eventually fall.

All People Are Worshippers

Right now, you may be feeling anything but peace in your life. Perhaps God seems distant or absent at the moment,

---

42 Tripp, 11.
43 F. F. Bruce, *The Epistles to the Colossians, to Philemon, and to the Ephesians* (Grand Rapids, MI: William B. Eerdmans Publishing Company, 1984), 408.

leaving you feeling spiritually depleted. Maybe the idea of experiencing settled peace in your life seems like a pipe dream because of the troubling circumstances you're dealing with. Health concerns, financial pressures, relational conflicts, work stress, past traumas, and a host of other problems may be strangling peace from your heart, leaving you fearful, discouraged, or spiritually numb. Add the shrapnel of spiritual warfare to the mix, and it's easy to see how so many Christians are feeling overwhelmed and exhausted. I wish I had easy answers to life's problems. Unfortunately, I don't. I do, however, know that what we worship greatly impacts how we handle the pressures of life and the spiritual conflicts we all face. When our worship is misplaced, joy, contentment, and peace evaporate. In the midst of the battle, it's easy for our hearts to slip into unfaithfulness to God and his wondrous word.

By nature, we are all worshippers. When most people hear the word *worship,* an image of congregants gathered together in a cathedral, country church, or some other type of worship center comes to mind. Maybe you think of monks chanting, devout people praying and singing, or someone dressed a certain way leading a group through religious rituals. Worship, however, is not limited to a particular place or time, so this image of worship is false and misleading.

Worship happens throughout each day in every place we go, in every conversation we have, and in every relationship we build. Hardwired into every human heart is the innate propensity to give our utmost adoration and adulation to something or someone. No matter how ardently people deny this fact, our hearts are always controlled by something, and we are placing the glory and honor God deserves at the foot of someone else's altar. This explains why laws are not always effective at eliminating harmful and immoral behaviors. Legislation is good and necessary, but no government can transform the hearts of sinners. Only God's grace, available through the gospel of peace, can produce permanent change in the hearts of people. Until our hearts fall in love with God and worship him above all else, we have no hope of genuine transformation of individuals or society. We will discuss this issue in more detail when we study the shield of faith in the next chapter, but for now we need to consider the ramifications of our susceptibility to worship idols rather than the one true God.

False Idols

We were created to worship the God who created us, but instead we readily shift our allegiance to some other god. Paul David Tripp writes, "A failure to obey God's commands is never just a breaking of some abstract moral code; it is a breaking of the worship relationship you were created to have with the Lord of lords."[44] Our ultimate shortcoming isn't that we violate God's rules. Although obedience to God's commandments is obviously of great importance, the challenge is significantly deeper than external actions. Based on the first two of God's Ten Commandments, we

---

44 Tripp, 106.

have a substantial problem with placing other gods before our Creator and a tendency to bow down in worship to images created with our own hands (see Exodus 20:3–6). It's significant that two of the Ten Commandments address worship practices and limit our worship to the one true God. Whenever we offer our hearts to another god, we have become guilty of spiritual adultery.

Over time, we eventually become like the object of our worship. When we choose to worship something in creation over the Creator, our hearts are darkened and our attention shifts away from our Heavenly Father. When this transfer of affection occurs, we become consumed with fear, anxiety, lust, selfishness, pride, anger, resentment, bitterness, impatience, hatred, and arrogance. These are all peace-robbers and place our feet on slippery ground. If we worship the true triune God, however, we increasingly become like Jesus, and the peace God offers keeps our feet set on the Rock of Ages (see Psalm 71:3). Standing firm on the Rock that is Christ keeps our footing steady and our hearts faithful to him (see Psalm 89:26; 1 Corinthians 10:4).

During Old Testament times, the worship of idols made of wood, stone, and rock was rampant. Even during the days of the apostles, gods and goddesses like Artemis were openly and passionately worshipped. While many believe idolatry is a practice limited to days gone by, I assure you, false worship is alive and well. Before introducing a few of the common idols people worship today, allow the words of Psalm 115 to sink into your heart.

"Their idols are silver and gold, the work of human hands. They have mouths, but do not speak; eyes, but do not see. They have ears, but do not hear; noses, but do not smell. They have hands, but do not feel; feet, but do not walk; and they do not make a sound in their throat. Those who make them become like them; so do all who trust in them" (Psalm 115:4–8).

The principle of this passage is clear. When people create idols in their own image, they become spiritually deadened like their false gods. Worshipping idols will steal our peace and leave us spiritually comatose. To state the obvious, there is no spiritual benefit to shaping an idol from metal, wood, or stone for the purpose of worship. Because these gods are created by the hands of men, they are incapable of providing salvation to those who venerate them. Because false worship is contrary to the gospel of Jesus Christ, Paul and the other apostles consistently condemned idolatrous practices throughout their ministries. Scripture repeatedly warns us that idols make promises they can never deliver, accentuating the importance of rejecting the gods of this age. Idols may promise the moon and the stars, but they are terrible taskmasters that will slowly rot the souls of those who worship them.

It's common for objections to erupt at this point in the idol discussion. Most westerners don't regularly fall to their knees before pieces of wood, metal, or rock. This doesn't negate, however, our natural God-given proclivity to worship. As sinners, we prefer to fashion gods that are willing to smile as we enjoy our vices and categorically overlook our blatant acts of immorality. Our natural tendency is to pull down God to coincide with our vain imaginations of who he should be, what he should allow, and how he should think. Pastor and theologian R. C. Sproul explains it this way: "We are by nature inventors, craftsmen who create for ourselves idols as substitutes for the living God."[45] Unfortunately, the inclination to replace the living God with the gods of our own creation doesn't stop when we accept Christ as Savior. According to Ezekiel 14:4–5, we're all prone to worshipping idols in our hearts, and arguably the most common god we prefer to worship is self. Rather than carving idols from physical materials like the pagans of ancient cultures, we meticulously craft our idols based on the patterns of our own self-exalting thinking, self-satisfying cravings, and self-adulating priorities.

Revisiting Heart Idols

Space doesn't allow for a lengthy discussion here on heart idols. But allow me to illustrate how these false gods work. An idol can be defined as anything or anyone that assumes God's rightful place in our hearts. Scholars Dan Allender and Tremper Longman write, "Sinful, selfish people do not like the idea of a God who is more powerful than they are. Through idolatry we try to pare God down to our size."[46] Because we prefer to crave gods we can control, and use to our

---

45 R. C. Sproul, *Acts* (Wheaton, IL: Crossway, 2010), 332–333.
46 Dan B. Allender and Tremper Longman III, *Breaking the Idols of Your Heart* (Downers Grove, IL: InterVarsity Press, 2007), 151.

own gratification, practically any created object or ideology can become a counterfeit god. While we are children of the light, we constantly feel the pull toward the darkness of idolatry. This is what makes our attraction to evil so powerful and why Satan's fiery arrows of temptation are so effective. Temptation to sin succeeds because it appeals to the residual sin nature living inside our idolatrous hearts.

In order to assess what is truly ruling and reigning in your heart, ask yourself three simple questions: One, what are you willing to sin against God to get? Two, what is it that you respond sinfully to when it's withheld from you? Three, what are you so desperate to have that you don't believe you can live without?

Answering these questions will provide a hint as to what counterfeit gods have taken up residence in your heart. The road to idolatry is slick, making our feet prone to slipping into false worship. It's significantly easier to recognize idolatry when we choose to worship something inherently sinful. But sin is often far more subtle. If we're not mindful of how quickly our hearts can wander off into idolatry, we unknowingly carve heart idols out of the good things God created for our enjoyment. When the good things of life, such as family, friends, a career, a hobby, or even a ministry, become ultimate things and consume our hearts and dictate our decisions, thoughts, reactions, and attitudes, they become a counterfeit god. Even something inherently wholesome, like loving our families, becomes sinful whenever it assumes God's rightful place of preeminence in our lives and drives all of our decisions, consumes all of our energy, and controls all of our thoughts.

When we think of counterfeit gods and their destructive role in our lives, we typically focus our attention on the symptoms of idolatry rather than on the actual god ruling our hearts. For illustrative purposes, consider seven common false gods of our age: appearance, success, acceptance, possessions, pleasure, comfort, and control. In my experience, sinful anger is one of the most common problems I address in personal discipleship settings. While anger is a God-given emotion, in fallen humanity it is rarely righteous and quickly deteriorates into sinful anger. Unrighteous anger typically takes one of two forms: (1) explosive anger, illustrated by those who fly off the handle, scream, cuss, throw temper tantrums, and punch walls (and sometimes people) or (2) seething anger, illustrated by those who keep their wrath under wraps and allow it to simmer beneath the surface, waiting to spew its molten lava once it reaches its boiling point. Sinful anger, like jealousy, envy, discontentment, covetousness, dishonesty, and so many other transgressions we struggle with, is an indicator that something in our hearts has gone awry. With the questions above—what are you willing to sin against God to get and what is it that you respond sinfully to when it's withheld—in mind, let's consider how the symptom of unrighteous anger develops when we worship one of the seven common idols.

1. Appearance: People are willing to deprive their bodies of proper nutrition and/or spend an exorbitant amount of time and money pursuing the culture's definition of the perfect appearance. Inevitably, they

fall short of their ideal, resulting in anger against God for not providing their idealized look, and resentment toward those who have seemingly attained the physical appearance they idolize.

2. Success: People are willing to lie, cheat, and steal to achieve the culture's definition of success. Inevitably, they fall short of their goals, resulting in anger against God for not providing what their hearts demand, and resentment toward those who have seemingly attained the achievements they idolize.

3. Acceptance: People are willing to manipulate, cater to the whimsical desires of others, and sacrifice their own spiritual well-being for the purpose of being accepted by those they believe will bring satisfaction to their souls. Inevitably, their relationships fall short of their romanticized ideal, resulting in anger against God for not providing the relationships they demand, and resentment toward those who have obtained the popularity they idolize.

4. Possessions: People are willing to sacrifice their relationships, families, and health on the altar of possessions when they believe material things will provide the contentment and respect their hearts demand. Inevitably, their desires are never satisfied, resulting in anger against God for not providing everything they crave, and resentment toward those who have acquired the possessions their hearts sinfully idolize.

5. Pleasure: People are willing to commit sexual sins, become gluttonous, and sinfully pursue any other imaginable pleasure for the purpose of finding lasting satisfaction and contentment. Inevitably, their sources of pleasure fail to deliver what they promise, resulting in anger against God for not providing all the pleasures they long for, and resentment toward those who are enjoying the pleasures they idolize.

6. Comfort: People are willing to go to great lengths to enjoy the comforts of modern society, oftentimes to the neglect of God-given responsibilities such as work, parenting, church involvement, and community service. Inevitably, the demands to always be comfortable will be disappointed, resulting in anger against God for bringing uncomfortable circumstances their way, and resentment toward those who create inconvenience and disrupt the pursuit of the comfort they idolize.

7. Control: People are willing to manipulate, gaslight, threaten, undermine, and dominate others when they demand to be the one in absolute command of people and circumstances. Inevitably, their attempts to control others and situations fall short, resulting in anger against God for not giving them the jurisdiction over others they demand or for not bending circumstances to their will, and resentment toward those who do not fall in line with their agenda and rob them of the control they idolize.

To be clear, there are aspects of our desire for a pleasant appearance, success, acceptance, possessions, pleasure, comfort, and control that are appropriate. We should practice good stewardship over our bodies by choosing a healthy lifestyle and looking the best we can. As good stewards of our God-given abilities, we should seek success in our endeavors for the purpose of God's glory and human flourishing. The innate desire to be accepted by our friends and family is because God created us as relational beings. Possessions can be a wise financial investment, produce happiness, and hold sentimental value. Enjoying the pleasure of life within God's boundaries is a gift from our Creator. Comfort can promote productivity and create opportunities that discomfort often eliminates. Humbly exerting our God-given authority for leadership in our homes, communities, churches, or places of business for God's glory and human flourishing is the right thing to do. The problem isn't that these are entirely wrong pursuits; it's that we have the sinful tendency to make at least one of these our ultimate reason for existence.

These desires become sinful when we make any one of them the center of our universe and build all of our hopes and dreams on them instead of on Christ and the gospel. Substantial, life-altering problems arise when we wrongly assume that these idols are worthy of our worship, and we grant them the control over our hearts they were never intended to have. Difficulties also arise when we look to people, such as a parent, a spouse, a child, a friend, or a person in leadership, to fulfill these desires. No individual can provide the satisfaction and contentment our hearts desperately crave. When we seek ultimate fulfillment in anyone or anything other than the Lord Jesus Christ, we have fallen in love with a false god.

The voices of this wicked age tell us that these gods can satisfy the deepest longings and cravings of our hearts, but they can't. In reality, not one of these false gods can provide the lasting meaning, significance, purpose, contentment, and peace our hearts are searching for. Based on years of personal and ministry experience, I'm guessing that you find at least one of the seven common idols appealing. Again, these seven pursuits are not inherently wrong. They only become sinful when they become our reason for living, when we can't imagine living without them, and when sinful actions and attitudes are flowing from our hearts when they are withheld.

For years, acceptance served as my god, and it still vies for attention on a regular basis. I also need to admit that I can be controlling in certain areas of my life, my schedule being my favorite.

In the reflection questions, I have included a short exercise that will help identify idols that are possibly ruling and reigning in your heart. Because Satan uses our tendency to worship these idols to craft and tailor his temptations, we must identify our false gods so we can prepare to guard our hearts against Satan's attacks.

Takeaways

God didn't send his Son into the world to satisfy our every need, to meet our every demand, or to scratch every itch. Jesus entered the world as a helpless child to live among men, to satisfy the righteous demands of God's holy law, and to take the Father's just wrath on our behalf. In light of our redemption, we must lace up God's shoes of readiness and make sure our feet are firmly set on the solid foundation of the gospel with these two takeaways in mind.

1. Because of our ravenously idolatrous hearts, we must put on readiness as clothing and tie the shoes of the gospel on our feet so we don't slip into sinning against God. The gospel isn't merely for securing our salvation or keeping us out of hell; it's essential for daily obedience and spiritual growth.

2. As heralds of the gospel, we must also take up readiness as an armament and run into the world with the lifesaving and life-changing gospel of peace. As finite beings, we are incapable of changing hearts and lives; only the power of the gospel can deliver people from their idolatry and provide freedom from sin. With our stances firmly set in the gospel, we are to faithfully live each and every day trusting in its power. The war for supremacy being waged on the battlefield of our hearts is far from over, making it necessary to plant our feet on the firm foundation of the gospel.

As we will learn in the following chapter, we need to trust in the gospel and allow it to change us and others by faith.

Key Point: Readiness is made possible by standing firm in the gospel of peace.

For Further Consideration

1. Read Psalm 37. Compare and contrast the righteous and the wicked.
2. Verses on peace:

    Psalm 4:8

    Psalm 29:11

    Psalm 34:14

    Psalm 72:7

    Psalm 85:8

    Psalm 119:57

    Proverbs 3:1–2

    Romans 1:7

    Romans 5:1

    Romans 15:33

    Ephesians 1:2

    Ephesians 2:14

    Philippians 1:2

    Hebrews 13:20–21

    1 Peter 1:1–2

    2 John 3

3. Verses on the gospel:

    Romans 1:7–17

    1 Corinthians 1:22–25

1 Corinthians 15:1–4
2 Corinthians 4:1–7
Galatians 1:6–12
Ephesians 1:1–14
Philippians 1:27–30
Colossians 1:21–23
2 Timothy 2:8–13

4. It's important to identify the potential idols reigning in your heart. Whatever fills the following blanks are your counterfeit gods. How would you fill in these blanks?

    As long as I have _____, I have meaning and significance.

    If I were to lose _____, I would lose everything.

    I will willingly sin against God to have _____.

    When I don't receive _____, I respond sinfully (e.g., anger, bitterness, jealousy, envy).

    If I only had _____, I would experience everlasting peace.

5. What steps can you take to replace your counterfeit gods with the one true God?

Shield: Live By Faith

In all circumstances take up the shield of faith, with which you can extinguish all the flaming darts of the evil one.
Ephesians 6:16

Health problems can occur at any moment. Medical issues take many different forms and impact people of all ages. At the age of sixteen, my life took a major detour because of a severe illness. It began in September of 1986. I was in the first few days of my junior year of high school preparing for the upcoming football season with great expectations for the team. I was in fantastic shape. Perfectly healthy. And putting in a lot of hard practice time with the team.

During one of our preseason practices, I began feeling unusually sluggish and found it difficult to run. In the middle of one of the drills, my legs felt abnormally weak. So, I did the unthinkable. I stopped running. One of the coaches blew the whistle and scolded me for quitting on the play. I told the coach I wasn't feeling well and was excused to the locker room. I had suffered dehydration in the past, so I assumed I only needed to get some water and get out of the heat for a while, and then I would be fine.

Over the next couple of days, I continued to feel weak and lethargic. Lacking the strength to practice, I was forced to sit on the sidelines and watch the team running drills. Friday after school, I drove home determined to rest up and return to normal on Monday. Although I spent the majority of the weekend in bed, by Sunday night I felt even worse. When my alarm sounded Monday morning, my legs were completely numb, and I was unable to stand.

Following a call to my pediatrician, I was referred to a neurologist for an evaluation. Using some old crutches from a previous knee surgery, I shuffled into the doctor's office and sank into a chair for an appointment that would drastically change my life. After a brief evaluation, the neurologist promptly diagnosed me with something called Guillain-Barre syndrome. Don't feel bad if you've never heard of the disease, few people have. Guillain-Barre is a rare neurological disorder, typically caused by a viral infection, in which the immune system begins attacking the person's nerves. As a result, patients experience muscle weakness, tingling in their hands and feet, and paralysis. Symptoms can range from relatively mild to severe. In extreme cases, Guillain-Barre can cause permanent paralysis, and sometimes it's fatal.

After the diagnosis, I was immediately admitted to a local hospital. As the hours ticked by, I grew progressively weaker. Stubborn to the core, I refused to be bedbound and continued getting out of bed on my own. After I collapsed on the bathroom floor, however, I was officially forbidden by the medical staff to get out of bed. Too weak to argue, I acquiesced. By midweek, my legs and arms were completely paralyzed and I could hardly speak. My eyes were also affected, making it difficult to see.

On Friday afternoon, I received an unexpected visit from my neurologist. To this day, I can still hear the strain in his voice as he explained that my case of Guillain-Barre was very severe, and he feared that I was heading down a long and troublesome road. Within an hour, I was airlifted to Johns Hopkins Hospital because the local hospital wasn't equipped to handle my care.

Once I arrived in Baltimore, I was admitted to the pediatric neurology unit and continued to decline. By Sunday afternoon, the paralysis had spread, leaving me paralyzed from my neck down and unable to breathe on my own. For the next eight days, I was mostly comatose and on a ventilator in the PICU with all kinds of lines sticking in my body. In a few short days, I went from playing football to lying helplessly in an ICU bed, completely paralyzed and being kept alive by a breathing machine.

Eventually, I was well enough to return to the general neurology floor. Weeks later, I was deemed strong enough to go home where I was scheduled to continue physical therapy to regain my strength. While my family and I pretended that I was improving, we all knew that I wasn't. By this time, the 195-pound football player was weighing in at a whopping 120 pounds. I went from bench-pressing over 200 pounds to not being able to lift a cane off my chest.

When I went back to Johns Hopkins for a follow-up appointment a few weeks after being discharged, my doctor took one look at my condition and immediately had me readmitted. By God's grace, my health didn't regress any further. There were no more ventilators or ICU stays, but the direction of my life took a radical turn. Eventually, I did regain feeling and some strength in my upper body. My legs, however, remained completely paralyzed.

I don't recollect the day of the week, but I vividly remember the morning when my team of physicians informed me that I had a chronic form of Guillain-Barre, and that I was never going to walk again. They predicted that I would gain more strength in my arms, but they said the paralysis in my legs was permanent. At sixteen, my dreams of playing sports in college or the pros were destroyed.

Destined to spend the rest of my life in a wheelchair, I began learning how to shift myself from the bed to a wheelchair. My parents were preparing to add ramps to our house so I could gain access more easily. No more dreams of playing professional baseball. No more football. My life goals were shattered like a thin piece of ice on the pavement. But I can honestly say, I was okay with what God was doing in my life. I trusted that what was happening was for my good. God was crushing my idols of celebrity, fame, and fortune, and he was doing so out of his love for me.

Late one night, while the neurology unit was quiet, I was lying in my room staring at the ceiling. I knew every stain in the tiles by heart, along with every imperfection in the craftsmanship. As I often did into the early hours of the morning, I was listening to the radio. An old '80s song was playing, one I had heard a million times.

The song is called "All Cried Out." It's a sappy '80s love song with questionable lyrics that I didn't really understand at the time. But the chorus struck deep inside my soul that night. I was all cried out. I had no more tears to cry; no more complaints to lodge, only prayers. My physical strength was spent, and I had no choice but to accept God's sovereign will for my life. All I could do was cry out to God for his grace to thrive in the circumstances he had orchestrated. Like any other person, I often prayed for healing—who wouldn't? But on that night, listening to "All Cried Out," I prayed something profoundly different.

On that quiet night in Johns Hopkins Hospital, I prayed a prayer that I still remember with crystal-clear clarity. I said, "Lord, if your will for my life is to be in a wheelchair, I'll do that. All I ask, God, is that you use me and this illness for your glory." That's all I knew to pray. Of course I wanted to walk again—and by God's grace I did—but at that tender moment, I was honestly all right if God didn't heal my legs. I was confident that God would be glorified if I walked again, and I also believed that he would be equally glorified if I never took another step.

It was during my long and horrific battle with Guillain-Barre that I learned how to apply my personal faith in Jesus Christ to the difficult situations of life. That painful lesson has served me well through the years, and I can honestly say that even if I could go back and change those events, I wouldn't change a thing. A part of me died that quiet night staring at the ceiling tiles, listening to the music I found comforting. While my dreams of an athletic career perished, my selfish aspirations gave way to God's greater purpose for my life. What I believed would be my road to fame, fortune, and admiration was washed away like a shattered shell in the ocean, and I am so thankful because my self-absorbed plans would have led to ruin. I didn't realize it at the time, but God was teaching me the importance of trusting him while bearing his impenetrable shield of faith.

The Shield of Faith

Like my graduation regalia, mentioned in chapter four, hanging in the back of my closet, most of us leave God's shield of faith hanging in our spiritual closet collecting dust bunnies. Whenever we need a dash of faith to get us out of a jam, we dust off the shield and put it to work until the problem passes. Once the skies clear and we're out of the tight spot, we put the shield back where we found it until rough waters come again. Faith isn't only for rainy days and troublous times. God's shield of faith is a piece of armor we need each and every day.

The common practice of keeping our faith locked away until it's needed is clearly not what Paul has in mind in Ephesians 6:16. This is made evident by the three important words, "In all circumstances." In times of blessing, we need faith. In times of trial, we need faith. In times of joy, we need faith. In times of discouragement, we need faith. In times of productivity, we need faith. In times of exhaustion, we need faith. When times are good, we generally ignore our need for faith. But we need faith even on the days when we are cruising along without any sign of problems.

Christians are often at great risk for surrendering to temptation during times of blessing, comfort, and ease. In God's wisdom, he knows that our flesh is vulnerable to sin during times of blessing. That's one of the reasons he uses trials to strengthen our faith. James writes, "Count it all joy, my brothers, when you meet trials of various kinds, for you know that the testing of your faith produces steadfastness" (James 1:2–3). When God lovingly tests our faith, we can confidently believe that he is using our trials for our spiritual growth. As Spurgeon writes, "Our Lord in his infinite wisdom and superabundant love, sets so high a value upon his people's faith that he will not screen them from those trials by which faith is strengthened."[47] God taught me more about faith during the weeks I was paralyzed than during the times my health was at its best. We all learn more about faith, trust, and hope through trials than during times of blessing. While trials are never an enjoyable experience, and their benefit may not be immediately evident, we must believe by faith that God is using the difficult circumstances of life for our spiritual good (see Romans 8:28).

In Ephesians 6:16, Paul used the Greek word *thureos*, translated as "shield." As you can imagine, a *thureos* was

---
47 Spurgeon, 495.

a basic and important means of defense for the Roman army. These shields were portable, maneuverable, capable of absorbing the impact of enemy weapons, and allowed soldiers to advance on their enemies quickly while being protected from the dangerous projectiles.[48] A *thureos* was a door-shaped armament, approximately four feet tall and two feet wide, providing the soldier with full body protection. A *thureos* also featured a locking mechanism, allowing an entire line of soldiers to lock their shields together, creating a united wall of protection. Prior to battle, soldiers soaked the leather straps on their shields with water, making them capable of extinguishing flaming arrows hurled in their direction.

Paul explains that we need God's spiritual shield of faith in all circumstances so that we can "extinguish all the flaming darts of the evil one" that are launched at our hearts. Taking up and equipping ourselves with the shield of faith will protect us from the violent attacks of the devil and keep our minds focused on God's glorious truth. Like a saturated *thureos* protecting a Roman soldier, our faith in Christ dampens Satan's spiritual arrows intended to drive us from the battlefield. Given our idolatrous hearts and fleshly desires, we need God's shield of faith protecting us from the schemes of the devil. Not only should we use this shield defensively, we must also use it to charge headlong into the spiritual warfare raging all around us.

---

48 Leland Ryken, James C. Wilhoit, and Tremper Longman III, eds., *Dictionary of Biblical Imagery* (Downers Grove, IL: InterVarsity Press, 1998), 45.

Old Testament Usage of Shield

Finding one particular Old Testament text that parallels Paul's shield of faith imagery is difficult because there are numerous passages where the word *shield* is used to refer to God's protection and strength. I will reference Psalm 91 as an example here, but I have also included more texts in the reflection questions. Psalm 91:2–6 reads, "I will say to the Lord, 'My refuge and my fortress, my God, in whom I trust.' For he will deliver you from the snare of the fowler and from the deadly pestilence. He will cover you with his pinions, and under his wings you will find refuge; his faithfulness is a shield and buckler. You will not fear the terror of the night, nor the arrow that flies by day, nor the pestilence that stalks in darkness, nor the destruction that wastes at noonday." In this text, the psalmist highlights faith, trust, shield, arrows, and God's protection; all of which are included in Paul's imagery found in Ephesians.

The beauty of Psalm 91 is the fact that it's not faith in and of itself that provides the spiritual protection we need. It's the object of our faith that protects us from spiritual harm. God is the one who serves as our shield against Satan's fiery darts (see Psalm 5:12). When our eyes shift away from this comforting truth, we're overcome by a whirlwind of negative emotions and feelings that tempt us to believe the deceiver's lies, leaving us spiritually exhausted and vulnerable.

During the times when we're feeling overwhelmed, the strength of our faith may ebb and flow like the tides on the seashore. But if our faith securely rests in the absolute finished work of Jesus on the cross of Calvary, we have no reason to fear. According to Paul, trusting in God's promises and power by faith is what extinguishes the devil's darts of deception that come at us each day. It's not necessary to have detailed knowledge concerning the darts or a full description of the evil forces firing them. What we need is Christ-centered faith that empowers us to trust that God will be our shield of protection when the great dragon's flaming arrows fly.

People of Faith

Personally, I find the phrase "people of faith" to be an interesting expression. The idiom insinuates that some people have faith while others do not. Christians, according to this line of reasoning, are people of faith. Atheists are not. In reality, however, all people are people of faith. Every person living on the face of the earth right now has faith in something or someone. People can have faith in their abilities, health, education, science, strength, money, wisdom, family, friends, celebrities, religious leaders, Artemis, and even Satan. As you can see, the list is long.

All of us have a worldview through which we see and understand the world, and this is influenced by the object of our faith. A worldview is the interpretive lens through which we make sense of what we see, hear, and think. Our perspective of the world isn't determined by logic per se but by what we believe to be true by faith. Our faith dictates how we think about the world and how we relate to it. Faith, along with the object of our faith, greatly impacts our daily decisions. We live, react, speak, and think according to our interpretive framework. Fostering a biblical framework, one founded on the gospel, helps keep us grounded in God's objective word while living in a culture that believes truth to be subjective.

Atheists and secularists boast about being "freethinkers" and above religion, believing they have no need for faith. But even the staunchest atheist's belief system relies on faith as much as the most fundamental Christian's. By faith, an atheist believes that there is no God and that the Bible is nothing but a fictitious collection of old fables that hold no authority, and they choose to live accordingly. By faith, a Christian believes that there is a God and that the Bible is authoritative and inspired by him, and they choose to live accordingly. While atheists and Christians appear to be on separate ends of the faith spectrum, they are actually closer than you might think. In fact, one could argue atheism is also God-centric since it focuses on the belief that there is an absence of God. Categorically dismissing God from the equation when trying to answer questions—such as what is the origin of the universe, where did humans come from, and how does the world operate—is a much bigger leap of faith than trusting in a God who created the universe, gave life to humankind, and lovingly rules all of creation.

I staunchly believe by faith that there is an almighty Creator who created this world and is the sovereign ruler over all of it. I find the belief in a sovereign God substantially more comforting and hopeful than believing that the world is nothing more than a disordered, chance-driven place where luck and fate reign supreme. Given all we know about archaeology, history, and the Bible, it's rational to believe that there is a God who has revealed himself through his Son. It's also perfectly reasonable to believe by faith that God sent his Son to die on the cross for our sins. And yes, it's also reasonable to believe that an all-powerful, preexisting God could raise from the dead.

If your faith isn't resting on a solid foundation, it's not only useless, it's fatal. The object of our faith determines our eternal destiny. In order to have redemptive value, our faith must rest upon the Lord Jesus Christ. A generic belief in God or some other type of deity isn't sufficient. People must have precise faith placed in a specific person—Jesus Christ, the Lamb of God who is the only one who can take away the sins of the world.

The Christian's best defense against the fire-tipped darts of the evil one is faith in the finished work of Christ. Confidently dress yourself in faith so that the enemy's arrows will be extinguished and your heart will be protected from evil. While standing your ground, take up faith as a shield so you can speak the truth of the gospel to the world. Once our faith is properly fixed on Christ, we must actively apply our salvation to the challenges of this age.

The Paralytic

It likely will not surprise you to hear that Matthew 9:1–8 is one of my favorite biblical accounts in the New Testament.

In this passage, some men bring a paralytic who is lying helplessly on a bed before Jesus. The Lord had already healed people with paralysis in Matthew 4:24 and 8:5–13. Based on the phrase, "when Jesus saw their [i.e., those who carried the paralytic] faith," we can assume these men had likely heard of Jesus's healing power and wanted the Lord to do for their friend what he had done for others.

Interestingly, Jesus didn't immediately heal the man. Instead, he said to the paralytic, "Take heart, my son; your sins are forgiven." Now, we must be hermeneutically and theologically cautious with Jesus's declaration. Sometimes in Scripture, sickness is directly related to a particular sin; other times it isn't. In this man's case, it's possible that Jesus's declaration of forgiveness indicates his paralysis was the result of a specific sin. In Matthew 9, a direct correlation is implied in Jesus's opening statement but not explicitly stated. Ultimately, all sickness and death are the result of the universal effects of sin.

Regardless of the specific cause of the paralytic's illness, Jesus is highlighting something substantially more important than the man's physical paralysis and its exact cause. Ultimately, this text is about faith and Jesus's authority to forgive sin. In order to prove his authority to forgive sin, Jesus told the man to pick up his bed and go home as an outward sign of his power. When the paralytic stood up and went home, Matthew tells us that the crowds were afraid and began glorifying God. Jesus not only had the power to heal the man of his physical needs, he possessed the authority to forgive his sin and spiritually deliver him from the powers of darkness. It was faith in Jesus demonstrated by the paralytic's friends that set these miraculous events in motion.

The word *faith* in Matthew 9 comes from the Greek word *pistis*, which is the commonly used term used in the New Testament for *faith*. The word refers to the "conviction of the truth of something." In the New Testament, *pistis* is used to describe the belief that God exists, that he created the world, that he alone is the sovereign ruler over all creation, and that he provides eternal salvation through his Son. The writer of Hebrews describes faith as, "The assurance of things hoped for, the conviction of things not seen" (Hebrews 11:1).

Based on the definition of faith in Hebrews 11:1, we learn that faith and hope are closely knit together. As John Calvin astutely notes, "Wherever this faith is alive, it must have along with it the hope of eternal salvation as its inseparable companion . . . Faith believes God to be true, hope awaits the time when his truth shall be manifested."[49] As an illustration of this dynamic, Noah once again serves as a worthy example. In Hebrews 11:7, we read, "By faith Noah, being warned by God concerning events as yet unseen, in reverent fear constructed an ark for the saving of his household. By this he condemned the world and became an heir of the righteousness that comes by faith." During the long, exhausting days of constructing the ark, all Noah had to base his unusual building project on was God's promise of a coming flood. By faith, Noah believed God's word

---

49 Calvin, 590.

and obediently began building the ark long before the first raindrop fell.

Because we walk by faith and not by sight, as indicated in 2 Corinthians 5:7, all of us have a decision to make. In Noah's case, the choice was simple. He could have chosen by faith to reject God's word as false with the hope that the floodwaters would never come to destroy him and his family, or he could have chosen by faith to accept God's word as truth with the hope that his family would be saved when the rains fell. Either choice was a decision based squarely on faith.

Today, we can choose to believe *by faith* that Jesus was a fraud and that the Bible is a hoax, leaving us free to live however we want, or we can believe *by faith* that Jesus Christ is God's Son sent to die on the cross for our sins and that Jesus is the only way to heaven. Jesus is either the way, the truth, and the life, or he isn't. The Bible is either inspired, infallible, and authoritative, or it isn't. Either the biblical writers recorded what actually took place, or they fabricated their accounts. The authors of Scripture suffered greatly for what they claimed. Many were martyred for what they believed. If they did so to defend a fabricated storyline, they were indeed fools. But if they spoke the truth, as I believe they did, they are to be highly regarded for their sacrifice. Either option has to be accepted by faith.

Faith of a Mustard Seed

There are times when we all believe our faith is insufficient and weak. Even those who followed Jesus during his earthly ministry had times when their faith was small. In Luke 17:5, the apostles pleaded with the Lord to "increase our faith!" In verse 6, Jesus answered them with an astounding hyperbolic statement. He replied, "If you had faith like a grain of mustard seed, you could say to this mulberry tree, 'Be uprooted and planted in the sea,' and it would obey you." In the context of this passage, Jesus was teaching the disciples that temptations to sin in this fallen world are inevitable. In verse 2, he issued a stern warning to those who encourage participation in sin, saying that it would be better for that person to be cast into the sea rather than cause someone to disobey God. The problem arose when Jesus added in verses 3 and 4 that the disciples were to radically forgive those who sinned against them. The disciples understood that they were incapable of fulfilling this commandment in their own strength. In order to obey Jesus's commandment to forgive those who repeatedly and deplorably sinned against them, they were in desperate need of greater faith than they could muster on their own.

Struck by Jesus's seemingly impossible instruction, the disciples were deeply troubled by what he demanded of them. To refrain from causing others to sin and to develop the spiritual fortitude necessary to forgive those who sinned against them, they needed the Lord to miraculously increase their faith. Professor David Garland observes, "Faith is a response to God's initiative that trusts that we are empowered to do what God requires. If we wait until we can say we have enough faith to do what Jesus asks, we will probably never do anything."[50] Obediently doing what God requires, no matter how big or small, requires faith. Like the disciples, we need to recognize our faith deficiency, otherwise we are liable to rely on our own strength and never get around to doing much for the Lord.

In Jesus's illustrious illustration, he teaches that faith is not a matter of quantity, but rather a matter of presence. Even a tiny amount of faith can do wondrous things, such as uprooting a mulberry tree and planting it in the sea (v. 6). These trees had a substantially deep root system, underscoring the difficulty of this accomplishment. Jesus's point is straightforward: even the smallest amount of genuine faith in God can produce remarkable results.

It isn't the size or amount of your faith that matters—it's the object of your faith that makes all the difference. Faith in Christ can move the mountain of our sin under his blood, allowing us to stand before our holy God adorned in his righteousness. Authentic, repentant faith, no matter how small and frail, is sufficient to eternally deliver anyone from their sin. By faith in Jesus, sinners are miraculously transferred from the kingdom of darkness to God's kingdom of light. Faith in Christ also protects us from Satan's ferocious attacks and keeps his fiery darts from piercing our souls.

---

50   David E. Garland, *Luke* (Grand Rapids, MI: Zondervan, 2011), 684.

Takeaways

Everyone places their faith in something or someone. No matter how vehemently people deny the existence of faith in their lives, it cannot be eradicated from the human experience. Rather than denying faith, we must evaluate our faith and assess whether it is Christ-centered or misguided. Before leaving this chapter, let's consider two important details concerning faith.

1. The object of our faith is a matter of life and death. Choosing who or what to trust by faith is an important decision that carries eternal consequences. Parents choose babysitters with caution. Employers make personnel decisions based on who they believe can be trusted. When it comes to religion, we face the most important decision of all. Who or what are we going to trust with our eternal soul? For Christians, the object of our faith is the triune God. We believe, by faith, that Jesus is the only way to heaven, and that all who believe in him will enjoy an eternity in God's presence. In 1 Corinthians 15:13–14, the Apostle Paul highlighted the importance of the resurrected Christ when he wrote, "If there is no resurrection of the dead, then not even Christ has been raised. And if Christ has not been raised, then our preaching is in vain and your faith is in vain." Faith in the resurrection of Jesus is only meaningful if it is based on truth.

According to Scripture, God created the world by his own volitional act. Out of his love, he sent his only Son to die on the cross for the sins of mankind. Jesus miraculously raised from the dead and made redemption possible through faith in him. By faith, you either believe this to be true or you don't. When we consider the object of our faith, we must have confidence that the recipient of our faith can deliver on its promises. From the opening verses of the Bible, we learn the importance of faith and trust in our Creator. The gods of this world cannot deliver on their promises of security, comfort, and peace. But Jesus can deliver on his promises. Like Noah, we must believe God's promises and faithfully obey his word so that we can be delivered from the penalty of sin and bring glory to his holy name.

2. When Satan's fiery arrows of temptation, doubt, discouragement, or exhaustion come our way, we must trust God's shield of faith to protect us. In ancient warfare, arrows were a deadly weapon to be reckoned with. In 1 Kings 22, King Ahab was killed when a man arbitrarily fired an arrow that struck him through the narrow joints of his armor (v. 34). Second Chronicles 35 records Josiah's death after being mortally wounded by an archer's arrow (vv. 20–24). On the physical battlefield, soldiers in ancient times took great precaution to keep themselves safe from flying arrows.

Spiritually speaking, we are to safeguard ourselves from Satan's hazardous arrows. God's shield of faith is an essential part of his armor because, as O'Brien writes, "The burning arrows depict, in highly metaphorical language, every kind of attack launched by the devil and his hosts against the people of God."[51] Satan is creative and will tailor temptations to reach our idolatry-prone hearts. As an expert in lying and deception, the great deceiver resorts to whatever means necessary to draw us in and open fire. In all circumstances, it's God's shield that keeps us safe from spiritual attacks.

Here are three essential practices that can help us stand firm in our faith when Satan's assaults come:

1. Allow faith to point us toward God's promises. Trusting in the Lord's promises provides the strength we need to stand against this crooked and perverse culture (see Deuteronomy 31:6).

2. Allow faith to point us toward the power and wisdom of God. The God who created this world is the same God who cares for you; find rest and peace in God's magnificent power and wisdom (see Psalm 147:4–5; 1 John 4:4).

3. Allow faith to point us toward obedience. Remaining faithful and obedient to God is difficult in a world where the majority rejects him and his word. By

---

51 O'Brien, 480.

faith, we obey God and trust that he is greater than the forces of evil (see Hebrews 11:6).

Our confidence, hope, and peace do not rest in the reading on our faith meters. There are days when our faith seems pretty weak when compared to the challenges of our time. When feelings of doubt, fear, and fatigue overcome us, we must remember that our security doesn't rest in our own fragile strength. We can courageously live an obedient life by trusting in the faithfulness of almighty God.

Key Point: In this sinful world, where the flaming arrows of our spiritual enemies will consistently come our way, we must put on and take up God's shield of faith daily so we can stand against the forces of evil with confidence, hope, and peace.

For Further Consideration

1. Verses that utilize shield imagery:
   Genesis 15:1
   Psalm 3:3
   Psalm 5:12
   Psalm 28:7
   Psalm 119:114
   Proverbs 30:5
2. Verses about faith:
   Psalm 23:4
   Joel 2:32
   Romans 1:17

2 Corinthians 5:7
1 Timothy 6:11–12
James 1:3
James 2:17–19
1 Peter 3:18
1 John 4:15
1 John 1:5–10

3. What are the circumstances in which your faith is often shaken?
4. How has God used the trials and struggles in your life to grow your faith?
5. Why do times of trial usually mature our faith in Christ more effectively than seasons of blessing?

Helmet: Apply Your Salvation

Take the helmet of salvation.
Ephesians 6:17

Life is sometimes filled with embarrassing moments—ones we wish we could take back and do over. In the fall of 2022, our church had the privilege of hosting Keith and Kristyn Getty. It was an incredible opportunity to have such talented musicians minister to our community. Joining the Getty team for the evening was Matt Papa, another gifted songwriter and musician. A few hours before the concert, Matt needed a ride to the hotel to prepare for the evening. I was given the address and name of the hotel, and promptly punched the information into my GPS. Minutes later, we were inching along through the traffic-infested streets of Wilmington.

Truth be told, I was overly confident that I knew exactly where the hotel was. Empowered by my self-confidence, I charged on like a navigator relying on the wrong map. When the GPS offered conflicting directions, I ignored the instructions and continued on my own way, believing that

I knew better than Google Maps. After all, I have lived in Wilmington for more than a decade.

Long humbling story short, I treated Matt to a meandering and misguided tour of Wilmington. Being the gracious man that he is, Matt never said a word about my ineptitude. He had no idea where he was going, and while I thought I did, I proved that I didn't have a clue how to get to the hotel. While I was sincere in my belief that I knew where we were going, I was sincerely and profoundly wrong. Oh, we never left Wilmington's city limits, but I repeatedly missed the mark.

Misguided and Lost

Like my wandering and misguided journey through Wilmington, there are many today who claim to know where they're going and sincerely believe they're on the right path to heaven. But they are lost and blindly traveling down what Scripture refers to as the path leading to destruction. In the Sermon on the Mount, Jesus said, "Enter by the narrow gate. For the gate is wide and the way is easy that leads to destruction, and those who enter by it are many. For the gate is narrow and the way is hard that leads to life, and those who find it are few" (Matthew 7:13–14). According to this teaching, the way leading to destruction is wide, easy, and well populated, many of them wrongly assuming they are heading in the right direction. Meanwhile, the path leading to life everlasting is narrow, difficult, and sparsely populated. While this relatively small group may be left out of the crowd and criticized for the path they have chosen, they are on the road leading to everlasting life. Because the two paths lead to vastly opposite destinations, it's imperative to know which path we're following.

Out of God's love for the world, he has provided road signs that tell people which road they are traveling. He wants us to know what path we're on. The majority find God's guardrails on the narrow road too restrictive, so they choose to follow the easy and popular route. Scores of people marching down the broad road believe they're on the right path.

Many of them earnestly practice some form of religion. But if they're not following the gospel of Jesus Christ, they're lost and destined for inevitable destruction. While many of these travelers are sincere in their religious efforts, sincerity alone isn't sufficient to lead them to heaven. Many religious people are sincerely wrong, and their sincerity is leading them straight to hell. That may sound harsh and unloving, but it's true. In fact, telling people the truth about what Jesus said concerning heaven and hell is an act of love.

In Romans 10:14, the Apostle Paul asked, "How then will they call on him in whom they have not believed? And how are they to believe in him of whom they have never heard? And how are they to hear without someone preaching?" The answer to these rhetorical questions is they won't. When we fail to speak the truth in love out of fear, we are admitting that we are more concerned about being rejected and ridiculed than reverencing and honoring God's holy name. Truly loving our neighbors means that we will tell them the whole truth and nothing but the truth, even when we are afraid they will dislike us or become angry. God's helmet of salvation keeps our minds focused on biblical truth so that we will lovingly speak it when given the opportunity.

As discussed in the previous chapter, the object of our trust and faith is what ultimately determines which eternal path we are following. As we read in the Gospel of John, "Whoever believes in the Son has eternal life; whoever does not obey the Son shall not see life, but the wrath of God remains on him" (John 3:36). As is typical in John's writings, this verse is extremely straightforward. Placing your faith in anyone or anything other than Jesus leads you down the pathway to eternal destruction. Contrary to the popular opinion of today's culture, faith in Jesus Christ is the only way to heaven. Those following any other path are misguided and lost. They may be sincere in their religious efforts, but their sincerity is deadly if their faith is not in Christ alone.

The Helmet of Salvation

Paul begins Ephesians 6:17 with a command aimed at Christians to take up God's helmet of salvation. On the battlefield, helmets protect soldiers from arrows, bullets, shrapnel, falling debris, and blows to the head. During biblical times, helmets were typically made of metal and worn into battle. Two biblical examples would be Goliath and King Saul, who both wore helmets composed of bronze (see 1 Samuel 17:5, 38). Because blows to the head from swords and other blunt objects can leave soldiers unconscious, permanently disabled, or dead, careful consideration was given to protective headgear.

Just as our physical hearts require protection, so do our minds. Our hearts are prone to idol worship; therefore, they need God's guidance provided by his breastplate of righteousness. Our minds are susceptible to all sorts of temptations and negative thought patterns. That's why our heads must be safeguarded by God's helmet of salvation. Two of the major battlefields of this spiritual warfare are our hearts and our minds. Left unguarded, both of these spiritual organs can lead us to grave danger. If the fiery darts of Satan can puncture the desires of our hearts and the beliefs of our minds, we're in deep trouble.

Concerning God's helmet of salvation, Paul seemingly draws his imagery from Isaiah 59:17, where we read, "He put on righteousness as a breastplate, and a helmet of salvation on his head; he put on garments of vengeance for clothing, and wrapped himself in zeal as a cloak." Don't miss the fact that the breastplate of righteousness, used to protect our idolatry-prone hearts, and the helmet of salvation, used to protect our information-processing heads, are closely connected in this verse. In order to successfully and consistently fend off Satan's attacks, both our hearts and minds must be adequately protected. If one is left unguarded and chooses to chase after sin, the other one will soon follow. When hearts wander from truth, our minds end up following. The thoughts we meditate on dictate what our hearts worship and what actions we perform. There is no way to separate the influence our hearts and minds have on the direction of our lives.

When it comes to God's helmet of salvation in Ephesians 6:17, there is another parallel passage in the New Testament we must also consider. In 1 Thessalonians 5:8, Paul writes, "But since we belong to the day, let us be sober, having put on the breastplate of faith and love, and for a helmet the hope of salvation." Notice in this text that the breastplate is described as faith and love, rather than righteousness. I like to think of the breastplate as the ancient equivalent of a bulletproof vest protecting our hearts.

In the Thessalonians passage, the helmet is described as the hope of our salvation. Unlike our flimsy and reckless usage of the word *hope* in English, the biblical understanding of hope does not imply uncertainty or lack of assurance that something is established. Paul uses the Greek word *elpis*, translated as *hope*, to describe the Christian's joyful and confident expectation of eternal salvation. *Elpis* is used to describe biblical hope that is confidently expecting something good in the future; there is a sense of moral certainty in *elpis* that should provide great encouragement to the believer. Hope, therefore, should be understood as a settled confidence in God and in the certainty of our salvation. Before applying God's helmet of salvation to our Christian walk, we must first consider what aspect of our salvation Paul is referencing.

A Biblical Understanding of Salvation

As previously mentioned, there are three dimensions to our salvation presented in Scripture. A brief review will hopefully clarify any lingering questions you may have regarding salvation and how it plays out in our lives.

First, when sinners place their faith in Jesus, they are *justified* before God and declared righteous. Those who reject Jesus as Savior will stand before God's holy judgment still under the condemnation of sin and will be held accountable for their choices. People who trust in Jesus's death, burial, and resurrection by faith will also stand before God, but they will be judged based on Christ's imputed righteousness, thus delivered from eternal judgment in hell. Ken Sande, founder of Peacemaker Ministries, beautifully writes, "Believing in Jesus means trusting that he exchanged records with you at Calvary—that is, he took your sinful record on himself and paid for it in full, giving you his perfect record, which opens the way for peace with God."[52] Faith in Christ alone saves sinners from the penalty of sin and allows them to experience eternal joy and hope, even while living in this evil world. In Romans 5:1, Paul writes, "Therefore, since we have been justified by faith, we have peace with God through our Lord Jesus Christ." For obvious reasons, the overwhelming majority of people hope to go to heaven when they die; after all, an eternity in heaven sounds a whole lot better than spending forever in hell. It's important to remember, however, that only Jesus can get you through the gates of heaven.

Second, not only are Christians justified, they are also in the process of growing in their salvation. In theology, this is the term we've considered previously: *sanctification*. This

---

[52] Ken Sande, *The Peacemaker* (Grand Rapids, MI: Baker Books, 2004), 45.

is the progressive process through which the Lord delivers us from our own sinful desires and lovingly molds us into his image. In Philippians 2:12–13, the Apostle Paul writes, "Therefore, my beloved, as you have always obeyed, so now, not only as in my presence but much more in my absence, work out your own salvation with fear and trembling, for it is God who works in you, both to will and to work for his good pleasure." Notice the theological balance recorded in this text. Christians are called to work *out*, not work *for*, their salvation. At the same time, it is God who is working in us to bring us to spiritual maturity. Over time, genuine believers progressively become more like Jesus. Through the working of the Holy Spirit, we become more obedient to God's commandments, and our sinful passions lose their hold on our hearts and minds.

Third, all of those who are justified and in the process of sanctification will one day be *glorified*. This is a reference to our future salvation that will occur when we enter the Lord's presence at the time of our death or upon the Lord's return. Glorification is the moment when our salvation is complete, and we are ultimately delivered from the curse of sin. In Romans 8:30, we read, "And those whom he predestined he also called, and those whom he called he also justified, and those whom he justified he also glorified." Faith and hope encourage us to keep our hearts and minds confidently fixed on the greater realities yet to come. One magnificent day, we will stand in the presence of our Savior fully glorified. When our salvation is complete, sin will no longer urge our idolatrous hearts to disobey God, and we will be liberated from Satan's schemes. Our sin nature will be eradicated, and we will enjoy unadulterated fellowship with our Heavenly Father. In our glorified state, there will be no more pain, sickness, heartbreak, or death. The hope of our eternal salvation is what protects us from the deepest and darkest valleys of life and keeps us faithful on the days when we would rather retreat to the couch and watch the battle on the news from a safe and secure location. As Christians, we are saved from our sin; we are also being saved daily from our sinful choices, and one sweet day, we will be decisively saved from sin and death for all of eternity. There will be no more tears. No more pain. And, all praise be to God, no more sin holding us in bondage.

Like Paul's reference to our ongoing pursuit of righteousness in Ephesians 6:14, in verse 17, he is referencing our ongoing pursuit of holiness through the process of sanctification. If you have been adopted into the family of God, you are already justified. Paul's emphasis concerning the helmet of salvation is on our sanctification. We need God's helmet of salvation if we're going to march forward in the process of living out our justification through daily obedience and the consistent pursuit of holiness.

Protecting Our Hearts and Minds

As Ralph Waldo Emerson famously said, "Sow a thought, reap an action; sow an action, reap a habit; sow a habit, reap a character; sow a character, reap a destiny." Although I would take great exception with much of what Emerson believed, I do agree with him on this point. How accurate it is that our thoughts precede our actions, and our actions quickly become habitual. Once thoughts and subsequent actions become engrained, they mold our character either to become more like Jesus or more like the fallen world. Over time, our habits set the course of our lives, and before long, we begin reaping the consequences of our choices. Developing habits can either create a lifestyle that brings honor and glory to God, or one that dishonors and grieves him. Because lifestyles begin with habits, and habits begin with the choices we make, we must diligently guard what takes root and grows in the soil of our hearts and minds (see Proverbs 4:23).

Because our hearts and minds set the course for our lives, we must be attentive to what information goes into our minds and what we habitually dwell upon. If we want to develop godly patterns of living, we must first develop God-honoring patterns of thinking. To ensure that our thoughts are consistent with Scripture, we must put on and take up God's helmet of salvation. Diligently protecting our minds against the flaming arrows of the devil is an essential part of our battle plan if we are to successfully stand against the forces of evil.

Addiction to sins such as idolatry, disrespect, negativity, bitterness, worry, covetousness, hatred, slothfulness, dishonesty, envy, and lust all begin in our minds. These thought patterns can entangle our minds and keep us spiritually anemic and isolated. Instead of refusing the temptation to meditate on sinful matters, we often make the spiritually damaging decision to allow our minds to wander into untruthfulness, unrighteousness, or vulgarity. While Satan may plant a seed of sinful thinking in our minds, we are fully culpable when we allow that seed to germinate, to grow, and to eventually dominate our thinking. Actions become reality only after we have pondered upon them for some time. Lust rouses adultery. Covetousness provokes stealing. Envy kindles gossip. Hatred incites slander. Before these sinful actions are committed, there are persistent thoughts of lust, covetousness, envy, and hatred that stir our fleshly desires. Our actions have consequences, and so do our patterns of thought. It's far more advantageous to defeat sin in our minds before we choose to carry out our sinful thoughts and fantasies.

As with any temptation, there are always plenty of exit ramps along the thought highway to help us reroute our minds to something lovely and honorable. All too often, we don't take the exit. Instead, we barrel along believing our habits of thinking are of little or no consequence. Once our thoughts become fixed upon our favorite sinful desire, we set up a lounge chair and stay for a while. Enjoying the view, we always stay longer than we should. It's like King David lusting after Bathsheba from his terrace. Rather than turning from her and refusing to dwell on her beauty, he entertained her image in his mind and lusted after her until he had to have her for himself, regardless of her marital status. When we accommodate sinful thoughts, they eventually produce sinful actions.

Once these patterns of thought become habitual, they often develop into strongholds that keep our hearts and minds in bondage for long periods of time (see 2 Corinthians 10:4). Correctly understanding the importance of right thinking, Paul wrote, "Do not be conformed to this world, but be transformed by the renewal of your mind, that by testing you may discern what is the will of God, what is good and acceptable and perfect" (Romans 12:2). Rather than leaving God's helmet of salvation in our spiritual closet collecting dust, we need it on our heads protecting our minds from the devil.

Takeaways

A major feature of Satan's sinister battle plan is relentlessly assaulting our minds with impurity; therefore, we must use God's helmet of salvation to do the following:

1. Protect our minds from ungodly content (see Psalm 101:3). Every day, our brains are bombarded with ungodly images, information, and influences. The material that comes into our minds through the internet, music, television, reading, and social media influences our thinking. Consuming a diet of ungodly content will make you spiritually ill and will eventually produce sinful actions. We must vigilantly guard the gates of our minds and only allow content

that honors and pleases the Lord into our minds. What we hear and see will influence our thought processes, which greatly impacts our decisions, habits, and lifestyle. Because of the constant attack on our minds through the messages, propaganda, and images of the culture, we must fervently guard our minds against ungodly and unwholesome content.

2. Redirect our thoughts to what is true, noble, just, pure, lovely, admirable, excellent, and worthy of praise (see Philippians 4:8). Far too often, we exchange "whatever is lovely" for "whatever I want" or for "whatever provides immediate gratification." We need God's glory to recalibrate our earthly cravings and thoughts so we only desire what glorifies him. When our minds slip into neutral, and we are not carefully guarding our thoughts, we typically dwell upon matters that are not true, filled with impurities, and less than praiseworthy.

   Rather than being molded by God's objective truth and verifiable facts, our narratives are usually imprudently driven by opinions, assumptions, and speculation. Because our thoughts are naturally drawn to what pleases our flesh and the false narratives we tell ourselves, we must fervently guard our minds against lies and impurities.

3. Remind ourselves that God loves us, even when we fail (see 1 John 3:1). As saved children of God, we must remember that our sin doesn't define us or cause God

to withhold his love. Because the person who speaks to us the most is ourselves, we must guard against the fictitious and exaggerated storylines that constantly consume our thoughts. All of us are well aware of our sins, even those we safely conceal from others, and Satan uses this to his advantage. Frequently, we ruminate over our sins and convince ourselves that God doesn't love us anymore. Satan makes matters worse by constantly reminding us of our failures and taunting us with accusations that only compound our guilt and shame. When we leave our minds open to these thought patterns, the fiery darts of Satan will burn holes in our hearts and minds, leaving us feeling discouraged and worthless. Because our thoughts can be drawn to self-deprecation and shame over our sins, we must fervently guard our minds against the devil's lies and consistently remind ourselves that God loves us even when we fail. God's love is constant and established. We can never do or think anything that would make him love us less.

4. Celebrate the victory that has already been won through Jesus Christ's death, burial, and resurrection (see 1 Corinthians 15:57). Given the daily ebb and flow of spiritual warfare, it's easy to forget that the ultimate victory in this war has already been secured through Christ. The constant barrage of cultural indoctrination that stands as an antithesis to God's truth wears down the minds of believers and makes it

challenging to keep the battle in perspective. Because our minds are prone to spiritual exhaustion, we must consistently remind ourselves that Christ has already won the war, giving reason to rejoice in his finished work on the cross.

5. Remember that God uses momentary affliction to prepare us for an eternal weight of glory that is beyond all comparison (see 2 Corinthians 4:17). Even God's own children are not spared the trials and tribulations that come with living in this crooked and wicked generation. Spiritual opposition in this world is inevitable. And while troubles are never enjoyable, we can remain hopeful because we know that God is working all things, even the difficulties, together for our spiritual benefit (see Romans 8:28). Because our minds are prone to spiritual discouragement in times of trial, we must consistently turn our attention to God's good and perfect purposes in our lives.

In order to keep our thoughts pure while swimming in the cesspool of a wicked culture, we must heed Paul's words in Colossians 3:2, where he writes, "Set your minds on things that are above, not on things that are on earth." Setting our minds on things above refers to our inner disposition. The Greek verb *phroneo* carries the idea of "to direct one's mind toward a thing." The present tense of the verb indicates an ongoing action. Paul commands us to set our minds on the things that bring glory and honor to God to prevent us from being pulled along by the current of worldliness swirling all around us. Heavenly, God-honoring, and Christ-centered meditations are to dominate our minds so that Satan's arrows cannot penetrate our thought patterns and lead us to dark and dismal places. The antidote for spiritual and mental exhaustion is to lift our eyes toward heaven and bask in the majestic glory of God.

Allowing the power of the gospel to change our hearts and minds will produce the joy, boldness, and confidence that comes from following the Lord. As Spurgeon wisely wrote, "The truth that we are sinners is painfully with us to humble and make us watchful; the more blessed truth that whosoever believeth on the Lord Jesus shall be saved, abides with us as our hope and joy."[53] When we spend our time dwelling on the things above, we are no longer enamored and entrapped by the glittering idols of this world. Putting on and taking up God's helmet of salvation will empower us to stand against the schemes of the devil by protecting our minds from disgraceful images, profane information, and ungodly influences. With our minds firmly fixed on the glory of God, we will be prepared to boldly proclaim the word of God to the world.

Key Point: Wearing the helmet of salvation will guard our minds from evil content and influences while keeping our thoughts centered on God and his holiness.

---

53 Spurgeon, 598.

Helmet: Apply Your Salvation

For Further Consideration

1. Passages for further study:

   John 3:1–21
   2 Corinthians 4:16–18
   2 Corinthians 10:1–6
   Galatians 5:22–26
   Ephesians 1:7–14
   1 John 5:11–13

2. For forty-eight hours, track your thought patterns in a journal. Take note of the destructive and sinful thought patterns infecting your mind. Once you have defined your sinful thought patterns, go to God's word and find verses that address your particular area of spiritual weakness.

3. Which of the following applications do you need to apply to your destructive or sinful thought patterns?

   a. Protect your mind from ungodly content (see Psalm 101:3).

   b. Redirect your thoughts to what is true, noble, just, pure, lovely, admirable, excellent, and worthy of praise (see Philippians 4:8).

   c. Remember God loves you, even when you fail (see 1 John 3:1).

   d. Celebrate the victory that has already been won through Jesus Christ's death, burial, and resurrection (see 1 Corinthians 15:57).

   e. Recollect that God uses momentary affliction to

prepare you for an eternal weight of glory that is beyond all comparison (2 Corinthians 4:17).

4. Make a list of Bible verses that will help you overcome any sinful thought habits you have identified.

Sword: Proclaim the Word of God

The sword of the Spirit, which is the word of God.
Ephesians 6:17

Our youngest son, Jordan, is a full-fledged stereotypical boy. From the time he could walk, he was drinking out of mud puddles (literally), hunting for critters, and making everything into a weapon. His weapon of choice was usually a sword or a lightsaber. Although his sword obsession was limited to toy swords, they still caused an awful lot of damage around the house. In fact, after he slashed the trampoline, the deck furniture, and the screen door, his swords were confiscated for a long period of time. To be clear, these swords were not battlefield caliber by any stretch of the imagination. But they were certainly sharp enough to poke holes in screens and trampolines.

Obviously, swords are dangerous weapons that can cause severe injury and death. They were the most important offensive weapon in the ancient Near East and in the Greco-Roman world. During the time of Paul, swords ranged from sixteen inches to three feet in length. In times of armed conflict, swords were used for stabbing and slashing opponents. The biblical writers employed sword imagery to portray the word of God and its impact on the human soul. One such example is Hebrews 4:12, which reads, "For the word of God is living and active, sharper than any two-edged sword, piercing to the division of soul and of spirit, of joints and of marrow, and discerning the thoughts and intentions of the heart." Here, the sword pictures how Scripture penetrates the human heart and reaches into a person's deepest thoughts, intentions, and motivations.

The Sword of the Spirit

In Ephesians 6:17, the sword of the Spirit completes Paul's depiction of God's armor. While described as the sword of the Spirit, it's specifically used to picture the word of God. Scholars and commentators debate the reason of the order in which Paul presents the armor of God; depending on who you read, you will likely find differences of opinion on the topic. I'll happily leave that discussion to others. I do, however, believe that it's significant that Paul begins this passage in Ephesians with truth and ends it with the word of God. God's universal and eternal truth, pictured by the belt of truth, is contained in the pages of Scripture, making the belt of truth and the sword of the Spirit, which is the word of God, equivalent.

The glorious church of Jesus Christ is called to wield the sword that makes the wounded whole, mends the brokenhearted, and liberates the captive soul. God's unchanging truth, recorded in the pages of Scripture, is what unshackles those held in bondage to sin, redeems the sinner from the clutches of Satan and hell, and promises eternal life in God's holy presence for those who believe the gospel. God's infallible word is forever settled and true. As Psalm 119:89 says, "Forever, O Lord, your word is firmly fixed in the heavens." God's eternal word has the answers to life's problems, and it's the church's responsibility to share the good news with the world. The only way to break the bondage of sin is justification by faith in Christ. Popular or not, only the truth of the gospel can change hearts, produce the fruit of the Spirit, and provide everlasting life.

It's safe to say that warfare has radically changed since the Greco-Roman period. Today, wars are primarily fought with long-range missiles and drones rather than with swords, arrows, and shields. The war in Ukraine has demonstrated this time and time again. But during the New Testament period, war was fought up close—face-to-face. On the ancient battlefield, it was two warriors locked in hand-to-hand combat until one maimed or killed the other. Soldiers fought close enough that the victor could hear the loser's final gasp of breath, feel the final twitches of their muscles, and watch as the life drained from their eyes. It was a brutal way to kill a human being and an agonizing way to die. Ancient battles often lasted most of the day, leaving even the survivors exhausted and injured.

Methods of warfare and torture have changed through the centuries. In recent decades, people have created new and improved ways to kill one another. No longer do we use swords, cannons, muskets, and bayonets on the battlefield. Instead, we use automatic rifles and weapons of mass destruction to kill as many enemies as we can as quickly as possible. We may try to convince ourselves that war will one day be eliminated from the face of the earth, but as long as this world is populated with sinners, the atrocities of war will continue.

Our oldest son is the proud owner of a really sweet drone. On one of our trips to western North Carolina, he was flying the drone over a nearby mountaintop to take pictures of the valley on the other side. I had to admit, it was very cool seeing how far the drone could fly without being detected by anyone on the ground. I don't know about you, but I sure wish God had inspired Paul to use the imagery of a more modern weapon rather than a sword. A drone of the Spirit would be far more convenient, and it would place us in less personal danger than wielding a sword. With a drone of the Spirit, we could fly it from one valley to another and carry out our mission without detection or personal risk. Our opponent would never see us coming, keeping us out of harm's way. Obviously, Paul had no concept of a drone when he wrote the book of Ephesians. Even if he did, the imagery of a drone would grossly miss the point Paul is making.

Spiritual warfare is exceedingly dangerous to our souls because it's a wrestling match that places us in extremely close proximity to our spiritual enemies. In order to use a sword on the physical battlefield, soldiers must stand eye-to-eye with their enemy and fight hand-to-hand. It's a nasty and bloody way to fight a war. Rather than picking off the forces of evil with a weaponized drone from miles away, we are called to wrestle against Satan and his forces of evil in an up-close and personal way.

Paul plainly states that the sword of the Spirit is a reference to God's word, indicating the importance of God's inspired and authoritative instruction. An Old Testament parallel is found in Isaiah 49:2, where we read, "He made my mouth like a sharp sword; in the shadow of his hand he hid me; he made me a polished arrow; in his quiver he hid me away." Isaiah 49 is a challenging text for several reasons, but the prophet penned these words in reference to the future Servant-Messiah. Isaiah offers an interesting description of his ministry, and I find two aspects of this verse particularly thought-provoking.

First, the Servant-Messiah's mouth being like a sharp sword indicates his ability to precisely and effectively speak the truth and function as a weapon against the lunacy of the world. His responsibility would be to pronounce God's judgment upon the wicked, call sinners to repentance, and proclaim peace to those with contrite hearts (see Revelation 1:16; 19:15). Second, the Servant-Messiah is pictured as a *polished arrow* equipped with the power to penetrate the hearts of people with God's truth. This arrow would fly true and straight, striking its target at the precisely correct moment.

As duly noted by commentators, the sword is the only distinctly offensive weapon mentioned in Ephesians 6:10–17. Swords are meant to kill. In Romans 8:13, Paul tells Christians to put the sinful deeds of the flesh to death by the Spirit. In Colossians 3:5, Paul instructs Christians to "put to death therefore what is earthly in you: sexual immorality, impurity, passion, evil desire, and covetousness, which is idolatry." When we lose contentment in God, our idolatrous hearts seek contentment in something else. Even good desires become sinful when they flow from a covetous heart that has exchanged God's rightful place in our lives with something found in creation. Because sin leads away from God, it can never be tolerated; profane actions, thoughts, and desires must be put to death by means of God's sword of the Spirit so that we can have an intimate relationship with the only one who can provide everlasting joy and peace. As we wrestle against the evil forces ruling this age, we must wield God's sword to put sin to death and push back hell's demons.

God's Inspired Word

In Matthew 16:18, Jesus promised to build his church and that the gates of hell would never prevail against it. Christ's work of building the church began on the foundation of Peter and the other apostles and has continued for thousands of years through the faithful proclamation of Scripture. In an attempt to rescue fallen humans from the clutches of Satan's deception and to build Christ's church, we are called to share the gospel with the world. All too often, however, the church fails to fulfill the Great Commission given in Matthew 28:18–20. As Sproul writes, "We have become in many cases, at least in America, the church quiescent as we just stand by and watch our generation give themselves, as the people of the ancient world did, to idolatry."[54] Christians are commanded to live separate from the wicked world, but believers are not called to isolation or indifference to what is taking place around them. In order to accomplish God's plan for the church, Christians must understand, know, believe, obey, and proclaim the whole counsel of God.

To gain a better understanding of the importance of Paul's instruction concerning God's revelation, let's consider a key verse that explains the importance of God's word. In 2 Timothy 3:16–17, Paul writes, "All Scripture is breathed out by God and profitable for teaching, for reproof, for correction, and for training in righteousness, that the man of God may be competent, equipped for every good work." In the pages of the Bible, God reveals his sovereign will over the world, his victory over the forces of evil, his glorious plan of redemption, his divine definition of right and wrong, and how his children can enjoy hope, courage, and peace while living in a sinful world.

During Jesus's earthly ministry, he regularly referenced the Hebrew Scriptures—what we call the Old Testament—and boldly asserted that these writings referred to him and that he came to fulfill the requirements of the law. Notice John 5:39–40, which says, "You search the Scriptures because

---

54 Sproul, 332.

you think that in them you have eternal life; and it is they that bear witness about me, yet you refuse to come to me that you may have life." Jesus recognized the Old Testament as a record of God's divine truth, and that he was the fulfillment of the law and prophecies recorded during the Old Covenant. Jesus, God's Son, recognized the authority of Scripture, and so must we.

The Bible isn't like any other book; it's not a science book, a psychology book, a math book, a history book, or a political science book. It's God's book. He is the ultimate author of Scripture. The Bible does not contain every piece of information about every known topic; otherwise we would need a U-Haul to lug our copy of Scripture to church. Instead, the Bible is a God-breathed book lovingly given to us by our Creator so we can personally know him and understand his will for our lives.

Second Timothy 3:16–17 is a key passage for understanding the nature of Scripture and its divine purpose. With that said, let's consider two characteristics of Scripture found in this passage. The first lesson we learn from 2 Timothy 3:16–17 is that Scripture is inspired by God. The word Paul uses here is *theopneustos*, literally meaning "breathed out by God," as indicated by the ESV. This is the only verse in the New Testament where this word appears. *Theopneustos* is a combination of two Greek words: *theos* (meaning "God") plus *pneustos* from the verb *pneō* (meaning "breathe or blow"). Author John Kitchen beautifully explains, "The Scriptures are not a preexisting body of human literature into which God breathed something divine, but rather they owe their very existence to the out-breathing of God's Spirit. Apart from God's out-breathing in time and space through specific human authors under the power of his Holy Spirit, the Scripture would not exist. It is the Scriptures, not the writers of the Scriptures, which are inspired."[55] Unlike believers living under the Old Covenant who were looking forward to the coming Messiah with only partial revelation, New Testament Christians living on this side of the Messiah's ministry have access to God's complete revelation. With God's completed word in hand, we must live obediently while patiently awaiting Christ's return.

Because the Scriptures are divinely revealed to humanity, they are unequivocally authoritative, sufficient, and preeminent over all other writings. Every word written on the pages of Scripture originated with God. The original manuscripts, known as the autographs, were written by the human authors without error. The autographs have been preserved for devoted Christians through the various scholarly translations of the Bible. Thanks to the faithful translators and copyists, we have accurate and reliable copies of God's eternal word in most of the world's known languages.

Through the power of the Holy Spirit, God miraculously governed the writing of Scripture without discounting the human author's personality, vocabulary, and style. As 2 Peter 1:21 says, "For no prophecy was ever produced by the will of man, but men spoke from God as they were carried along

---

[55] John Kitchen, *The Pastoral Epistles for Pastors* (The Woodlands, TX: Kress Christian Publications, 2009), 419.

by the Holy Spirit." While the biblical authors recorded the words God inspired them to write in their own style, and in different genres of literature, it is God who was the ultimate author of Scripture.

God's Profitable Word

The second lesson we learn from 2 Timothy 3:16–17 is that God's word is profitable. All of Scripture, both the Old and New Testaments, is equally inspired by God and is authoritative and instructive for his people. By *profitable*, the Apostle Paul means that the Scriptures are spiritually beneficial, applicable, sufficient, and advantageous to those who obey them. In the powerful introduction to his book *Providence*, John Piper writes, "The profit lies not mainly in the validation of a theological viewpoint but in the revelation of a great God, the exaltation of his invincible grace, and the liberation of his undeserving people."[56] The main purpose of Scripture, therefore, is for God to personally show himself to us through his special revelation, which is the supernatural communication from God to us to explain the narrow path leading to salvation. The truths revealed through special revelation cannot be known through any other source but Scripture; we cannot obtain special revelation by enjoying a sunset, viewing a mountain range, or watching a mighty river flowing inside its banks.

With our senses, we can observe what theologians call God's general revelation; this is a reference to all aspects of

---

56 Piper, 13.

the marvelously created order that we can see, touch, taste, smell, and hear. General revelation is directed to everyone and is widely experienced. Because general revelation does not reveal Jesus Christ or his redemptive work on the cross of Calvary, it is insufficient to provide the specific knowledge of God necessary for justification. In the pages of God's inspired word, we are told how to personally know God and how to please him. Through the redemptive power of God's special revelation, the Scriptures, we are enabled to live obediently and productively in today's sin-stained culture.

Given what Paul wrote in 2 Timothy 3:16–17, let's consider six specific God-ordained purposes and practical benefits of the Bible regarding holy living.

1. Teaching: includes instruction in biblical doctrine and principles, used to implant knowledge and understanding of God's divine Scripture and will. The Bible, carefully interpreted and applied, must be the content of the church's teaching. The Bible must not only be read, it must also be taught through doctrinally sound instruction.

2. Reproof: a rebuke given for the purpose of convicting sin and misbehavior, used to admonish disobedient Christians when they are out of line with God's word. The Bible is the standard by which the church is to lovingly rebuke one another.

3. Correction: the restoration to an upright or proper state, used to mature a believer's character for the purpose of restoration. The Bible is the source

through which the church restores and rebuilds disobedient and disorderly Christians.
4. Training in righteousness: the cultivation of a godly mindset and morality, used to increase the believer's virtue and to develop a Christ-centered worldview. The Bible is the God-breathed curriculum for righteous living. It's the primary means through which the church prepares believers to walk in righteousness.
5. That the man of God may be competent: he is complete, capable, and fit for service. Understanding, believing, and obeying the Bible will adequately prepare Christians for the challenges of life and ministry.
6. That the man of God may be equipped for every good work: he is sufficiently prepared to perform whatever ministry God may ask him to do. Diligently studying the Scriptures will equip Christians for whatever areas of service the Lord may call them to undertake.

According to 2 Timothy 3:16–17, the Bible provides a comprehensive and complete collection of divine truth necessary for Christians to live a righteous life. God does not call the perfectly equipped and exceptionally prepared to ministry. Instead, he uses his inspired word to equip and prepare those whom he calls to service and to grow them in righteousness.

Physical swords are used to pierce the body to kill. The sword of the Spirit, however, is used to pierce the heart for the purpose of instruction in righteousness, rebuke, and correction. Theologian Millard Erickson writes, "Scripture is our supreme legislative authority. It gives us the content of our belief and of our code of behavior and practice."[57] Rather than using a physical weapon used to kill, God's sword is a spiritual weapon used to restore, mend, and give life to those who believe the gospel.

Fighting Evil with Scripture

Many years ago, I scheduled a guest chapel speaker at one of the Christian high schools where I served. Minutes into the sermon, the pastor had the teenagers roaring with laughter. The room was abuzz with enthusiastic energy and belly laughs. While the entire student body was enjoying the chapel message, I was not. Other than a cursory Bible verse or two, the kids were never asked to open a Bible or to read a particular text of Scripture.

Afterward, I heard the students practically screaming over how much they loved chapel that morning. During lunch, I ventured into the cafeteria to ask some of the students what they thought of the chapel speaker. The praise was unanimous: according to the students, it was the best sermon they had ever heard. Unsurprised by the sermon's warm reception, I had a list of follow-up questions. I asked the kids what Bible text the speaker preached. They had no idea—because there wasn't one. I asked them to explain how the sermon called them to grow and change. Again, no answer.

---

57 Millard J. Erickson, *Christian Theology* (Grand Rapids, MI: Baker Book House, 1985), 257.

After asking a couple more questions, every student shared the same ultimate conclusion about the message. In one way or another, they said, "All I know is it was funny." That was why they enjoyed the "sermon." They gave the sermon rave reviews because it was funny, comfortable, entertaining, and exciting. The problem was there was no biblical text, no truth, no call to action, and no encouragement to grow in their faith. The kids gave the sermon an A. I gave it an F and never invited the speaker again. Like those teenagers, I'm afraid too many adult Christians score sermons based on the same criteria. If a message keeps us entertained, doesn't ask us to make any sacrifices, and doesn't ask us to change anything, then it's good. The problem is that style of preaching will never help us mature in our faith.

How important is Scripture to you? Before you answer, let me ask a second question. I have chosen to include a number of Scripture references in this book and in the reflection questions; how many have you skipped? Too often, I'm afraid we skip the Bible verses and focus more on what the book's author has to say. I know I'm guilty of that sometimes. In our rush to gain practical insights, we often neglect the words God recorded for us to read. Remember, the words of God carry far more weight than the words of any human author.

Hiding Scripture in our hearts keeps God's sword available at all times. It is God's inspired word that effectively cuts through the schemes of the devil and protects us from the kingdom of darkness. Even Jesus faced temptation, and when he did, he used the Scriptures to resist the tempter. In Matthew

4:1–11, Jesus journeyed alone into the wilderness where he was tempted by Satan. In response to each temptation, the Lord quoted from the book of Deuteronomy. Each time, "the devil left him" (Matthew 4:11). Likewise, God's word protects us from temptation and spiritually refines our hearts.

From Paul's writing, we learn the true nature of spiritual warfare. We are not knights in shining armor riding in on pristinely white horses to claim an easy victory over the forces of evil. We're soldiers fighting against rulers, authorities, cosmic powers, and the evil forces influencing this present darkness. As we wrestle in the messiness of this fallen world, we're left bloodied, dirt-stained, perspiration-drenched, and gasping for air. We're spiritual warriors, standing firm in the gospel and upon the eternal and absolute truths of Scripture in a culture that despises the idea of a sovereign God who has total authority over the world. Our armor is scratched and dented. The flaming arrows fired by the devil's forces have left their marks. But through it all, God's armor holds. Every time. Despite the conflict, and no matter how fierce the battle may rage, the armor of almighty God will keep his children safe and empower us to defend his kingdom and promote the good news of Jesus Christ.

Takeaways

No soldier in Paul's day would have considered entering the battlefield without his sword. Protective armor is one thing, but to be militarily successful, a soldier needs an offensive weapon capable of defeating the enemy. This principle carries over to the spiritual warfare we fight against the schemes and forces of the devil. We must protect ourselves from temptation and spiritual assaults, but we must also proactively launch a counteroffensive against the roaring lion seeking to devour us. In order to stand our ground and regain lost territory, we must be armed with God's sword. Without the sword of the Spirit, we're on dangerous ground. To be sufficiently prepared, we must implement three important practices.

1. We must daily feast on God's word. As Kitchen writes, "Godliness comes to characterize a life that feasts on the Scriptures."[58] Because we're all forgetful, it's essential that we consistently read the Scriptures and allow the truths of God's word to settle into our souls through meditation. By God's grace, owning a copy of Scripture isn't illegal in the United States. We're free to worship, free to read the Bible, and free to pray. And yet, we're typically too distracted and busy to immerse our minds in private Bible reading. The devil hates truth and will do all he can to prevent us from reading God's word. If Satan can keep our swords securely in their sheaths, he knows we're dangerously vulnerable to his attacks.

   Not only does the devil work hard to keep us from reading Scripture, he also tries to undermine its authority. One of Satan's favorite tricks is to convince us that Scripture is too restrictive or sections are no longer culturally relative. The deceiver wants us to

---

58 Kitchen, 422.

believe joy and contentment are found living on our own terms rather than within God's boundaries. Should the evil one convince us to believe a watered-down version of Scripture, he knows we will be rendered useless in the spiritual warfare he's raging against God and his church. A perfunctory reading of the Bible merely to check it off our to-do list is insufficient. Bible study should not be reduced to an academic exercise that allows us to simply collect more data or to a mindless routine that has no spiritual impact on our lives.

2. We must regularly be under the influence of doctrinally sound teaching and preaching. I've met people who claim they can grow spiritually with their Bible, their pen, and their coffee. Up to a certain point, I suppose that's true. But we all need consistent exposure to biblically minded preachers and teachers. While the truths of Scripture never change, hearing God's word presented from various speakers who use diverse illustrations and applications is extremely helpful. To mature in our faith, we need consistent instruction. None of us, no matter our level of theological training, are capable of coming to a mature understanding of God's word all on our own. While illustrations and applications may differ in various settings, the meaning of the text is already determined by God. If a pastor is preaching something profoundly different from what other theologically conservative people are

preaching, he is more than likely profoundly wrong. Weigh the accuracy of all teaching against Scripture, then allow God to expand your understanding of his word (see Acts 17:10–12).

In today's church culture, it is increasingly challenging to find pastors who consistently preach the whole counsel of God. Passages that deal with sin, hell, damnation, God's expectations for holiness, God's moral boundaries, and the exclusivity of Jesus as the only way to heaven often remain unaddressed in pulpits all over the world. In 2 Timothy 4:3–4, Paul warned, "For the time is coming when people will not endure sound teaching, but having itching ears they will accumulate for themselves teachers to suit their own passions, and will turn away from listening to the truth and wander off into myths." Today's health-and-wealth gospel, entertainment-driven worship, and pep talk sermons are failing when it comes to the consistent preaching and teaching of the whole counsel of God's word. It is Scripture that changes hearts, not engaging personalities, entertaining performances disguised as worship, or superficial sentimentalism.

While addressing the Ephesian elders in Acts 20, Paul proclaimed, "I did not shrink from declaring to you the whole counsel of God" (v. 27). Unlike the false apostles who were disguising themselves as disciples of Christ and deceiving people through proclaiming a false gospel, Paul unapologetically preached the entirety of God's truth (see 2 Corinthians 11:13). Rather than selecting portions of Scripture that are popular, culturally palatable, or politically correct, pastors and teachers are commanded to lovingly and compassionately proclaim the whole plan of salvation. Apart from faith in Jesus, people are facing God's judgment. In a culture that absolutely despises the concept of absolute truth, we must consistently and graciously proclaim the whole counsel of God.

3. We must continuously combat temptation with the sword of the Spirit. Everywhere we look, we find the lure of temptation. If you're drawn to alcohol, it's easy to find. If your downfall is anger, there are plenty of reasons in the world to be mad. If your struggle is with too much sugar, there are a lot of unhealthy choices at your local Walmart. If you crave material possessions, your local bank has a variety of loan options. If your hook is sexual temptation, there's an abundance of illicit materials readily available for free. Thanks to the evil forces of our age, opportunities to sin against God are always available; that's why Christians must be armed and ready with the sword of the Spirit.

Now that we have a better understanding of God's armor, we must turn our attention to what makes these armaments effective on the spiritual battlefield.

Key Point: The inspired Scriptures are the primary offensive piece of armor God has provided for Christians to stand firm against the cunning schemes of the devil and his forces of evil.

For Further Consideration

1. Psalm 19 is a key portion of Scripture because it describes God's majesty and the power of his word. Look up Psalm 19:7–9 in the ESV translation and fill in the blanks below. Beside each point, write a personal response to the truths found in these verses.

   The law of the Lord [God's word] is _____, _____ the soul.

   The testimony of the Lord [God's word] is sure, making _____ the _____.

   The precepts of the Lord [God's word] are _____, _____ the heart.

   The commandment of the Lord [God's word] is _____, _____ the eyes.

   The fear of the Lord [God's word] is _____, enduring _____.

   The rules of the Lord [God's word] are _____, and _____ altogether.

2. Do you have a consistent private time each day when you read and meditate on Scripture?
3. Are you regularly exposed to doctrinally sound preaching and teaching of Scripture?
4. Name some of the common lies Satan uses to deceive people and undermine the authority of Scripture.

5. How have the diabolical schemes of the devil influenced the preaching and worship in today's churches?
6. Read Luke 4:1–13 and describe the temptations Jesus faced and how he withstood them.
7. Read Acts 17:10–12 and explain how you can become more like the Bereans.
8. Verses for further study:

    Nehemiah 8:1–6
    Isaiah 55:10–11
    Luke 24:25–27
    John 1:1–18
    Acts 2:42
    Ephesians 1:13
    2 Timothy 4:1–2
    Hebrews 4:12–13
    Revelation 19:11–16

Strategy Six
Pray Without Ceasing

Praying at all times in the Spirit, with all prayer and supplication. To that end keep alert with all perseverance, making supplication for all the saints.

Ephesians 6:18

Once upon a time, when our children were younger, we all ate dinner together each evening. Part of our dinner routine included reading from a devotional and a time of family prayer. These days, however, our daughter is in college, our oldest son is working full-time, and our youngest son is involved in various and sundry activities like most teenagers. Needless to say, our family schedule has changed a great deal over the years, making regular family meals difficult.

Nowadays, dinner is left to each person to make when their schedule allows. Whenever our daughter ventures into the kitchen to make something to eat, it's normally a misadventure to behold. She's notorious for the mess she leaves behind. She often uses the griddle to prepare her meals. Protein pancakes are one of her favorites. When she makes them, she makes them big. Like Frisbee big. After a few minutes, looking at the stubbornly gooey batter oozing over the edge, Jaelyn wonders why her pancakes aren't cooking correctly. Each time this happens, I ask what seems to be an obvious question: "Did you plug in the griddle and turn it on?" Of course, I always know the answer. Every time her food isn't cooking, it's because the plug is either hanging off the counter, nowhere close to the power outlet, or it's plugged in but not turned on. I'm no chef, but I know pancake batter cooks much better when the griddle is heated.

A griddle without a power source is useless for cooking. Likewise, the Christian life without a power source is lethargic and lifeless. For the Christian, prayer plays an essential role in standing against the forces of evil. Although prayer is not another piece of God's armor, it's the means through which the whole armor of God is made effective. If you're familiar with the Marvel character Iron Man, you know that Tony Stark's suit of armor is powered by a reactor capable of producing massive amounts of energy. This supercharged device supplies Iron Man with superhuman strength and abilities, enabling him to fight the world's most heinous enemies. Prayer will not provide Christians with the ability to fly or fight mighty titans like Iron Man, but it will empower us to stand against Satan and his forces.

Armed with Prayer

For those faithfully standing against the schemes of the devil, it's not enough to mindlessly put on the armor of God and take up its pieces. In order for God's armor to enable us to fight, we need a power source, and that power source is prayer. As Warren Wiersbe writes, "Prayer is the energy that enables the Christian soldier to wear the armor and wield the sword. We cannot fight the battle in our own power, no matter how strong or talented we may think we are."[59] There isn't sufficient strength, wisdom, or talent in any human being to withstand Satan's malicious attacks on their own. Because of our finiteness, Paul instructs us to constantly pray in the Spirit and rest in the Lord's power.

Sadly, many Christians often live days, weeks, months, or even years without speaking to the Lord in prayer. This is why we all need to be reminded about the power of prayer. While Scripture doesn't prescribe a particular format or formula for our prayers, communicating with our Heavenly Father is to be a regular part of the Christian life. Regular prayer seeks communion with God and acknowledges our absolute dependence on him. When we fail to pray, we're proclaiming an attitude of prideful self-reliance that denies our need for divine strength and intervention. When we believe that we know better than God, that we can provide for our own security, answer all of our own questions, solve every problem, withstand temptation, and make all of the right decisions without God's input or guidance, prayer will

---
[59] Warren Wiersbe, *Be Rich* (Colorado Springs, CO: Victor, 2004), 172.

be forsaken. A consistent lack of prayer is admitting that we believe God's strength, wisdom, guidance, or protection against temptation is unnecessary. A life without prayer is one on the verge of falling prey to Satan's flaming arrows.

On the Battlefield

While standing against the schemes of the devil wearing the belt of truth, breastplate of righteousness, shoes of readiness, shield of faith, helmet of salvation, and the sword of the Spirit, we must remain in constant prayer. Like soldiers on the battlefield who require uninterrupted communication with their commanders, we need constant interaction with our Heavenly Father through reading Scripture and prayer. Pastor and author A. W. Tozer writes, "Prayer is not a work that can be allocated to one or another group in the church. It is everybody's responsibility; it is everybody's privilege. Prayer is the respiratory function of the church; without it we suffocate and die at last, like a living body deprived of the breath of life."[60] No matter how smart, strong, and sufficient we may think we are, prayer is our communication lifeline in the midst of the battle.

More often than we wish to admit, our times of prayer are reduced to a grocery list of demands that we bring to the checkout counter, insisting God provides everything on our list free of charge. But prayer isn't an occasion to redeem "coupons" and place demands before God's throne. Prayer is a conversation with our Heavenly Father in which we have

---

60 A. W. Tozer, *Prayer* (Chicago, IL: Moody Publishers, 2016), 159.

the privilege of humbly coming before him to bask in his majesty, to seek his wisdom, to be strengthened by his power, and to receive guidance through Scripture and the Holy Spirit. As Tozer said, prayer is a privilege afforded to each follower of Christ; we would be wise to make full use of this opportunity.

On the spiritual battlefield, it's tempting to take matters into our own hands, devise our own plans, and fight trusting only in ourselves. But as authors Kent and Barbara Hughes caution, "Those who would minister for God, regardless of how well they have put on the gospel of peace, regardless of how well they wear salvation, truth, righteousness and faith, must make prayer the first thing. The Christian soldier—each person engaged in Christian ministry—fights on his knees!"[61] Without time on our knees in prayer, we will be no match against the forces of darkness. We can be dressed and ready to fight, but apart from prayer, we will become spiritual casualties in this war.

During Jesus's earthly ministry, he consistently communed with the Father. One example of Jesus praying is found in the opening chapter of Mark's gospel. In verse 35, we read, "And rising very early in the morning, while it was still dark, he departed and went out to a desolate place, and there he prayed" (Mark 1:35). In this verse, we are told that Jesus went out to pray before sunrise and sought out an isolated place. In order to spend uninterrupted time conversing with

---

61 Kent and Barbara Hughes, *Liberating Ministry from the Success Syndrome* (Wheaton, IL: Crossway Book, 1987), 78.

his Father, he found a quiet place where there would be no distractions, and where he could be away from the crowds and his disciples. Jesus's actions optimized his private time with the Father, leaving for us a wonderful example worthy of emulating. No matter what time of day your schedule allows for prayer and devotion, you must set aside a few purposeful minutes each day to spend private time with the Lord.

The four verbs in Mark 1:35 are also worth exploring. Mark tells us that Jesus rose. Departed. Went out. And prayed. Interestingly, the first three verbs are in the aorist tense, denoting simple action. Prayed, however, is in the imperfect tense. Bible scholar James Brooks observes, "The imperfect tense suggests prolonged prayer."[62] Jesus, the divine Son of God, rose early in the morning, departed into the darkness, went out to a secluded place where he could be alone, and spent an elongated time communicating with his Father. Later that morning, when Jesus was nowhere to be found, Simon and the others were forced to search for him. Apparently, he had been gone for a long period of time, causing his disciples to wonder what had happened to him.

As Christians, we talk an awful lot about prayer. We study prayer. Read books about it. We say grace before meals. We pray when the world is seemingly caving in around us. But how many of us actually seek the Lord on a consistent basis? If prayer was of such great importance to Jesus, it should be to us as well. That's why Paul's instruction in Ephesians 6:18–20 is so significant and worthy of our immediate attention and action.

---

62 James A. Brooks, *Mark* (Nashville, TN: Broadman Press, 1991), 53.

At All Times

In Ephesians 6:18, Paul pleads with the church at Ephesus to concentrate on prayer. Working from the ESV translation, we see that the word *all* occurs four times in the verse. These four *all*s provide us with a nice primer on the issue of prayer. In the first *all*, Paul encourages Christians to pray at all times in the Spirit. Because the forces of evil are an ever-present danger, and a spiritual attack is always possible, it's essential to remain in a constant state of communication with our Heavenly Father.

The call to persistent prayer is seen elsewhere in Paul's writings. In Romans 12:12, Paul writes, "Be constant in prayer." In 1 Thessalonians 5:17, we read, "Pray without ceasing." The meaning of these two verses is straightforward: there is no time in which followers of Jesus should not be praying. Consistently communing with our Creator should characterize all of God's children. Rather than limiting prayer to times of trial, meals, or when we want something, prayer should be present in our lives daily, in the good days and the bad.

Far too often, we treat God more like a Magic 8 Ball or the genie in Aladdin's lamp than the sovereign ruler over all of creation. Expressing our thankfulness for the little blessings of life, the accident that didn't happen, the convenient parking space that opens up when we're running late, the kind deed done by a stranger, the smile of a friend, or the five-dollar bill we find in our jacket pocket are simple ways to develop a habit of prayer. Spurgeon writes, "Earth should be a temple filled with the songs of grateful saints, and every day should be a censor smoking with the sweet incense of thanksgiving."[63] As redeemed sinners adopted into the family of God, we have much to praise the Lord for. Every day is an opportunity to thank God for his goodness, mercy, provision, and grace. Because of our new life in Christ, prayers of thanksgiving should roll off our tongues each time we see the traces of God's hand in our lives. We regularly pray for the big matters of life, but because we're called to pray at all times, our prayers should include the seemingly insignificant ones too.

In August of 2021, my entire family came down with COVID-19. My wife's case was mild. Our three kids felt slightly sick for, like, four hours. Then there was me; I definitely got the sickest. I don't get ill often, but when I do, it hits me hard. By far, my worst symptom was brain fog and confusion. Early one Saturday morning, I had to drive our daughter to work. At the time, she was working downtown. Because her shift started early, I could typically drop her off and get out of town before the traffic picked up. But on this particular morning, traffic was already heavy due to a race taking place downtown. People were everywhere, and in my brain fog, I was having a difficult time concentrating on the road.

For the safety of the runners, some streets were blocked off, forcing me to take an alternate route out of the city—one that I wasn't particularly familiar with. Thanks to my COVID brain, I got confused and a little lost. When I finally

---

63   Spurgeon, 650.

came across a street I recognized, I got my bearings enough to know where I needed to turn. The problem was I failed to remember that I was traveling on a one-way street. As a result, I made a left turn directly in front of an oncoming vehicle. It was only by God's grace that the other driver did not hit my car.

About a quarter of a mile up the road, I pulled into a parking lot to rest my anxious mind and to praise God. Amazingly, because of God's providence and protection, what could have been a terrible accident was avoided. I know there are times accidents do happen, and that in no way changes God's character or the fact that he is sovereign over the affairs of men. But on that particular day, I fully believe God spared me from a potentially lethal accident. Many, many times since that frightening Saturday morning, I have verbally thanked God in prayer for his protection.

Each day, we all have reasons to praise God in prayer and to thank him for the blessings we enjoy. When we intentionally take the time to look for God's hand in the little matters of life, it's not hard to find reasons to sing hallelujah to the King of Kings and Lord of Lords. God is good all the time. That's why we as followers of Jesus, above all people, should always have a song of praise on our lips. For obvious reasons, none of us can formally pray with our heads bowed, eyes closed, and on our knees all the time. Nor can most of us spend several hours a day praying in isolation. While this type of prayer is sometimes untenable, we are commanded to always display a prayerful attitude of dependence on almighty God.

In the Spirit

Recognizing that prayer is simply a conversation with our Heavenly Father makes it no longer seem overly difficult or daunting. This is especially true when we remember that we are to pray "in the Spirit." I don't believe that this phrase is a reference to speaking in tongues but rather instruction to pray under the guidance and power of the Holy Spirit. I believe there are three important observations to make concerning Paul's instruction to pray in the Spirit.

First, praying in the Spirit is only possible for those who have been adopted into the family of God through justification by faith in Jesus Christ. It's interesting to me how even people who question or outright reject God's existence quickly offer up "thoughts and prayers" for those in crisis. Certainly God is capable of hearing any prayer he chooses to entertain, but only true believers in Jesus have the Holy Spirit as our advocate and intercessor before the Father. As Paul writes in Romans 8:14–16, "For all who are led by the Spirit of God are sons of God. For you did not receive the spirit of slavery to fall back into fear, but you have received the Spirit of adoption as sons, by whom we cry, 'Abba! Father!' The Spirit himself bears witness with our spirit that we are children of God." All people who call upon the name of the Lord for salvation receive the Holy Spirit, and he empowers our prayer lives.

In verses 26 and 27, Paul adds, "Likewise the Spirit helps us in our weakness. For we do not know what to pray for as we ought, but the Spirit himself intercedes for us with groanings too deep for words. And he who searches hearts knows what is the mind of the Spirit, because the Spirit intercedes for the saints according to the will of God." One of the most comforting truths found in the pages of Scripture is that the Holy Spirit prays and intercedes for us. Even when we don't know how to express our needs or lack the strength to pray much beyond a few feeble words, we have an intercessor who communicates with the Father on our behalf.

Second, praying in the Spirit keeps us from laying a laundry list of demands and expectations at God's feet, insisting him to bow to our wishes and bend his will to meet ours. When I was kid, we received Christmas catalogs from Sears, Montgomery Ward, and JCPenney in the mail. If you're too young to know what these were, you can google it later. Once we received these large catalogs, I would spend hours flipping through their glossy pages making an extensive list of everything I wanted for Christmas. From toys to T-shirts to sports equipment, my list was exhaustive. Through the weeks leading up to Christmas, I would write multiple revisions of my list. With each revision, I would submit it to my parents, fully expecting to receive everything my little covetous heart desired. Some years I received many of the items on my list, but to my recollection, I never found *all* of them under the tree on Christmas morning. Like most kids, I focused more on what I didn't get than what I did. This sounds an awful lot like our view of prayer. We regularly overlook God's provisions and blessings, and instead we focus on the prayers God doesn't answer according to our desires. This leaves us feeling discouraged and convinced that prayer doesn't actually work.

Like my Christmas list, we meticulously craft our list of demands, make the necessary edits, submit it to God, wait twenty seconds for our heavenly genie to do his magic, then expect God to provide everything our selfish little hearts desire. When our wishes don't come true, we're disappointed, angry, bitter, or questioning God's love. But when we pray empowered by the Spirit, we don't come before God with a list of anything but reasons to praise and thank him. We also come before his throne believing that he will answer our prayers according to his perfect will and in accordance with his knowledge of what is best for us. More often than not, what we believe would be best would bring nothing but destruction to our lives. God knows us better than we know ourselves, and he sees where our lives would go should he grant every foolish request we make. Our Heavenly Father loves us enough to tell us no and to provide what is best for us in the long run.

Third, praying in the Spirit keeps us from empty and ritualistic prayers like those offered by the Pharisees. In Matthew 6:5, Jesus taught, "And when you pray, you must not be like the hypocrites. For they love to stand and pray in the synagogues and at the street corners, that they may be seen by others." By no means is Jesus forbidding public prayer, but he is warning against praying publicly for the purpose of being seen and applauded by men. Hypocrites, like the Pharisees, long to have the attention of people so they receive the glory that rightfully belongs to God. Instead, we are to humble ourselves before the Lord and prayerfully submit our lives, plans, and will to him, making certain that he receives all the glory, praise, and honor.

All Types of Prayer

In the second *all* used in Ephesians 6:18, Paul uses two Greek words translated as *prayer* and *supplication*. The first word is *proseuche*, meaning "a prayer addressed to God." This word can be used to describe any general request. The second word is *deesis*, meaning "a need or want." This word seems to indicate a more specific request brought before the Lord. Parsing these two words too finely would likely be pressing them further than Paul intended. The usage of these two words together, however, seems to indicate that the Father wants his children to bring all types of prayers to him. Regardless of context or form, God wants us to pray with all sorts of petitions.

As the father of three children, I want my kids to come to me with big matters and small ones. I want to hear all about their challenges and blessings, and the things that bring them joy. Because I want to know all I can about our kids, I'm always willing to listen to what they have to share so I can learn what's on the forefront of their minds. I believe our Heavenly Father feels the same when we come to him with our deepest thoughts, concerns, and enjoyments. Yes, he knows everything there is to know about us, but he is still pleased when we open our hearts to him.

Persevere in Prayer

In the third *all*, Paul directs us to pray alertly with all perseverance. The subject of perseverance is found in multiple passages of Scripture and underscores the importance of remaining resolutely faithful to Christ even when times are difficult. When it comes to prayer, we're to remain devoted, consistent, and steadfastly attentive, and we're not to allow ourselves to grow weary in the battle. In Colossians 4:2, Paul encourages us to "continue steadfastly in prayer, being watchful in it with thanksgiving." It's important to highlight the combination of prayer and watching found in Ephesians 6:18 and Colossians 4:2. While we're commanded to consistently pray during the spiritual battles we all endure, we're also to remain awake and alert on the battlefield.

During the early days of the church, prayer was of great importance (see Acts 2:42). The early Christians readily devoted themselves to the apostles' teaching, to fellowship among the brethren, to the breaking of bread, and to concentrated times of prayer. Likely because of the intense persecution they experienced, the early church understood the importance of prayer. By God's wisdom, we have record of an occasion in which God answered the prayers of his people even when their faith was weak (see Acts 12:1–16, specifically v. 5). We can have volumes of biblical knowledge stored in our minds, but without prayerful watching and obedience to God, it's useless.

While it sometimes feels like our prayers are worthless, we must persevere in our heavenward communication. I particularly like James 5:16 in the King James Version. It reads, "The effectual fervent prayer of a righteous man availeth much." Biblical prayer isn't a mystical incantation that can be used to manipulate God, as the itinerant Jewish exorcists were trying to do in Acts 19. It's the process through which God uses his word and the Holy Spirit to shepherd us through the valleys, comfort us in times of pain, provide wisdom in times of confusion, and change our hearts to increasingly resemble his. Biblical prayer is also not a guarantee of healing, deliverance, security, or removal of all trials. According to James, however, fervent prayer offered by a genuine Christian is powerful and effective.

For All the Saints

In the fourth and final *all*, Paul instructs us to make supplications for all the saints. The word *saints* is a translation of the Greek word *hagios*, meaning "dedicated to God" or "holy." In the New Testament, *saint* is applied to all genuine believers, rather than to a select few who have been assigned the status of "sainthood" by a church for certain religious acts. In effect, the word *saint* serves as a synonym for Christian. Those who are positionally in Christ are considered holy in the sight of God and are appropriately referred to as saints. Paul's use of *hagios* doesn't imply sinlessness or a special class of believer, but rather it's a reference to those "who have been separated from the world and consecrated to the worship and service of God."[64] So when Paul tells the Ephesians to pray for all the

---

64 Youngblood, 1113.

saints, he is calling the church to pray for all people who have professed Christ as Savior.

As part of the body of Christ, we're expected to pray for family members, friends, all believers, and even our enemies. As of this writing, two good friends of mine are attending to some serious issues with their daughter. The more I have prayed for this family, the deeper my concern for them and their little girl has grown. Prayer does that; it knits our hearts to other believers in ways we could never imagine. It has always been interesting to me that most of our prayers focus on physical problems and circumstances with little to no regard for spiritual needs. As I pray for my friends, there are undoubtedly physical issues to pray for, but the deepest problem is spiritual in nature, requiring supernatural intervention that only comes from God. No one can fix the situation in their own power and wisdom, but God can.

In spite of Paul's imprisonment and difficult circumstances during the time he wrote the book of Ephesians, he emphasizes praying for other believers over asking the church to pray for him and his needs. Although the apostle had a long list of challenges, he was more concerned with the welfare of others than his own. This is a lesson for all of us to learn when it comes to our private times of prayer. Rather than spending our prayer time counting off self-centered demands and wants, we must use our time with the Lord to carry others before his throne of grace.

In verses 19 and 20, Paul does finally ask the church in Ephesus to pray for him in one specific area. Rather than asking the body to pray about his physical needs, his imprisonment, or his ailments, he asked the saints to pray for boldness in gospel proclamation. When he was tempted to remain silent, he needed the Lord's strength to courageously speak the truth—like he did while ministering in Ephesus. In Paul's mind, his circumstances were incidental when compared to his greater calling of being an apostle called to proclaim the whole counsel of God.

Takeaways

In times of deep heartache or intense hardship, I often hear Christians say with a sigh of defeat, "Well, I guess all we can do is pray." Based on Ephesians 6, is that how we should view prayer? Are we to wait until we've exhausted all our wisdom, ideas, energy, and attempts to fix the problem, then, and only then, resort to prayer as a last-ditch effort? Is prayer only applicable when we're at wit's end and have no place else to turn? Based on Paul's teaching, this is a profoundly skewed concept of prayer and one that must be corrected if we're going to consistently pray as God intends.

In all circumstances, we are to pray without ceasing. Throughout the course of the day, we're called to communicate with our Heavenly Father through continual and watchful prayer. We are to praise him, thank him, and bring our concerns and needs before him. The following twelve examples of times when we should earnestly pray will help you realize that there is always a reason to pray.

1. When we're tempted, we can pray for the Lord's deliverance.
2. When we're afraid, we can pray for the Lord's courage.
3. When we're weak, we can pray for the Lord's strength.
4. When we're confused, we can pray for the Lord's wisdom.
5. When we're hurting, we can pray for the Lord's comfort.
6. When we're weary, we can pray for the Lord's endurance.
7. When we're anxious, we can pray for the Lord's peace.
8. When we're angry, we can pray for the Lord's grace.
9. When we're lonely, we can pray for the Lord's care.
10. When we're insecure, we can pray for the Lord's assurance.
11. When we're filled with joy, we can offer praises to the Lord.
12. When we're blessed with even the smallest blessing, we can offer thanksgiving to the Lord.

We can always bring our needs, complaints, fears, concerns, struggles, and praises before God's throne. Apart from Christ-centered, Holy Spirit–empowered prayer, we're bound to be a casualty in the spiritual war raging in this evil age. God's armor can protect us, but we also need the power of the Holy Spirit and prayer to get us safely through the battles. Prayer should never be a tack-on at the bottom of our to-do list. Nor should prayer be an empty ritualistic routine that we perform simply to check it off our list of religious duties.

Prayer should never be hidden in a box labeled, "Use only in case of an emergency," nor should it be used as an attempt to manipulate God to our own plans and will. Having ongoing conversation with our Heavenly Father should be a vital part of our lives, because without it, we're prone to caving to the temptations of the evil one.

Our final strategy for staying spiritually fit for this battle is refusing to walk the path of obedience all alone. To be spiritually successful, we need the body of Christ.

Key Point: Praying at all times is key to standing against the schemes of the devil and for maintaining an intimate relationship with our Heavenly Father.

For Further Consideration

1. Scriptures for further study:
   Psalm 39:12
   Psalm 54:2
   Psalm 55:16–19
   Psalm 66:19–20
   Luke 21:36
   1 Corinthians 14:15
   1 Timothy 2:8
   James 5:13–16
   Jude 20–21
2. Do you consistently set aside time each day for the purpose of prayer?
3. What keeps you from praying consistently?

4. When you read the twelve examples of prayer above, which ones do you need to keep in mind? Can you list other areas in which you need to consistently pray?
5. How can you pray more effectively for the saints in your local church?

Strategy Seven
Stay in the Body

So that you also may know how I am and what I am doing, Tychicus the beloved brother and faithful minister in the Lord will tell you everything. I have sent him to you for this very purpose, that you may know how we are, and that he may encourage your hearts. Peace be to the brothers, and love with faith, from God the Father and the Lord Jesus Christ. Grace be with all who love our Lord Jesus Christ with love incorruptible.

Ephesians 6:21–24

Michelle and I married in January of 1995. A few weeks later, Michelle was accepted into a doctoral program at the University of Vermont. After Michelle finished her undergraduate degree in May, we moved from Maryland, minutes from our families in Delaware, to Vermont, some five hundred miles away. Needless to say, we were facing a lot of changes, and we suddenly found ourselves all on our own. That is one of the reasons we knew that we needed to find a good church. Before long, we were plugged into a local body of believers and serving wherever we could. Throughout our nearly three decades of marriage, the church has been an indispensable part of our lives. Whether you're serving in vocational ministry like we currently are or not, the local church must be a key part of your walk with Christ.

Two of Satan's Favorite Strategies

Organized religion has increasingly earned a bad reputation over the last several years; sadly, Christian churches have been no exception. In some dreadful cases, for good reason. Sexual abuse scandals and other moral failures have ruined the testimonies of ministries and church leaders alike. Because churches are filled with sinners, we shouldn't be shocked by the decadence of humankind, even of those in positions of church leadership. We should, however, be brokenhearted over these horrid events and filled with righteous anger over those who have disparaged God's holy name. I believe Satan is using two specific strategies to limit the church's influence in the world.

First, the great dragon is firing his flaming arrows at church leaders, attempting to disqualify them from ministry and destroy God's reputation in the process. Satan knows that if he can trip up pastors, deacons, or other church leaders and get them to choose immorality, many other believers will be harmed in the process. Temptations in ministry come in all shapes and sizes, but there are common pressures that come with leadership. Knowing what buttons to push, the deceiver enjoys capitalizing on these challenges to cause ministries to implode. I know Christians who have been so deeply wounded by the moral failure of their pastor that they are no longer part of a local assembly. Some may still be attending a local church but distance themselves from the other Christians and refuse to trust another pastor. Understanding that the moral failure of one leader can hinder a local church body for many years, Satan aggressively tempts people in leadership with the twisted hope of trapping them in a life-dominating sin.

The second strategy Satan uses is insistently undermining the importance of local church involvement. Despite the church being God's program for the New Testament age, many believers are no longer faithful to a local gospel-centered assembly. While COVID-19 compounded the problem, it didn't begin with the pandemic and its subsequent shutdowns. Increasingly, because of numerous other commitments and distractions, many Christians no longer consider intentional connection to a local church important to their spiritual well-being. Consumed with careers, sports, hobbies, vacations, and any number of other activities, serving in a local church has become expendable. Most Christians who are not committed to a church family are not distracted by anything inherently sinful, but they have placed good, and even commendable, activities over the corporate worship of Christ. Understanding that these distractions hinder a church body from being all it can be for Christ, Satan is pleased knowing that scores of believers are too preoccupied with acceptable things to have any meaningful ministry in a church. In Psalm 122:1, David writes, "I was glad when they said to me, 'Let us go to the house of the LORD!'" It is a sad testimony that so few New Testament Christians share David's enthusiasm. Rather than being excited about local church involvement, many Christians look for excuses to ignore God's commandment for Christians to consistently gather together (see Hebrews 10:24–25).

While Satan's schemes are wreaking havoc in many churches, we must never forget that God intends for his saints to be an active participant in ministry. Understanding the importance of God's people meeting together for worship and service, the writer of Hebrews warns, "Let us consider how to stir up one another to love and good works, not neglecting to meet together, as is the habit of some, but encouraging one another, and all the more as you see the Day drawing near" (10:24–25). Regularly meeting together as the body of Christ is an essential part of standing against the devil's tactics.

The Bride and Body of Christ

Beginning in the second chapter of Acts through the rest of the New Testament, we see God's love for and protection of the church. The book of Ephesians was written to the church in the city of Ephesus. Like all local congregations at the time, the church in Ephesus had its share of strengths and weaknesses. Not much has changed in over two thousand years of church history. Commensurate to the congregations in the first century, today's churches are also filled with

Stay in the Body

strengths and weaknesses. There is simply no such thing as a perfect church because all of them are filled with sinners who perpetually bring their sinful attitudes, actions, habits, and motivations to every gathering. Nonetheless, God expects those who claim the name of Jesus to be active participants in a local assembly of believers. In the New Testament, the church is referred to as the bride of Christ. As Christ's lovely bride, God loves his church; therefore, Christians should love her as well.

I have been married for a very long time, but I still remember our wedding day like it happened last week. Had I attended the ceremony, exchanged vows and rings, kissed my wife, and then run off to live on my own, my bride would have been greatly grieved. Similarly, many Christians like the wedding ceremony—the moment when they are adopted into God's family by faith—but don't particularly like being committed to Christ as his bride. And yet, that is exactly how God has commanded us to love the body of Christ. As a husband, I vowed to remain faithful to my wife through the thick and thin. In sickness and in health, in times of prosperity and hardship. When the skies are blue or when they're darkened by heavy clouds, I promised to love and support the woman I married. Likewise, Christians are expected to find a doctrinally sound local church, become a committed member, find a place to serve, and use our gifts to make the body the best it can be.

Christ's love for the church is pictured in Ephesians 5:29–30, where Paul writes, "For no one ever hated his own flesh, but nourishes and cherishes it, just as Christ does the church, because we are members of his body." Despite the church's imperfections, Jesus loves his bride and cares for her. Jesus sacrificially shed his blood on the cross of Calvary to redeem the church, to make her his own, and to lovingly shepherd her. Notice Paul's usage of *we are*. Concerning Paul's use of the first-person plural, New Testament scholar Andrew Lincoln suggests that this "May well be intended to underline for the letter's recipients their own participation in the reality of Christ's loving care for his body and to emphasize that what has been said in the preceding argument about the church applies to them, because they are, in fact, members of this privileged community, Christ's body."[65] Any privilege we enjoy as part of the church is because of God's grace, not because we are inherently deserving of this honor or because we have any hope of reciprocating. It's through a common faith in the Lord Jesus Christ that we have been adopted into God's family and incorporated into the body of Christ.

Not only does the New Testament refer to the church as the bride of Christ, it also uses the imagery of the human body. In Paul's lengthy and insightful discussion concerning the body of Christ found in 1 Corinthians 12:12–31, he writes, "For the body does not consist of one member but of many" (1 Corinthians 12:14). As Paul paints the picture of Jesus's body, he reminds us that, as all the organs of our physical bodies have a particular function, we all have a specific part to play in the body of Christ. Bible commentator

---

[65] Andrew T. Lincoln, *Ephesians* (Dallas, TX: Word Books, 1990), 380.

Stay in the Body

John Phillips observes, "No more intimate relationship could be imagined than the organic relationship that exists between one member of a physical body and another member. Each member of a body shares the same life, is controlled by the same spirit, is washed by the same blood, and is ruled by the same brain."[66] Within the church, we all have a function to perform, and the body suffers when a part fails to fulfill their responsibility. It's ludicrous to believe an eye, a foot, a hand, a nose, an ear, or a mouth could ever function apart from the rest of the physical body or that one part could assume the responsibility of the others (see 1 Corinthians 12:12–31).

Have you ever tried tying your shoes with your eye or writing a letter with your ears? God designed the various parts of our physical bodies with particular responsibilities, and when we try to use them in a manner in which they were not designed, we are unable to thrive. Similarly, a Christian cannot properly function apart from the body of Christ, and a local church cannot flourish without the faithful support of its members. Because we all have differing and limited gifts, we're incapable of functioning in isolation from the church. Livers, lungs, hearts, brains, kidneys, along with all the other organs, cannot survive outside of the human body for very long. Disconnected Christians, those who try to live independently from the body of Christ, are equally unable to spiritually survive for very long. Despite its imperfections and periods of dysfunction, the church is still God's plan for this

---

[66] John Phillips, *Exploring Ephesians and Philippians* (Grand Rapids, MI: Kregel Publications, 1995), 167.

age. To stay spiritually healthy, we need the caring support, faithful exhortation, loving rebuke, and sympathetic encouragement found in the body of Christ. We cannot thrive in the claustrophobic den of isolation; that's why we're commanded to surround ourselves with other devoted members of God's church.

As Paul brings his epistle to the church at Ephesus to a close, he mentions his dear partner in the ministry, a man by the name of Tychicus. In the final verses of Paul's letter, we gain great insight into what serving Christ looks like. From the magnificent example of Tychicus and Paul, we learn the characteristics of a faithful and sacrificial church member. From the final verses of Ephesians, let's consider the example of Tychicus and Paul and pray that we are equally committed to the gospel as these two faithful servants.

Tychicus, a Servant of Christ

Tychicus served as the courier of Paul's letter to the Ephesians, along with the apostle's letters to the church at Colossae and to Philemon. In Colossians 4:7–9, Paul offers a similar description of his highly regarded coworker. From the Ephesians and Colossians passages, we learn that Paul deeply respected Tychicus. Judging by the responsibilities entrusted to Tychicus, he was clearly a man of character. Let's consider Paul's description of this faithful Christian and gain some insight into how members of Christ's body are expected to function.

First, Tychicus was termed a beloved brother. *Beloved* in Ephesians 6:21 is translated from the Greek word *agapetos*, meaning "esteemed, dear, favorite, worthy of love." As members of the family of God, we are brothers and sisters in Christ. The expression *beloved brother* underscores the close, reciprocal relationship that existed between Paul and Tychicus. Sending Tychicus to deliver news and letters was of great personal sacrifice to Paul. With Tychicus traveling, Paul was left to deal with the challenges of being in captivity without a colleague he obviously appreciated. The relationship between these two men serves as a powerful illustration of how individuals within the body of Christ can quickly become closer to us than even our natural siblings.

Second, Paul describes Tychicus as a faithful minister. Given his proven track record, Paul deeply trusted him to fulfill the ministerial responsibilities delegated to him. *Minister* comes from the Greek word *diakonos,* meaning "one who executes the commands of another, such as a servant or attendant." *Diakonos* can be understood as a waiter of tables or one who serves food and drink. Over time, the word became the technical term for the office of deacon. In the church, deacons are those called to serve the body by performing the menial tasks of the ministry, such as *waiting tables*. Every local church needs members like Tychicus, individuals willing to serve even in obscure and menial ways with no concern for public attention, accolades, or praise. Ministers who serve with no concern for personal glory are invaluable to a local body of believers.

Third, Tychicus was a reliable messenger. Since he had firsthand knowledge of Paul's situation, he was an obvious choice to send to the churches. With Paul still imprisoned in Rome, he sent Tychicus to provide a detailed update concerning his welfare and circumstances. In order for the body of Christ to pray more precisely for Paul's needs, they had to have more information. While the church can always pray for one another in general terms, detailed prayer requests allow the body to pray more specifically. Tychicus was Paul's chosen man who could provide the necessary details of Paul's situation in Rome, including the apostle's particular circumstances, legal standing, financial situation, physical health, and ministry developments.

Fourth, Tychicus was considered to be a dependable encourager. It's likely that he was well known by the recipients of Paul's correspondence. One of the reasons Paul sent his dear brother to Ephesus was because of his ability to provide much-needed encouragement to other believers. The word *encourage* is translated from the Greek verb *parakaleo*, meaning "to call to one's side" or "to comfort, instruct, admonish, exhort." In John 14:26, we find the noun *parakletos* used in reference to the Holy Spirit. The ESV translates the word as *helper*. Translators of the NIV chose the English word *counselor*. While all of these translations are correct, I prefer the KJV's choice of *comforter*. Like the Holy Spirit serves as our helper, counselor, comforter, and encourager, Tychicus was to serve as Jesus's mouthpiece and provide these important spiritual gifts to the church.

Paul, an Apostle of Christ

Throughout Paul's epistle to the Ephesians, he has presented doctrinally rich material without sharing much information about personal matters. Before mentioning Tychicus's duties, Paul asked the church to pray for boldness as he proclaimed the mystery of the gospel (see Ephesians 6:19–20). Rather than concerning himself with his difficult circumstances, Paul turns his attention to the believers in Ephesus and their spiritual needs. As he brings his letter to a conclusion, Paul offers his final words of encouragement for the church. From Paul's concluding prayer, we learn four desires the apostle had for the church in Ephesus. From this final petition, we also learn four valuable practices of committed church members.

Paul's first desire was that the church would experience peace and live peaceably in a violent and antagonistic world. In the book of Ephesians, peace is closely associated with reconciliation (see 2:14–18). The peace of God, which was theirs through the finished work of Christ, was to flow through the members of the body and permeate the congregation. Concerning God's peace, Ken Sande writes, "As the supreme peacemaker, Jesus sacrificed his life so we could experience peace with God and with one another now and forever."[67] God's children are to be promoters of peace; therefore, Paul urges the Ephesian church to faithfully pursue peace with their Heavenly Father and with one another.

Despite the spiritual warfare raging around us, we can experience peace with God through Christ. As Jesus promised

---
67 Sande, 44.

in John 14:27, "Peace I leave with you; my peace I give to you. Not as the world gives do I give to you. Let not your hearts be troubled, neither let them be afraid." As followers of Jesus, we must also be people who purposefully seek peace with others. In Matthew 5:9, Jesus said, "Blessed are the peacemakers, for they shall be called sons of God." Living in an evil age where many stand in opposition to the gospel makes experiencing peace a challenge. In Christ, however, we can experience the peace of God, even while serving in this turbulent age.

Second, Paul desired that the church would experience and dispense love. The necessity of love for God and others is seen throughout the book of Ephesians. Concerning the love of God, Paul writes, "But God, being rich in mercy, because of the great love with which he loved us" (2:4). Concerning mankind's love for one another, Paul commends the church at Ephesus when he writes, "For this reason, because I have heard of your faith in the Lord Jesus and your love toward all the saints" (1:15). Because Jesus loves us and gave himself for us, we are to bow in submission to him and love others as he loves us.

In Ephesians 6:23–24, and in the select passages listed in the previous paragraph, Paul uses either the noun or verbal form of the Greek word *agape*, translated as "love" in each of these verses. Unlike the English language, which uses essentially one word for love, Greek implements four different words to express the idea of love. In the New Testament, *agape* is one of the primary words used to describe love. It can be thought of as self-sacrificing love for the spiritual benefit of another. The point of *agape* is to sacrificially place the needs of others above our own.

Stay in the Body

When we use the English word *love,* we typically mean something to the effect of, "I love mango," meaning "I love to eat mango because it tastes good to me." Of course when I eat a mango, I peel off the skin, spit out the parts that aren't ripe or are starting to rot, and avoid the pit. I chew up the parts I like and throw away the rest. This sounds a lot like how we generally treat one another. The parts of people that satisfy our cravings, we consume for our selfish desires. Whatever parts we find distasteful, we discard. This type of ungodly behavior can leave those we are called to love wounded by our unkindness. This is not how agape love works. Christians motivated by *agape* volitionally choose to die to themselves and serve others as Jesus did during his earthly ministry. People are not consumables expected to please our every whimsical craving; they are individuals, wonderfully created in the image of God, and deserving of our sacrificial love and respect.

Serving others isn't always easy, and it can be amazingly inconvenient at times. When all three of our kids were working their way through grade school, quiet moments in our house were difficult to find. As you can imagine, as the pastor of a church and the president of a Christian school, I don't get much time at home with my family. Spending time alone is an even bigger challenge. One Friday evening, the boys were off someplace, and my wife and daughter were camping at a beach located in the southern part of our county. I planned my evening alone very carefully, including a major cheat meal and a movie that wasn't animated. I sat down at our kitchen table and prepared to take my first bite when my wife called. With hesitation in her voice, she announced that my daughter had accidently locked the keys in the van. Again, it was a Friday night in a beach town, meaning the traffic would be more awful than usual. On top of the traffic, the campsite wasn't exactly close to our house.

With the smell of my dinner in my nostrils, I had three choices: (1) I could tell my wife to figure something out on her own, (2) I could get angry and begrudgingly drive to the campground and unlock the van, or (3) I could die to myself, sacrifice my evening alone, and joyfully serve my wife and daughter. I would love to say that I praised Jesus for providing the opportunity to serve my family, but that would not be exactly accurate. Truth is, my response landed somewhere between options two and three. Out of love for my two favorite girls in the world, I put aside my plans and my disappointment, and drove to the campground and unlocked the van. That's what sacrificial service looks like.

As Christians, we are called to serve one another as Jesus served the disciples when he washed their feet and how he served us when he laid down his life on the cross. By nature, we're all selfish and generally frustrated when inconvenienced; that's what makes serving others so difficult. And yet, Jesus commanded us to live very differently from what comes instinctively. The Lord teaches us to "love one another as I have loved you. Greater love has no one than this, that someone lay down his life for his friends" (John 15:12–13). Only a small percentage of Christians will be martyred for their faith, but one hundred percent of Christians are commanded to die to ourselves and actively serve the body of Christ.

Third, Paul desired that the church's love would be accompanied by faith. Like love, faith is another common theme found in Ephesians. As a staunch promoter of perseverance, Paul prayed that the Ephesian church would remain steadfast in their faith. In the opening chapter of his epistle, Paul acknowledged their faith in Christ and love for one another when he wrote, "For this reason, because I have heard of your faith in the Lord Jesus and your love toward all the saints" (1:15). Knowing faith can be rattled in times of trial, Paul beseeched the church at Ephesus to remain faithful to the Lord, even when wrestling against the schemes of the devil. They needed to take up the shield of faith so they could withstand the flaming darts of Satan (see Ephesians 6:16).

Fourth, Paul desired that the church would experience and dispense grace. Throughout the book of Ephesians, Paul taught his audience about the blessings that come from being the undeserving recipients of God's favor through his grace (see Ephesians 2:4–5). As a promoter of grace, Paul wanted the church to rest confidently in this precious truth while dispensing Christlike grace to those living in their midst.

One area in which the church is commanded to show grace is in our speech. In Colossians 4:6, Paul writes, "Let your speech always be gracious." Paul uses the same Greek word for grace in both Ephesians 6:24 and Colossians 4:6. The word is *charis*, meaning "that which affords joy, pleasure, delight, sweetness, charm, loveliness." Paul uses *charis* in Ephesians 4:29 when he writes, "Let no corrupting talk come out of your mouths, but only such as is good for building up, as fits the occasion, that it may give grace to those who hear." As we rest in God's amazing grace, we must also speak with God's grace in mind. Being gracious with our words doesn't always come naturally. But obedience to God means that we use our tongues to speak God's grace to those around us.

Living peaceably, lovingly, faithfully, and graciously in the midst of this spiritual warfare will empower us to stand firm against the schemes of the devil and to experience consistent victories over his evil forces. Paul's desire is that within the body of Christ, there is a spiritual climate that mirrors these qualities.

Together in Gospel Ministry

In physical warfare, soldiers who fight alone typically don't last terribly long on the battlefield. Likewise, Christians who engage in spiritual warfare without support from others tend to fall into sinful and destructive patterns of living in relatively short order. God didn't redeem us from our sin so we could live isolated from the body of Christ. Standing against the forces of evil isn't an individual effort. The writer of Hebrews cautions, "Take care, brothers, lest there be in any of you an evil, unbelieving heart, leading you to fall away from the living God. But exhort one another every day, as long as it is called 'today,' that none of you may be hardened by the deceitfulness of sin" (Hebrews 3:12–13). Christians who refuse to build community in a local church are in danger of developing a hardened heart, resulting from sinful choices that cause them to fall away from fellowship with God and his people. In Galatians 6, Paul commanded believers to bear one another's burdens (see Galatians 6:1–2). It's impossible to bear the burdens of another when there is no relationship or knowledge of one another's afflictions. Part of loving and assisting one another is supporting each other through hardships, trials, temptations, and moral failures.

The church is not a club, nor a social, religious, or political organization. It's a body of redeemed people coming together for the purpose of gospel ministry. As creatures created in the image of God, we are created for community. It was not good that Adam was alone in the garden; therefore, God created Eve. Even in our age of radical individualism, it is not good for us to be alone. No place in the New Testament do we find an isolated believer standing all alone, trusting in their own power and strength. In Ecclesiastes 4:9–10, Solomon wisely taught, "Two are better than one, because they have a good reward for their toil. For if they fall, one will lift up his fellow. But woe to him who is alone when he falls and has not another to lift him up!" While this text is often referenced in the context of marriage, this isn't a marriage text. It certainly applies to marriage, but it's not limited to husbands and wives. This is a people text. People who try to live apart from the support and encouragement of others are in deep trouble when Satan's flaming arrows fly.

As I've heard it said, if you want to go fast in life, go alone. But if you want to go far, go as a team. To Christians I would say, if you want to fall prey to Satan's schemes, go alone. But if you want to effectively serve Christ with your life, serve within the body.

A number of years ago, I was hiking in the mountains of western North Carolina with two friends. We were hiking to a beautiful waterfall hidden deep in the woods. Getting to the falls required a journey along some tough terrain, including one particularly steep bank leading down to the water. Getting down the hill was one thing, but climbing back out was another matter. On our way out, I was the first to make the climb, followed closely by one of my friends. With two of us back on the trail, we waited for our other friend. When he didn't appear, we went to check on his progress. Unable to scale the incline, he was stranded at the bottom.

After our friend failed at a couple of attempts to climb the hill, I went down to help. With my other friend still at the top, and me at the bottom, we came up with a plan to rescue the one who couldn't climb out on his own. It took some teamwork, but we finally pushed and pulled our friend up the slope and back to the trail. Two, or in this case three, are better than one because if left to ourselves, we're in serious danger. I have often wondered what would have happened to my friend had he hiked that trail on his own.

DesiringGod.org writer Marshall Segal explains it this way: "If we try to live and work alone, we'll stumble and fall alone. And when we fall alone, we won't have the encouragement, correction, and support we need to get back up and press through our failures, sorrows, and trials."[68] There

---

68 Marshall Segal, "Why Don't We Have Good Friends?," accessed November 7, 2022, https://www.desiringgod.org/articles/why-dont-we-have-good-friends?utm_campaign=Daily%20Email&utm_medium=email&_hsmi=232395506&_hsenc=p2ANqtz-_mXvtpfBJJH39W8ULFNm0bcph8hy40jHx66Fog9V7u6aG30hZwmqk4KIdAP875omfWVqnT5pYDDw0Go1lZ7edX-y_PQA&utm_content=232395506&utm_source=hs_email.

is simply too much at stake to attempt entering the spiritual battlefield alone. Whether you want to admit it or not, you need the support found in a gospel-centered local church. As messy as churches can be, faithfully serving in a local body of believers is God's will for your life. The local church should serve as an earthly foretaste of what God's kingdom is like. Churches on this earth are filled with sinful people, making them an imperfect representation. We are, however, called to live by kingdom ethics today so we can picture, albeit imperfectly, life in God's kingdom. To reach the world with the gospel, God needs all of his people sacrificially engaged in ministry. Yes, that includes you.

Since its inception, the church has been a place of relational intimacy and spiritual reinforcement. Even during Jesus's earthly ministry, his relationship with his disciples included time on lonely roads, visiting with people, eating meals with friends, and sailing and fishing together. Jesus and his disciples prayed together, worshipped together, served together, and shared the bumps of life together. These men journeyed through life together and grew closer as a result. They knew each other's strengths and weaknesses. They saw each other at their best and their worst and had their fair share of disagreements. The disciples even watched as Jesus was brutally beaten, humiliated, and crucified. It was a tough road they traveled together. But they walked the road one step at a time. Side by side, heart to heart, they lived and served together.

Despite many Americans' unwavering commitment to individualism, Christians have never been expected to wrestle against evil alone. Like the interlocking shields used by the Roman soldiers to create a united wall of protection, Christians must also band together, hand in hand, and create a spiritual barricade that is capable of fending off Satan's fiery arrows. Even the Apostle Paul didn't rely solely on his own strength and abilities to stand against Satan's opposition. To stay devoted and effective in gospel ministry, Paul needed other faithful believers at his side. Devoted men like Tychicus were valuable to Paul, providing a powerful illustration of the type of relationships required to faithfully serve Christ over a long period of time.

Takeaways

Without sacrificial involvement in a gospel-centered church, Christians will be vulnerable to spiritual attacks and will not consistently mature in their faith. Ever since the Garden of Eden, Satan's malicious tactics have remained the same. When he tempted Eve, he waited until she was alone before enticing her with his lies. To this day, Satan prefers to isolate us, weave his tangled web of lies, and then tempt our idolatrous hearts with something our flesh already craves. Take a moment to consider your pet sin. How often do you engage in your favorite sinful activity when you're surrounded by faithful Christians who love and care about you? I'm guessing your answer ranges from rarely to never. Blatantly disregarding the body of Christ leaves us isolated, ill-prepared, and incapable of standing against the wiles of the devil. Whether we recognize our desperate need for support from a local church or not, God's truth remains the same: followers of Jesus need the spiritual refreshment and refinement that takes place in the context of a local body of believers.

Tychicus serves as an exemplary model of a Christian who was greatly respected and useful in gospel ministry. From Tychicus's example, we learn four characteristics that every Christian should develop. We must do the following:

1. Intentionally develop close, transparent, and God-honoring relationships within the body of Christ: if you have been attending a church for any length of time but remain unknown and inactive, with possibly a few exceptions, the absence of meaningful relationships probably says more about your lack of engagement than the church's hospitality.
2. Actively seek opportunities to faithfully minister in a local church: if you are not consistently investing time, talent, and treasure into serving the body of Christ, it's time to find a place to use your giftedness for the cause of Christ.
3. Purposefully serve as reliable messengers: part of body life is keeping one another informed about the blessings and concerns of life so we can appropriately rejoice, encourage, support, and pray. We are also called to consistently and graciously share the gospel message.
4. Sacrificially encourage and support others: some Christians are naturally gifted at providing encouragement and support. For those lacking in this area,

you must deliberately develop the skills necessary to become a dependable encourager, comforter, supporter, and helper.

Tychicus was a significant part of Paul's ministry team, and he likely learned much from the apostle's pattern of living. Unquestionably, the Apostle Paul serves as one of the most remarkable examples of a faithful Christian servant found in Scripture. From Paul's life and ministry, there is much to emulate, even his prayers are immensely instructive. In his closing prayer for the church at Ephesus, we glean four characteristics Christians should develop. We must do the following:

1. Humbly be peaceable: redeemed by the shed blood of Jesus, we enjoy eternal peace with God. As we rest in God's peace, we are commanded to persistently pursue peace with others, particularly with other members of Christ's body.

2. Sacrificially love others as Christ loves the church: while the American version of love typically focuses on emotions and feelings, the New Testament focuses on the volitional choice to sacrificially serve others and to treat them in accordance with 1 Corinthians 13.

3. Unwaveringly remain faithful: facing Satan's flaming darts can become spiritually exhausting and leave us vulnerable to discouragement. For our faith to remain strong, we must take up the shield of faith and rest in God's strength and protection.

4. Patiently practice graciousness: it's disingenuous for us to boast about our salvation being the result of God's grace and yet treat our families and neighbors with rude impatience and inconsiderate unkindness. Being patiently gracious demonstrates our love for God and others.

Consistently living up to these eight characteristics is a tall task. Nevertheless, the testimonies of Tychicus and Paul serve as powerful reminders that these characteristics should be evident in every Christian's life. Although they will all be imperfectly present, each one should be increasingly evident in our sinful lives. The closer we draw to Christ and obey his commandments, the more pronounced these characteristics will be manifested in our lives.

Key Point: Consistent involvement in a gospel-centered local church is essential for Christians to grow spiritually and stand against the schemes of the devil.

For Further Consideration

1. Read through the book of Ephesians and take note of the principles discussed in this chapter.
2. Read Proverbs 18:1 and explain why isolating from others is unwise and dangerous. Compare the teaching of Proverbs 18:1 with Proverbs 15:22.
3. Verses for further study:
   Matthew 5:9
   John 14

Acts 20:1–6
Romans 12:14–21
1 Corinthians 12:12–31
1 Corinthians 13
2 Corinthians 5:18–21
Colossians 4:7–9
2 Timothy 4:12
Titus 3:12

4. From the testimony of Tychicus, assess your current level of spiritual maturity when it comes to being a . . .

   Beloved brother or sister
   Faithful minister
   Reliable messenger
   Dependable encourager

5. From the testimony of Paul, assess your current level of spiritual maturity when it comes to being . . .

   Humbly peaceable
   Sacrificially loving
   Steadfastly faithful
   Patiently gracious

Conclusion

The LORD lives, and blessed be my rock, and exalted be the God of my salvation.

Psalm 18:46

During the weeks of working on this project, I had numerous discussions with people caught locking horns with the devil and fighting against his deceptive schemes. Despite the spiritual opposition that always hovers over ministry like a threatening thunder cloud on a hot summer day, people still came to faith in Jesus and obediently took their next steps in following him. Several individuals followed the Lord in baptism. New families became members of our church body. Several large events were held on campus without a glitch, and God was glorified in the process. God blessed our ministry in measurable ways, and we were seeing plenty of fruit from our labor.

And then . . . the inevitable spiritual opposition came in with a heavy hand. Satan's flaming arrows flew at us fast and hard, and some people were wounded in the battle. Because of illness and sinful choices, several families were thrown into disarray and crisis. On top of the major challenges, other people responded in sinful anger over minor issues, making these issues larger than they needed to be. Like gasoline thrown on a fire, small issues became explosive because of hateful and sinful responses.

What was once a period of smooth sailing and joyful ministry quickly deteriorated into a tempest of sinful decisions, heartbreak, and conflict. That, my friend, is how life happens in this sinful world. Whenever Christians attempt to obey God and live in accordance with Scripture, spiritual opposition from Satan and his forces of evil is to be expected. The devil's schemes always become more aggressive when Christians serve and ministries are bearing good fruit for the Master.

Meliorism was introduced in the opening pages of this book. To refresh your memory, it means, "The doctrine that the world tends to become better or may be made better by human effort." For thousands of years, humanity has tried to make the world a better place where wars are never fought, death is eliminated, global harmony rings in the air, no one is hungry, and people no longer sin against one another. This utopian fantasy has never happened—and never will until Christ sets up his eternal kingdom. In the meantime, we are to serve as salt and light in this dark world while standing strong against the schemes of the devil. To do so, we need God's strength, power, and armor.

In this fallen world where evil is called good and good is called evil, we will experience trouble. Jesus promised. But he also promised that he has overcome the world and that the gates of hell will never prevail against the gospel and his church. Living in this fallen age is spiritually exhausting. But, by the grace of almighty God, we have Spirit-infused resolve to fight the good fight of faith for his glory. God is purposefully sovereign, and he is faithfully working all things together on this earth so that his perfect and glorious plan will be accomplished. Our responsibility is to live righteously by obeying God's authoritative word while standing against the forces of evil.

In this battle, there can be no backing down. Hearts and minds protected, feet ready to run, God's truth in hand, an attitude of prayer keeping us focused, and God's shield of faith extinguishing Satan's flaming arrows, we charge forward, with no thought of surrender.

Appendix: How Does Someone Become a Christian?

You may be wondering how someone becomes a Christian. According to the Bible, Christians are those who have admitted that they are sinners, repented of their sin, and called upon the name of Jesus to redeem them from their sin. Salvation is not the result of performing good works, being a good person, going to church, being baptized, or observing the Lord's Supper. These are important for Christians, but these actions do not make someone a Christian. In other words, you cannot enter heaven through what you do. God's word teaches that only those who trust in what Jesus did on the cross and through his resurrection can be saved from their sin and from hell.

Important Bible verses would include:

1. "All have sinned and fall short of the glory of God, and are justified [i.e., saved] by his grace as a gift, through the redemption that is in Christ Jesus" (Romans 3:23–24).

2. "For the wages of sin is death, but the free gift of

God is eternal life in Christ Jesus our Lord" (Romans 6:23).

3. "God shows his love for us in that while we were still sinners, Christ died for us" (Romans 5:8).
4. "If you confess with your mouth that Jesus is Lord and believe in your heart that God raised him from the dead, you will be saved. For with the heart one believes and is justified [i.e., saved], and with the mouth one confesses and is saved" (Romans 10:9–10).
5. "For God so loved the world, that he gave his only Son, that whoever believes in him should not perish but have eternal life. For God did not send his Son into the world to condemn the world, but in order that the world might be saved through him" (John 3:16–17).
6. "Jesus said to him, 'I am the way, and the truth, and the life. No one comes to the Father except through me'" (John 14:6).
7. "Whoever confesses that Jesus is the Son of God, God abides in him, and he in God" (1 John 4:15).

You cannot become a Christian through good works, religion, or high moral standards. As a sinner, no matter what you have done, you can be saved by humbling yourself before God, repenting of your sin, placing your faith in Christ alone, and calling upon his name to redeem you by his grace. Through humble faith in Jesus, God will adopt you into his family and make you a new creature. In 2 Corinthians 5:17, the Apostle Paul writes, "If anyone is in Christ, he is a new creation."

There are no magic words that you have to say to be saved. If you come humbly before God with a truly repentant heart, God will save you. Remember, no sin is too big for God to forgive.

If you would like to receive Christ as your Savior, here is a sample prayer of how you can ask Jesus to save you:

> "Lord, I come humbly into your presence, admitting that I'm a sinner. I have been living a life of rebellion against you and your word. I know that I can't save myself from my sin. I also know that I can't earn my way to heaven through my good works or by keeping a list of rules. That's why I'm calling upon the name of the Lord Jesus Christ right now to redeem me. I confess that Jesus is the Lamb of God, the one who died on the cross to pay the penalty for my sin. Jesus is the true Son of God who rose from the dead. I believe that only the shed blood of Jesus can wash away my sin. So, God, I repent, and accept the truth by faith that Jesus is the only way to heaven. Forgive me of my sin, God, and save me. Adopt me into your family by your grace and become my Heavenly Father. Amen!"

Acknowledgments

I have always believed that writing a book is a community project, but now that I have accomplished the goal of publishing one, I am even more aware of how desperately an author needs a team to mold a rough draft into a finished product. I would like to express my sincere appreciation to some special people who helped breathe life into this book.

First, I want to thank my workout partners: Adam Tartt and Jeff Fox. Over coffee one morning, I begged these two men to talk me out of publishing a book. Instead, they relentlessly encouraged me to go for it. During the following months, they listened to my wandering thoughts and ideas about what I would write. Once I started putting words on the page, they demanded constant updates on my progress. By the end of this project, I believe they were more excited about this book being published than I was. Their encouragement always came at the right time, and their enthusiasm kept me moving forward.

Second, I want to thank Kerk Murray for his wisdom and guidance. Finishing a dissertation is one thing, but publishing a book is far more difficult. I was a little nervous about the publishing process, but Kerk patiently walked me through it step by step. Someone told me before I met Kerk that he was one of the kindest people on earth, and that if I had an issue with him, the problem was with me. That turned out to be a profoundly accurate assessment.

Third, I want to thank my marvelous editor, Carly Catt, for her expertise and insight. From Carly's attention to detail, I learned firsthand that editors make writers into authors. By asking great questions and identifying weaknesses in the first draft, Carly skillfully helped craft my sometimes-rambling manuscript into a cohesive book. I always enjoy working with people who are professional, timely, kind, and direct. Carly is all four. Without question, she was the editor I needed to make this project a reality.

Fourth, I want to thank Joanna Kneller for her careful proofreading and kind words of encouragement. Joanna did a great job refining my manuscript into its final form. Books are definitively a team effort, and I am thankful Joanna was part of mine.

Most importantly, I want to thank my beautiful wife, Michelle, for all of her support. As a college professor, she reads a lot of papers. In addition to her grading responsibilities, I pile pages upon pages on her desk for proofreading. I value her opinion above all others, and I am so thankful that she supports my desire to write and publish books. Michelle reads my work when it is raw and always provides the honest input needed to refine my ideas. In many places I have read that your spouse should never be your first reader. I, for one, am proud to have my wife as both my first and final reader. Rather than telling me what I want to hear, Michelle points out what is good and what needs to be improved. There is no way *When Flaming Arrows Fly* would have ever been written without the support of my amazing wife.

To God be all the glory!

Oh, taste and see that the LORD is good! Blessed is the man who takes refuge in him!

Psalm 34:8

URGENT REQUEST!

Thank You For Reading My Book!

I value all of your feedback and I look forward to hearing what you have to say about *When Flaming Arrows Fly*!

Your constructive input will help make any future editions of this book and my upcoming books better.

Please take a few minutes right now to leave a helpful review on Amazon letting me know what you think of *When Flaming Arrows Fly*.

I Sincerely Appreciate Your Kind Support!

- Jay Knolls

About The Author

Jay Knolls is a Delaware native, but has also lived in Maryland, Vermont, Pennsylvania, and Florida. He currently resides in Wilmington, North Carolina where he serves as the lead pastor of Grace Baptist Church and as the president of Wilmington Christian Academy. He is also the founder and president of Wondrous Word Ministries. Jay enjoys reading, writing, preaching, teaching, weight training, and exploring the mountains of North Carolina. He is an avid Carolina Panthers and Hurricanes fan, and roots for the Baltimore Orioles and Philadelphia Phillies during baseball season. *Les Misérables* by Victor Hugo is Jay's favorite novel. Before entering pastoral ministry in 2002, he spent more than a decade working in the health care industry as a respiratory therapist. With over twenty years of preaching and pastoral experience, he offers a seasoned perspective on Scripture and gospel ministry. Jay holds a BS from Salisbury University, and an MDiv, and DMin from Calvary Baptist Theological Seminary. Jay is available for podcasts, interviews, and speaking engagements upon request. Please visit his website at https://wondrousword.com for more information.

Made in the USA
Middletown, DE
23 July 2025